The
Japanese
in
Hawai'i

Okage Sama De

Dorothy Ochiai Hazama

Jane Okamoto Komeiji

3565 Harding Ave, Honolulu, Hawai'i 96816
(808) 734-7159 fax (808) 732-3627 www.besspress.com

Executive Editor: Dr. Ann Rayson
Index: Jody A. M. Hansen
Cover Photo courtesy of the Komeiji family
Cover Design: Carol Colbath

Cataloging-in-publication data

Hazama, Dorothy Ochiai.
  The Japanese in Hawai'i : okage
sama de / Dorothy Ochiai Hazama
and Jane Okamoto Komeiji ; foreword
by Senator Daniel K. Inouye ; afterword
by Congresswoman Mazie K. Hirono.
        p.   cm.
  Includes illustrations and appendices.
  ISBN: 978- 1-57306-286-2
  1. Japanese Americans – Hawaii – History.
2. Japanese Americans – Hawaii – Social
life and customs. 3. Japanese Americans –
Hawaii – Ethnic relations. 4. Hawaii – Ethnic
relations. I. Komeiji, Jane Okamoto II. Title.
DU624.7 J3 H39 2008 996.9-dc22

To our mothers who nurtured a love of things Japanese:

Shigeyo Ochiai
Kame Okamoto

and our children who inspired us:

Cathy and Neal Hazama
John, David, and Paul Komeiji

Table of Contents

Tables

Foreword

By Daniel K. Inouye
United States Senator

For most residents and visitors in Hawaii, sugar plantations are an Island vista viewed only as we speed by on freeways and byways. These vast green acreages and quiet towns are gradually receding from the landscape of our Islands, as they blur in the general consciousness of our community.

It would be well for generations long separated from the hardships of the plantations to realize the message that the passing of our sugar plantations carries in the legacy of the Hawaiian Islands.

For groups imported as a cheap, reliable source of field labor- Chinese, Japanese, Portuguese, Filipinos- these plantations were islands themselves. There were not static places to be viewed with detachment from afar, rather they were tightly regimented societies seen from inside, looking out. At the beginning, for most, they were the footstep in the door to a better tomorrow, to an American society that promised unlimited opportunity for the daring and dedicated.

The experience of Japanese in Hawaii is a commentary on the realization of this American dream. The publication of OKAGE SAMA DE: THE JAPANESE IN HAWAI'I adds valuable volume to our existing literary works on Japanese in Hawaii. Its historical narrative and personal anecdotes present a new and welcome dimension to the current body of recorded knowledge on this segment of Hawaii history.

Its original printing during the centennial celebration of the arrival of the first Japanese laborers was a timely coincidence. I hope that will make OKAGE SAMA DE even more widely read throughout our community. Surely long-time Hawaii resident and newcomer alike will find much that is informative and entertaining in this book.

OKAGE SAMA DE brings alive the hardships and sacrifices endured by the Japanese in Hawaii in the struggles to work their way out of the plantations, and open the plantation power structure to non-white management. The road to success was a rocky one. We can learn from this book that in many ways, the trials and progress of the Japanese in Hawaii mirrored the changes of Hawaii society as a whole, during its transition from subsistence to plantation to contemporary technological society.

I commend the authors for presenting such a comprehensive and authoritative history. It is a poignant tribute to lives and times long past that even today influence the goals and lifestyles of modern Hawaii.

Preface

The need for a book about the Japanese experience in Hawai'i first dawned on us separately but vividly when we came to the realization that being American and being Hawaiian were matters of the heart and not of physical characteristics or backgrounds. It was O.K. to be Japanese Americans in Hawai'i. Having spent the greater part of our impressionistic years during the war and post World War II years, we were robbed of the opportunity to know and to comprehend our Japanese heritage. For many of us, perhaps, being deprived of the ability to speak and write Japanese was our greatest loss. We were conditioned to consider anything having to do with our enemy, the Japanese, as inferior and old-fashioned. When our parents put away their Buddhist and Shinto shrines, burned their kimonos and family photographs, forsook their language and customs, we thought that we had also discarded our Japaneseness.

But, such was not the case. For one thing, although we tried to emulate the Caucasians, we could alter our beings only super-ficially. We still looked Japanese. We went to Christian churches, spoke the English language, dated men of our choice, and even talked back to our parents. However, deep down we were not comfortable with ourselves. Within us we still harbored concepts preached to us from birth – *on* (obligation to others), *giri* (recipro-cal obligations), *haji* (shame), and *oyakōkō* (filial piety) among others. During the war we missed the opportunity to fly carps on Boys' Day, the excitement of joining other family members at the Shinto Shrine to greet the New Year, as well as the subsequent festivities that lasted for a week.

At school we studied the coming of the Pilgrims, the French, and the Irish to American shores and of their help in building our great nation. In Hawaiian history, we learned about the role that the missionaries played in the development of the Islands from a Kingdom to a Territory of the United States. The Hawaiian history books did briefly note the coming of the various immigrant groups, including the Japanese, to work in the sugar fields. Therefore, we knew that our parents had come to Hawai'i from Japan as laborers. But we did not know when they came, why they came, what they did specifically, nor how they felt about their experiences. They may have tried to tell us, but we turned our deaf ears to them for we wanted more than anything else to be accepted as mainstream Americans. Consciously and unconsciously, we denied our heritage. Not knowing our roots, we could not identify ourselves and our own beings. We could not answer the question, who am I?

As mothers and as teachers, we found this lack of identity also evident in our children. By then we had grown to realize that America, generally, and our beloved Hawai'i, specifically, were ethnically and culturally pluralistic societies. There was lots of room for the various groups to retain their ethnicity and yet to be united as people under one flag. Having a Japanese or any other heritage did not make us less American.

The original need then became an urgent one, and we decided to work on a history that would give the young people, as well as our fellow Nisei, some idea about their backgrounds which in turn could help them fathom their identities to function as confident Americans, proud and appreciative of their Japanese heritage. We also hoped that this history would enable other Americans to better understand us Japanese Americans. We further hoped that it would enable everyone to conclude that white, black, brown, or yellow we are all human beings with the same basic needs and hopes.

The process of researching, interviewing, discussing, and completing this project has been an exciting, challenging, and fulfilling experience for both of us. There were many times that we both exclaimed, "Oh, I didn't know that," or "Now I understand why we did that!" As we ourselves became immersed in understanding our Japanese heritage, we became intensely aware of our deeply ingrained sense of appreciation which is frequently expressed through a common saying, "Okage sama de." This prefacing phrase used in conversations and speeches means, "I am what I am because of you," or "My accomplishments, big and small, have been made possible because of you (individually or collectively)." Implied in "Okage sama de" is the belief that all of what you have done for me in the yesteryears has left its mark on all of my todays. We are indeed grateful to be a part of the people of Hawai'i, and we are most appreciative of our parents and peers who have made it possible for us to enjoy the quality of life we have today.

State of State Address to the Legislature.
John A. Burns, Governor of Hawai'i
February 20, 1969

To be perfectly candid, I sense among some elements of our community – particularly those who are descended from our immigrant plantation workers – a subtle "inferiority of spirit," which is totally unwarranted and which becomes for them a social and psychological handicap in life.

You who have grown up with me here in the Islands and who remember the pre-World War II climate know full well what I mean. You know, too, that there should be no basis for this feeling.

On the contrary, our people are equal to and in my judgment superior in many ways, to their counterparts anywhere. They should be proud of their ethnic roots, of the riches and treasures of their Pacific and Asian cultures. . . .

I submit further that they should be given every opportunity – even in our public school system – to learn more about their own people's rich past, to understand the sources of inspiration which motivated their fathers and their ancestors before them.

The undercurrent of uncertainty simmering beneath our affluent surface has been articulated in expressions of concern that Hawai'i stands in danger of losing its unique characteristics.

These concerns are well founded. . . .

We need now to focus our attention on the significance of the past to keep our future secure. . . .

The contributions to our society of the Chings and the Lums, the Cravalhos and the Henriques, the Kahanamokus and the Kealohas, the Tanakas and the Oshiros, the Samsons and the Menors, the Kims and the Ahns, the Cooks and the Judds – their stories – and thousands of other stories like them – are an integral part of Hawai'i's real history.

Acknowledgements

Okage sama de . . .

Because of the help of many, many people, we have been able to see the completion of our book. Although we have expressed our appreciation through credits to many Issei and Nisei relatives and friends throughout the text, we would like to thank the following people in particular for their help:

Etsuo and Tatsuyo Hazama, Uncle Philip Ninomiya, and Dr. Dennis Ogawa for their encouragement, suggestions, and invaluable assistance.

George Bacon and George Yoshishige who generously and graciously provided their photographic expertise.

Dr. Glen Grant, Cathy Hazama, Dr. Teruo Ihara, Kate Inokuchi, Jane Kinoshita, Pat O'Connell, and Kay Yamada for reading and critiquing the manuscript.

Goro Arakawa, Dr. Bernice Hirai, David Kittelson, Dr. Laurence Kolonel, Dr. Yasumasa Kuroda, Leighton Liu, Dr. Y. Scott Matsumoto, Dr. Gerald Meredith, Bishop Dwight Nakamura, Eleanor Nordyke, Robert Schmitt, Evelyn Shintani, Jane Wakukawa, and Dr. Katsuhiko Yano for providing help in their fields of specialization.

The staffs of the following institutions for their assistance:

Bishop Museum, Library and Photo Collection

Hawaii State Archives

Hawaiian and Pacific Collection, Hamilton Library, University of Hawaii

Hawaiian Room, Hawaii State Library

Oral History Project, Social Science Research Institute, University of Hawaii

U.S. Army Museum of Hawaii

Waipahu Cultural Garden Park

War Records Depository, University of Hawaii

Susan Hayama, Elaine Mezurashi, Cheryl Otani, Gail Shimabukuro, Sherl Shimokawa and Flo Tanigawa for typing.

Our husbands, Richard and Toshio, for being our sounding boards and for sustaining us with their love and encouragement throughout our project.

Arigato Gozaimasu,
Dorothy Ochiai Hazama
Jane Okamoto Komeiji

Introduction
JAPANESE AMERICANS IN HAWAI'I TODAY

The Japanese Americans or Americans of Japanese Ancestry (AJAs) are highly visible among the people of Hawai'i today. They are a part of the mainstream of the life in Hawai'i. They live on all the major islands, in the city and the suburbs, in lower income housing and elite neighborhoods. They work in occupations from the unskilled to the professional. Many are involved at all levels in business as owners, as management level personnel in big companies, and as secretaries and sales clerks. There are leaders among them as well as members of the rank and file of the labor force of Hawai'i. More recently, they have also ventured into creative endeavors as artists, musicians, and dancers. They are an integral part of Hawai'i's multi-ethnic community.

The Japanese have always placed a high value on education, and education has been the ladder they have used to succeed in all areas available to them. Many individuals have attained prominence in government, politics, and the professions such as law, medicine, dentistry, ministry, and education. For example, the two Senators representing Hawai'i in Congress in the early 1980s were Japanese Americans. Senator Daniel K. Inouye and Senator "Spark" M. Matsunaga had served as Representatives to Congress before they became Senators. Former Representative Patsy T. Mink, who became Chairperson of the City Council of the City and County of Honolulu in 1982, was the first woman of Asian ancestry to be elected to Congress. Governor George R. Ariyoshi was the first Japanese American and the first person of Asian ancestry to be elected Governor of the State of Hawaii or of any other state in the union. Part Japanese American, Jean Sadako King, the first woman ever to be elected to the office of Lieutenant Governor, served in that capacity from 1978-1982. She, like all the others mentioned, began her political career by serving in the State Legislature. Almost half of the elected Senators and Representatives of the Hawai'i State Legislature in the early 1980s were of Japanese American descent. Many others served in the county governments and in the grassroots activities of political campaigns.

In other branches of government, the Japanese Americans have served as judges and lawyers at all levels in the Hawai'i State and County Court Systems. In 1959, Wilfred Tsukiyama was appointed Chief Justice of the Supreme Court of Hawai'i, the first AJA to be so honored. In 1984, three out of five Supreme Court Justices were Japanese Americans.

Many, many others have chosen education as their profession. About 60 percent of the teachers and administrators of the State Department of Education in the early 1980s were of Japanese American descent. Dr. Fujio Matsuda was the first Asian American and the first person born in Hawai'i to be named President of the University of Hawaii.

The Japanese Americans vary in age and differ widely in their lifestyles. The Issei are those who migrated from Japan. Their children, the Nisei, are the first generation to be born in the United States in addition to being the second generation to live here. The Nisei now have children and grandchildren of their own, the Sansei and Yonsei, the third and fourth generations.

While most of the elderly Issei still adhere to Japanese traditions and enjoy activities centered around their Buddhist temples, many Nisei and especially the Sansei and Yonsei are more American in lifestyle and values. Many of the later generations no longer are able to converse in Japanese. However, as young adults, a number of Sansei and Yonsei are showing an increasing interest in regaining a knowledge of Japanese customs and language.

"Things Japanese" have become a part of the multi-ethnic cultures of Hawaii's people regardless of background. Hawai'i's people enjoy Japanese foods at home, in restaurants, and at lunch wagons. The ingredients for Japanese cooking can be found in any supermarket. The zōri, or Japanese sandal, is popular among all people, and the Japanese custom of leaving footwear at the doorstep has been adopted by most households. The martial arts, flower arrangement, and architectural styles are but a few of the other contributions from the Japanese to Hawai'i's lifestyle today. In turn, most Japanese Americans have adopted many of the customs of the other ethnic groups into their way of life.

Therefore, it was surprising to many people to learn that the Japanese, according to the U.S. Census of 1980, constituted only 24.9 percent of the total population of Hawai'i; 239,748 out of the total population of 964,691 were of Japanese descent.[1] Although there were more Japanese Americans in Hawai'i than ever before, the percentage had declined over the years from a high of over 40 percent in the early 1900s.[2] While the overall population of Hawai'i had increased rapidly, very few Japanese entered the state as immigrants, and the Japanese Americans who were already citizens had one of the lowest birth rates in the state. Therefore, although the Japanese Americans have become highly visible and frequently prominent as citizens of Hawai'i, they made up only about a fourth of the total population of Hawai'i in 1980.

This is a story of Hawai'i's people from Japan – how and why they came, their struggles to find their place in their new homeland, and their contributions to the lifestyle of Hawai'i today.

Chapter I
EARLY ARRIVALS

Storms at sea may have been the cause for the first Japanese to have landed in Hawai'i many years before Captain Cook's arrival in 1778. It is thought that they were drifters, fishermen whose ships were blown off their course or shipwrecked. Some reports tell of two separate occasions of Japanese landing in Hawai'i in the 13th century at Makapu'u Point on O'ahu. Soon after, another group of two men and three women of fair skin was said to have landed at Kahului, Maui. It was reported that the two men wore swords on their hips. Neither of these stories can be confirmed because although the Hawaiians had a rich oral tradition, they did not have a written language, and the incidents were recorded in Japan long after they happened. However, beginning in the early 1800s there are first-hand, written accounts of Japanese arrivals in Hawai'i. Most noteworthy among these was fifteen-year-old Manjirō Nakahama who was shipwrecked with four fishing partners on a tiny island inhabited only by birds. The five lived on the island for six months until they were rescued by Captain W.H. Whitfield of the whaling ship *John Howland* on June 27, 1841. Five months later they sailed into the Port of Honolulu.

Of the five, four remained in Hawai'i. Denzo worked for awhile at the Hawaiian Chiefs' Children's School while his brothers, Jusuke and Gorouemon, were taken into the household of Dr. Gerrit P. Judd, a medical doctor and a prominent government official. However, Jusuke died from dysentery and complications from an injured foot. His two brothers then moved to Kāne'ohe to be near Jusuke's grave and became farmers on land granted to them by Governor Kekūanaō'a. The fourth man, Torauemon, became a carpenter and a boatbuilder.

Manjirō, the fifth rescued fisherman, was adopted by Captain Whitfield and sailed with him aboard the *John Howland*. The Captain taught him many things including the English language, geography, map reading, and navigational skills. Manjirō took a new name, John Mung, and lived and studied for three years in Fairhaven, Massachusetts, before returning to Honolulu in

1

A daguerreotype of Manjirō Nakahama. E.V. Warinner, Voyager to Destiny. Compass-America Productions, Inc.

September, 1846 where he renewed his friendship with the three surviving members of the original group.

After further travels throughout the Pacific on whaling cruises, Manjirō made arrangements for his return to Japan. Japan at that time was ruled by the Tokugawa Shogunate, and the ports had been closed to foreign ships for two hundred years. No one was allowed to enter or to leave Japan. During his travels Manjirō had learned enough to realize that Japan could benefit from foreign contacts. He wanted to help his country establish foreign trade.

Manjirō, therefore, approached his friends with his plans to return to Japan. Torauemon, who had married a Hawaiian girl, decided to remain in Hawai'i; but Denzo and Gorouemon consented. The three obtained passage on the merchant ship *Sarah Boyd*. Because of the Shōgun government's Seclusion Edict, they were worried throughout the trip. They were not certain whether they would be welcomed. When they reached one of the islands of Okinawa, they were immediately taken as prisoners. However, there was great interest in them as they related their adventures and their knowledge of the outside world.

The officials were very suspicious of the trio's loyalty to Japan. The final clearance for re-entry came when the three stepped on a metal crucifix, thus proving that they had not been converted to Christianity and were still loyal to Japan. They were then allowed to return to their home villages. Soon afterwards, Manjirō was called to Edo, the capital of Japan, to help in the meeting between Commodore Matthew Perry of the United States and Lord Abe, head of the Shōgun's cabinet. Commodore Perry had brought an official letter from the President of the United States demanding better treatment of shipwrecked sailors and suggesting a commerce treaty. Manjirō used his experiences and knowledge and served as advisor and interpreter. A treaty of amity and peace was signed by the United States and Japan in 1854. A commercial treaty between the two countries was signed later.

Thus it appears that during the centuries before the mid 1800s, individual drifters from Japan, especially shipwrecked fishermen, were brought to Hawai'i's shores by the strong ocean currents.

Chapter II
THE GANNEN MONO

Sugar is believed to have been first milled in Hawai'i on the island of Lāna'i as early as 1802, by Wong Tse Chun from China. But, his project ended in failure and he returned to China. The first successful attempt was begun in 1835 at Kōloa on Kaua'i; however, it was not until the late 1840s that the sugar became a major crop. *Haole* (Caucasian, originally any foreigner) businessmen realized that sugar could be marketed profitably in America, but there were some major problems to overcome.

Land ownership was a prime concern. The foreigners did not want to invest large amounts of money and time needed to grow sugar unless they owned the land. The Great Māhele of 1848 established land ownership for the first time, and the land was divided among King Kamehameha III and 245 chiefs. By 1850, through subsequent acts, native commoners and foreigners were able to own land in fee simple. This enabled the haole business-

At an early sugar mill, a carabao turned stone grinding wheels to extract the juice from the sugar cane. The juice was then boiled down to molasses.

men to purchase land to set up plantations in order to grow sugar on a large scale.

But labor was another big problem. Native Hawaiians were first hired to do the growing, harvesting, and milling of sugar; but as more and more sugar was produced, there was an acute shortage of Hawaiian laborers. Young Hawaiians were lured to the Mainland by the Gold Rush, and now that the natives could own their own land, some preferred to cultivate their own *kuleana* (property). Compounding the problem was the fact that thousands of Hawaiians had been dying from diseases introduced by foreigners. The number of Hawaiians dropped greatly from 130,313 in the 1831-32 census to 65,647 in 1860. Thus, getting workers for the sugar plantations became a serious problem.

By the mid 1800s, worried plantation owners began thinking of importing workers from other countries. The Masters and Servants' Act passed in 1850 by the Hawaiian government established the legal basis for the contract labor system. The Act made it lawful for any person twenty years or over to bind himself by written contract to serve another for a term not exceeding five years. It further declared that contracts made in a foreign country for labor in Hawai'i would be binding, but not for a period longer than ten years. It contained a penal code in which the worker who refused to serve according to the terms of the contract could be committed to prison at hard labor. On the other hand, any master guilty of cruelty or violations of any of the terms of the contract could be fined up to a maximum of one hundred dollars which, if not paid, could mean imprisonment. The Masters and Servants' Act of 1850 became the basis upon which labor was supplied to the plantations for the next fifty years. The planters were interested in obtaining hard working immigrants who would work at low wages. They hoped that these immigrants, preferably single males, would serve out their contracts and then sign another contract or return to their homelands. Workers with families were not sought for they would involve additional concerns and expenses. In 1852, the Chinese became the first group of laborers to be brought to Hawai'i. They worked hard and were good workers. However, they were miserable under the crowded and unsanitary living conditions and the harsh working conditions. Therefore, many of them stayed on the plantation only until they fulfilled their contracts and moved out to the villages and towns as soon as they could to start their own farms, stores, and other businesses.

Ten South Sea Islanders were imported and employed at Kōloa

Plantation, but they did not work out as laborers. The need for workers as well as people to replenish the population was a serious enough problem as to be discussed by King Kamehameha V's cabinet soon after he came to the throne. Meanwhile, a "Planters' Society" composed of planters, plantation agents, and others interested in agriculture was organized in 1864. A committee of the "Planters' Society" and a committee of ministers appointed by the King held several conferences exploring various sources for labor recruitment from Polynesia to Europe. By the end of 1864, a Bureau of Immigration was created by law. It was authorized to promote immigration from abroad, to supervise the importation of foreign laborers, and to regulate contracts with laborers.

The Bureau of Immigration acted immediately and its agent recruited more workers from China. Priority was given to bringing in more Polynesians; but when the efforts resulted in the arrival of only 126 men, women, and children, this idea was abandoned. Europe was eyed as a source, but it was too expensive to import European laborers. Not only was the cost of importing them great because of the distances, but they had Western views on wages and demanded more money and better living conditions. Therefore, the planters turned to Japan.

Meanwhile, W.C. Wyllie, a sugar planter who was also Foreign Minister under Kamehameha V, wrote to Eugene Van Reed, an American businessman in Japan, about importing laborers. Van Reed, who had been given the title of Consul General for Hawai'i, met difficulties as he tried to arrange a treaty which would allow him to recruit workers for Hawai'i's sugar plantations.

The Shōgun's (general's) government did not recognize him as an official of the Kingdom of Hawai'i. Japan was also still under the Seclusion Edict and any Japanese caught leaving the country was under penalty of death. Changing strategies, the Hawaiian Kingdom asked the U.S. Minister, General R.B. Van Valkenburgh, to deal with Japan on its behalf. Van Valkenburgh succeeded only in getting a temporary friendship treaty between Japan and Hawai'i.

Although he was without a treaty of emigration, Van Reed signed 300 men and women in the port city of Yokohama and got them their passports from the Shōgun's government. He was ready to ship them to Hawai'i when the Shōgun's government was dissolved after two centuries of being in power. Imperial rule was restored under Emperor Meiji in 1868.

The sailing vessel, Scioto, *transported the first group of Japanese plantation laborers who became known as the Gannen mono.*

From Y. Baron Goto's Gannenmono.

Van Reed was in a tight spot for a British ship, the *Scioto,* which he had chartered for $10,000, had already waited for ten days and each day's delay cost him more. The new government would not give him permission to sail. Neither did it recognize him as Consul General or the 300 passports that he had gotten from the old government.

The *Scioto* finally slipped out of Yokohama Bay without lights on the dawn of May 17, 1868. On board, bound for Hawai'i as the first Japanese plantation laborers, were 153 of the 300 people who had signed up. Among these Japanese immigrants were 146 men, five women who accompanied their husbands, and two teenage boys aged thirteen and fifteen. These 153 became known as the *Gannen mono,* meaning people of the first year of the Meiji era. They included a gardener, an artist, a wood cutter, a cook, servants, as well as fish and vegetable dealers, a few samurai or warriors, and only a few farmers. During the stormy voyage of thirty-five days, one man died; but a baby, Yotaro, was born so the total reaching O'ahu on June 19, 1868, remained 153.

The Japanese were taken to the immigration station for a physical examination. After processing, they were allowed a few days of rest and sightseeing in Honolulu. A few were employed as household servants in Honolulu homes, but the majority were

7

then assigned to plantations on different islands in groups of ten to thirty persons. The employers paid the Bureau of Immigration $70.00 for each worker in addition to the $10.00 they had paid in advance.

The agreement in the contract was:

> Three years service at monthly wages of four dollars per man, the thirty-six months to be counted from the day they arrived in Honolulu; . . . On the first of every month, counting from the day they left Yokohama, one half of their wages was to be paid to them and the remaining half paid by a note; but if the laborer should desire to receive this remainder, he was to make known his wish to his employer through the head man, and the money should be paid over to him in exchange for the note. Whatever was due to them at the end of their term was paid on their arrival at Yokohama, by the Hawaiian Consul General, who was to receive and care for them, until they returned to their homes.[1]

Tomisaburo Makino, the leader of the group, wrote to Yokohama saying, ". . . Since leaving the ship here, we have been treated with exceptional kindness, including gifts of food. We are all finding out for ourselves that Honolulu is a much better place to live than we had been told in Japan."[2]

The Japanese immigrants thought Honolulu in 1868 looked like a sleepy fishing village. They saw narrow streets lined with brick and wooden buildings – small Chinese shops, a fish market, a blacksmith shop, a post office. They saw taro patches, Chinese rice paddies, and groves of trees.

The *Hawaiian Gazette* in its June 24, 1868 issue described the way the people in Hawai'i saw the Gannen mono:

> At first glance these Japanese looked like good people. They were brimming with vigor and zest. These people from the Empire of Japan did not appear to have visited foreign countries before and strolled through the streets as if they were enjoying the novelty of it all very much.
>
> They are of a very polite race. They quickly took to our greeting, "Aloha!" and repeatedly returned the courtesy with "Aloha, Aloha."
>
> In spite of their shabby clothing, they did not appear to be timid in the least. On the whole they created a favorable impression and were greeted warmly by white residents and natives alike. It is hoped that they will turn out to be amiable and useful workers.

However, when the Japanese began working on the sugar plantations, the Islands were not as pleasant as they had first thought upon arrival. They had to work from dawn to dusk – twelve hours a day or more at jobs they were not acustomed to. They were not used to the scorching hot Hawaiian sun. One fourth of a day's work was subtracted from their pay for ten to fifteen minutes of tardiness, and two days' wages were deducted for each day's absence.[3] They did not know the land, nor the people. They had expected members from their own group to be their *lunas* (field bosses), but such was not the case. They did not understand the orders from the lunas because they were in English. They were often lashed with bullwhips for not obeying commands and when they did not keep working continuously. Even illness, if not severe, was not accepted as an excuse for staying away from work. They also found the price of goods to be very high. They were not able to save as much money as they had hoped; their wages were very low.

Stories of their mistreatment and troubles reached Japan. More than a year after the arrival of the Gannen mono in Hawai'i, the Japanese government sent a young man, Kagenori Uyeno, as a special envoy to Hawai'i to look into the welfare of the laborers. In talking with the workers on the plantations, he found most of the troubled stories to be true. He asked for the return of the laborers, especially because they had been brought to Hawai'i illegally without the Imperial Government's permission. The workers were badly needed on the plantations so the Hawaiian Kingdom assured better treatment including wages during illness, an increase in wages, and fines for whipping. Any unhappy Gannen mono was allowed to return to Japan. Forty out of the 153 decided to do so.[4]

In 1871, at the end of the three-year contract, thirteen more Gannen mono returned home. About ninety asked the Japanese government for passports to remain in Hawai'i. The experience of the Gannen mono was not the fully successful enterprise that the planters and laborers had hoped for, and seventeen years were to pass before another boatload of Japanese workers would disembark in Honolulu.

Grandfather
Toyokichi Fukumura

Father
Solomon Kenn

Son
Charles Kenn
Kenn Collection

Charles William Kenn
Grandson of a Gannen mono
and Hawai'i's First Living Treasure

Charles Kenn, a grandson of a Gannen mono, was selected in 1976 as the first "Living Treasure" by the Honpa Hongwanji in recognition of his unique accomplishments and contributions. Considered by many as a man who was decades ahead of his time in promoting and preserving Hawaiian culture, Charles Kenn is a highly respec-ted historian, teacher, translator, author, and poet, who is cited in thirty-eight *Who's Who* listings.

Part Hawaiian-Japanese-German, Charles Kenn is a direct descendant of Toyokichi Fukumura, a six-foot-tall son of a samurai, who migrated to Hawai'i in 1868. Toyokichi's father had fallen into disfavor because he had defended the Shōgun when the Emperor was restored to the throne. Eighteen-year-old Toyokichi, the eldest of five sons, was fearful of persecution by the Emperor's forces so he left their 800 acre farm in Edo, Japan, and migrated to Hawai'i on the *Scioto.* Eventually, like many members of the Gannen mono, he married a pure Hawaiian, Kahā Lu'ukia.

Toyokichi and Kahā had two children, Solomon and Mary. Solomon married Hawaiian-German Mine Haines and fathered six children. Their youngest child, Charles, was born on January 2, 1907. In 1916, when Charles William Fukumura was still in elemen-tary school, Solomon changed the family name to Kenn.

10

Charles Kenn graduated from McKinley High School in 1927 and from the University of Hawaii in 1931. He then attended Whittier College as the first exchange student from Hawai'i. While serving as an Associate Editor of the campus newspaper *Ka Leo,* at the University of Hawaii, he wrote articles on aspects of Hawaiian culture at a time when few, if any, realized the value of preserving the Hawaiian heritage. He also studied Hawaiian *ha'a* (called hula today) and performed at the Royal Hawaiian Hotel.

Charles Kenn served for many years as a parole social worker and a parole officer for juveniles for the Territory of Hawaii. He was appointed as the first Director of Hawaiian Activities for the City and County of Honolulu and was Vice-Chairman of the first and second Aloha Week Committees.

Today, Charles Kenn is recognized for his depth of knowledge about ancient Hawai'i in such divergent areas as religion, hula, and sports. He is considered the greatest living expert on the secret art of *lua,* ancient Hawaiian martial arts, and holds the distinction of being the last consecrated "Firewalker" left in Polynesia. Charles William Kenn is truly a "Living Treasure."

Charles Kenn
Interviewed in 1983

Chapter III
WAVES OF IMMIGRANTS

Meanwhile, the Hawaiian sugar planters became increasingly concerned with the high tariff that the United States government was imposing upon sugar. It mounted to as high as 30 percent. After much politicking, both in Hawai'i and in Washington, and after King Kalākaua's trip to Washington, D.C., the Reciprocity Treaty of 1876 was signed by the two countries. By terms of the Treaty, Hawaiian exports, including sugar, were to be allowed tariff free entry into the United States. Certain U.S. exports into Hawai'i would receive the same privilege. An important provision of the Treaty was that the Kingdom of Hawai'i would not make similar agreements with any other nation. Thus, Hawai'i became closely tied to and economically dependent on the United States.

With the Reciprocity Treaty, the Masters and Servants' Act, and the revolutionary laws pertaining to land ownership, the Hawaiian sugar planters were in a good position to conduct profitable operations. However, the securing of cheap labor in quantity continued to be a problem. From 1870 through 1884, the Japanese government did not permit any of its people to come to Hawai'i because of the problems encountered by the Gannen mono, its need for settlers in the newly developed northern province of Hokkaidō, and its desire to amend its unfavorable treaties with the Western nations which cast the Japanese as inferior people.

Chinese laborers were available and continued to migrate to Hawai'i, but soon there was concern because of their independent nature and their increasing numbers. By 1872, there were almost as many Chinese as Caucasians.

Portuguese, Pacific Islanders, Norwegians, Swedes and Germans were brought in to work on the plantations. For various reasons such as the cost of transportation and the selection of workers unsuited for field work, the planters looked to other sources for labor. Hence, efforts were continued to persuade the Japanese government to allow emigration.

It was within such an environment that King Kalākaua in 1881 stopped in Japan on his voyage around the world. He was

Map of Japan depicting prefectures from where many of Hawai'i's immigrants came.

Jane Komeiji

King Kalākaua and his party were photographed with Japanese dignitaries in Tokyo during his 1881 world tour. Seated left to right: Prince Yoshiaki Komatsu, King Kalākaua, Minister of Finance Tsunetami Sano. Standing left to right: Chamberlain C.H. Judd, First Secretary of Finance Ryosuke Tokuno, Foreign Minister and Commissioner of Immigration W.N. Armstrong. Hawaii State Archives

delighted to receive a royal welcome by Emperor Meiji. The two even shook hands – the first time in the history of Japan that the Emperor had shaken hands with a foreign ruler.

During a secret meeting that he had arranged with Emperor Meiji, King Kalākaua discussed some of the problems facing the Kingdom of Hawai'i and sought Japan's cooperation. He asked that:

1. Japan allow her people to emigrate to Hawai'i. Not only were they needed to supply labor on the sugar plantations, but they could augment the diminishing Polynesian population.
2. Japan join Hawai'i to organize a confederation of Pacific Area nations to strengthen and develop their governments and their economies.
3. A marriage arrangement be made between Princess Ka'iulani, his niece, and Prince Yamashina. Princess Ka'iulani was then five and the Prince was fifteen years. This action, he felt, would cement the relations between Hawai'i and Japan.[1]

Although the Emperor sent word politely declining the marriage proposal and postponing the opportunity to organize a confederation, the two nations developed a relationship of trust and friendship as a result of King Kalākaua's visit. In addition, after consulting his advisors, the Emperor sent word that Japan would be willing to insert a clause about the emigration of her people to Hawai'i at the revision of an earlier 1871 Friendship and Commerce Treaty. This, however, would have to wait until treaties with other Western nations, currently disadvantageous to Japan, were also revised.

The treaty revisions were accomplished in 1884. Captain Curtis I'aukea, Special Envoy to Japan from the Hawaiian Kingdom, received word from the Japanese government that arrangements could now be worked out for emigrants to be sent to Hawai'i for certain periods of time.

Special Envoy I'aukea rushed back to Hawai'i in June of 1884 and met with a group which included a representative of the plantations, two representatives from the Japanese workers, Consul Irwin, and himself to work on a contract proposal. The worker representatives spoke of their hardships such as the harsh terms of their contract, poor housing conditions, the lack of understanding by the employers, and the poor pay they received in comparison to workers from other racial groups.

The contract agreed upon in September, 1884, included the following: [2]

1. The Hawaiian government would pay for the transportation costs of the laborers and their families from Yokohama to Honolulu.
2. Contracts with the plantations were to be signed in Hawai'i.
3. Each immigrant was guaranteed three years of work at $9.00 per month for males and $6.00 a month for females. In addition, each male worker was to be given $6.00 and each female worker $4.00 per month for living expenses; thus the total monthly income for males was $15.00 and $10.00 for females.
4. The immigrants were to work for ten hours per day in the fields or twelve hours per day in the sugar mills for 26 days per month. Any person working for longer periods was to be given extra pay. Time required for travel to and from the work site was to be part of the working day.
5. The workers were to be given free medical care, housing, and firewood.
6. Twenty-five percent of each worker's pay was to be put into the bank. This money was to be used for emergencies or for their return to Japan.
7. The Hawaiian government would guarantee that rice would cost no more than five cents per pound.
8. The workers did not have to pay a head tax for three years.

Although the Japanese government agreed to the terms of the contract, it was made known that the agreement was not between the two governments, but between the individual emigrant and R.W. Irwin, a representative of the Hawaiian government. The planters were delighted, for at long last, they felt they could count on a supply of cheap, hard-working laborers.

In soliciting emigrant applications, the Japanese government sent out information about Hawai'i, its geography, its people and their feelings towards the Japanese, living conditions and the terms of the contract. Prospective workers were told that they must stay for the three-year duration of the contract, but that they could also stay for longer periods or become permanent residents, should they so desire. Transportation back to Japan was the responsibility of the worker. The information even included a list of articles each emigrant might find useful to take:

> Three sets each of ordinary wearing apparel, a short-sleeved kimono, a pair of tight fitting trousers, a set of summer nightwear, summer bedding and mosquito netting, miscellaneous personal items and perhaps pots and pans. (Information Regarding Emigration - Foreign Ministry, Japan-December, 1884). [3]

The Japanese government had expected about 600 persons to apply. Instead 28,000, particularly from Hiroshima and Yamaguchi Prefectures, applied. Conditions were especially bad in these two prefectures in Central Japan at that time. The price of rice had dropped, and many farmers were unable to pay their taxes and their land rentals. Many did not have enough to eat. Some had already left their homes to work in other parts of Japan, so emigration was not a new idea. The government selected 676 males, 150 females, and 110 children. Almost one-half of them were from the poor Yamaguchi Prefecture.

This group of *kanyaku imin* (contract immigrants), made up mostly of farmers, boarded the *City of Tokio* in Yokohama on January 20, and arrived in Honolulu on February 8, 1885, seventeen years after the Gannen mono. Also aboard was Jiro Nakamura, who was sent by the Imperial Government to establish a consulate in Hawai'i to oversee the welfare of the emigrants.

The immigrants were warmly welcomed – by the haoles, the Hawaiians, as well as by the Japanese who had been living in Hawai'i. King Kalākaua personally visited the new arrivals at the immigration facilities in Kaka'ako and even invited them to 'Iolani Palace to put on a kendō or fencing tournament for him. For this he gave each participant a silver dollar! Native Hawaiians greeted them with shouts of "Aloha" and gifts of clothing and food. They

1885 Kanyaku Imin Arrivals by Prefectures

During the first year of the Government Contract Period, 1885-1894, there were two vessels that arrived in Honolulu. On board were the following number of immigrants grouped according to their emigrating prefectures.

February 8, 1885	Vessel - City of Tokio	June 17, 1885	Vessel - Yamashiro Maru
Yamaguchi	428	Hiroshima	390
Hiroshima	222	Kumamoto	270
Kanagawa	214	Fukuoka	149
Okayama	37	Shiga	74
Wakayama	22	Niigata	37
Mie	13	Wakayama	33
Shizuoka	11	Kanagawa	12
Shiga	5	Gumma	10
Miyagi	1	Chiba	8
	945		983

Statistics from *Hawaii Nippon Jin Imin Shi*, 1964, pp. 313, 314.

Immigrants at landing as they embarked from the Miike Maru *in 1893.*

Hawaii State Archives

were processed in a speedy organized manner by the immigration officials. Plantation representatives were on hand at the immigration compounds to facilitate placement.

While waiting for the signing of the contracts on the various plantations, the immigrants were allowed to go sightseeing. Honolulu was then a quiet town with no horse carriages or railroads. According to Consul Nakamura's March 11, 1885 report to the Japanese government, some of the immigrants even went into the Royal Hawaiian Hotel,

> . . . shed their wooden clogs, sandals, slippers, shoes or whatever else they were wearing, arranged them in neat rows near the entrance, bowed low and went on a tour of the second and third floors, acting as if they were visiting a public hall. It is said that no one stopped or questioned them.

> . . . Although a few from the Tokyo and Yokohama areas wore Western style suits, the majority of them, being farmers from the rural districts, are completely indifferent as to the manner in which they are attired. Some wear hats, some drape bandanas over their heads to avoid the sun, while some carry fans to cool themselves with while walking. Women generally wear light kimonos, white short Japanese socks, and parasols to ward off the sun. I cannot but feel ashamed when I meet them on the streets. However, there is no class distinction in this country and the local residents seem to have accepted our peoples' peculiar attire and actions. Children do not tease or chase them on the streets.

17

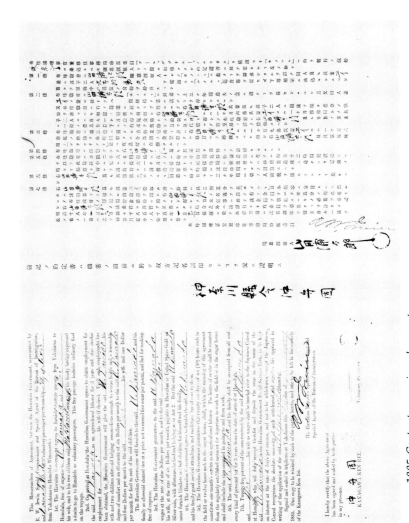

1885 Contract, a precious document.
This contract was issued to U. Yamada and wife who were members of the first kanyaku imin group.
Yamada Collection

By the 26th of February, all of the immigrants had signed their contracts, and had left Honolulu for their jobs. Many employers could not sign up as many workers as they desired, so anxiously awaited the arrival of the next shipload.

The Hawaiian government sent out a circular to the plantations with information about the Japanese people, their customs, and ways of dealing with them. It was suggested that the employers provide five gallons of hot water daily per person for bathing. They were not to place white or native lunas over these workers. It was noted that most of the workers were willing to work an extra 30 minutes per day if they were allowed to grow vegetables on a quarter of an acre each. Consul Nakamura of the Japanese Consulate and Consul Irwin of the Hawaiian government made an inspection tour of the various plantations on Maui in March and found that both the planters and the workers seemed happy.

However, in a short while, the situation once again deteriorated. The workers found the planters ignoring the provisions of the contract. Neither were they heeding the suggestions of the Hawaiian government. They had reverted to employment conditions under the Masters and Servants' Act in which they wielded total control over the lives of the laborers. Because some of the workers had been educated and were aware of the contract terms,

A group of field workers of mixed ethnicity paused to have their picture taken. Most of the Japanese women have their sickles in their hands. The luna remains in his usual stance on his horse.   Ethnic Studies Oral History Project

19

The Last Survivor Among the First Shipload of Kanyaku Imin

When Hazel Ume Yamada passed away on May 26, 1976, Hawai'i lost the last survivor from the group of 945 immigrants who had come aboard the *City of Tokio* in February, 1885. She arrived as a two-year-old and lived in Hawai'i for ninety years. She was the widow of George Mankichi Yamada who had also come on the same ship as a six-year-old.

Ume-san arrived in Honolulu in the arms of her parents, Torano-suke and Saka Suenaga, and the family was sent to Makee Plantation on Kaua'i to fulfill their contracts. In an interview in 1960, she recalled how her mother worked as hard at night as during the day. Saka endured strenuous physical labor on the plantation during the day, fed the family and took care of the household chores after work, and sewed late into the night.

After leaving the plantation, the Suenagas used their savings to start a grocery store in Kalihiwai on Kaua'i. Ume-san attended English school, but her parents' greatest concern was that she receive a proper Japanese education. On his buying trips to Honolulu as a successful businessman, Toranosuke met a highly respected wholesaler and intellectual, Saiji Kimura, and broached the subject of entrusting his daughter in his care so that Ume could study the Japanese language and learn manners befitting a well-bred Japanese lady. So, at age thirteen, Ume-san became Hawai'i's first Japanese "school girl," which later became a very common way for non-Honolulu students to work toward a Japanese or English education. When not in Japanese school, she was expected to do the chores in the Kimura household.

The first Japanese language school was begun in the parlor of a large two story structure which served as a classroom for Kazuo Kuwahara Sensei and his pupils. Thirty students of all ages were taught together. Most of them like Ume-san were arrivals on the *City of Tokio* in 1885 or born soon after their parents' arrival. A few younger immigrants, however, were superior academically because they were more recent arrivals and more proficient in Japanese from their schooling in Japan. The school became the Hawaii Nipponjin Gakkō (Hawaii Japanese School) and was later renamed Hawaii Chūō Gakuin. Ume's classmates included the older children of Reverend Okumura as well as Michie Okamura who later became the wife of Kinzaburō Makino.

When Mrs. Kimura decided to return to Japan, Ume could no longer reside in their household so she returned to Kaua'i. By this time, her parents were rice growers in Hanalei; and she returned to English school for a year. She had eight years of English schooling

George Mankichi and Hazel Ume Yamada. Their marriage brought together two people who came to Hawai'i as young children on the first 1885 shipload of kanyaku imin.

Yamada Collection

which was more than most girls received at that time. Because of this educational background, anyone meeting Ume for the first time was always impressed if not startled by her excellent pronunciation and fluency in English. In fact, many years later, at the age of seventy-seven, when she took the naturalization test, unlike most Japanese immigrants, she took it in English because her Japanese was rusty.

At age sixteen, Ume became the bride of twenty-three-year-old Mankichi Yamada. In those days Japanese girls married at around fourteen or fifteen. George Mankichi Yamada had also spent his youth on Kaua'i. He had graduated from Honolulu High School on Emma Street and was employed by Hawaii Ballast Company as an accountant when he married Ume. He was later appointed for a brief time as an interpreter for the traveling court. He finally became a contractor and the proprietor of a flourishing business. Ume and Mankichi were happily married until his death in 1926 at age 47. By this time he was well known as a contractor throughout the islands. The ensuing years were difficult ones for Ume, who was left with six children to raise. However, by careful management of the inheritance that her husband had left her, especially the rental units on their property, she survived to enjoy her children and her grandchildren for many years.

From information provided by Ed and Kay Yamada.

21

they led their fellow workers in complaining and demanding that the employers adhere to the agreements. Individual workers protested by feigning illness, engaging in slowdowns, setting fires to fields and mills, and occasional acts of violence. Small localized work stoppages were held protesting the lack of water, beatings, and being driven to work without rest. However, the protests fell on deaf ears and conditions did not improve. In fact, in some instances protestors were fined $6.00 for the first offense and $8.00 for subsequent offenses.

Morale was low among the workers. Many drank and gambled to ease the pain of hard work and the emptiness of their lives. Others deserted the plantations, only to be caught by the police and to be whipped, fined, imprisoned, and returned to work.

The Japanese government, upon learning of these conditions, sent Special Commissioner Katsunosuke Inouye to Hawai'i. Commissioner Inouye noted the workers' grievances which resulted in Japan's threat to stop sending more workers unless something was done immediately to protect the laborers. It even threatened to return to Japan the 988 immigrants who had just arrived on June 17, 1885, aboard the *Yamashiro Maru*.

Frightened by the possibility of termination of this labor source, the Hawaiian government quickly entered into an agreement with Japan and made the immigrants wards of the Hawaiian government and the planters its agents. It was further agreed that no ward of the government could be physically abused. Neither could he be arrested for breach of contract without the government's approval. Mr. Nakayama of the Bureau of Inspection was designated to make all necessary investigations and to handle the problems of the Japanese immigrants.

Japan did not allow further emigration until the conditions of the agreement were satisfactorily implemented. The next shipload, therefore, did not arrive until February 14, 1886, on the *Peking Maru*.

Between 1885 and 1894, which is known as the Government Contract Period, 29,069 kanyaku imin came on twenty-six sailings. Those who had come with the idea of returning to Japan rich after their three-year contracts found it increasingly difficult to do so. Wages were lower because of a tighter sugar market, the cost of living was high, and repayment to planters for transportation had to be made by those arriving after 1887. Many were forced to remain in Hawai'i upon expiration of their contracts, thus increasing the total Japanese population in the Islands. This unexpected increase of permanent residents worried the authorities. Of the 29,069 that had come during the Government Contract Period, only 8,171 had gone back to Japan. There were 1,773 deaths and 1,305 births, leaving the number remaining at 20,430. [4]

There was conflict between the needs of the planters and those of the Hawaiian government. The plantations needed large numbers of cheap workers while the government was now concerned about Hawai'i being taken over by the large number of Japanese and becoming Japan's colony. It was this fear that prompted the Hawaiian officials to once again tap China as its source of labor in 1892.

In March 1894, the Provisional government passed an act which required contract laborers to have written contracts and written approvals before being allowed to land. "Free Laborers" (those recruited by private immigration companies) were required to have $50.00 and visible means of support before being allowed entry. Furthermore, in June of 1896, in an effort to limit Japanese immigration, the government adopted a policy of requiring plantations to ask for laborers in the proportion of two-thirds Chinese to one-third Japanese.

Because of the increase in the number of emigrants to Hawai'i and an attendant increase in administrative work, the Japanese government turned over the recruiting and processing of workers to private emigration companies. The first group of emigrants to sail to Hawai'i under this new system consisted of 150 individuals who came on the *Ume Maru* through Itōhan, an importing firm. They were forced to sign three-year contracts with the plantations.

The Hawaiian government enforced the restrictions on subsequent arrivals. It questioned and examined each immigrant before issuing bangos (from the Japanese word *bangō* meaning number), metal tags on chains with identification numbers, to those meeting the provisions and denying others from entry. In 1897, over a thousand immigrants were thus returned to Japan! The Japanese government protested the denials on the basis of an earlier treaty and demanded compensation.

The Republic of Hawai'i was pressured by its desire to settle the issue before the passage in the U.S. Congress of the Newlands Resolution which provided for its annexation to the United States. It, therefore, paid an indemnity of $75,000 to the Japanese government. The Newlands Resolution was signed by President McKinley on July 7, 1898. Transfer of sovereignty took place on

per ss Kinau   Honolulu, HI   June 2 1890, /88

Mr C McLennan.
Laupahoehoe Sugar Co.

Dear Sir,

We have yours of 29th ult.

Lease Kua has been sent for record and will be returned to you when we get it back.

Japanese. Another small lot is coming but only enough to give about 75% of the balance due on old orders, and no new orders have the slightest chance of being filled. You cannot therefore count on getting the 50 that you wish for. On your original orders for 60 there is a balance of 11 due so you may expect about 8 more.

Goods ordered. These all go by ~~separate~~ invoice (herewith)

~~enclosed.~~ We cannot get the American Chow-chow, nor No 5 Frying pans, although we have some of the latter on our English Ship now discharging and will send the same as soon as possible. Kindly order again. Such cheap Cruppers as you name cannot be got in town. About $9 per doz is the lowest. At your price they would be worthless. With regard to the brake blocks we would say that we understand from your order that they are to be the same size as sample, but on the sample is a card on which is written 2" thick which we suppose that you wish them of this thickness. Please let us know if they are to be exactly as sample or to be 2" thick. We are unable to find any 2 star Hennessy Brandy. Will we send 3 star?

Coin ordered goes by bearer. Receipt enclosed. Note you order $15,000 silver, but this is of course meant for $1500 which we send.

We cannot get any 1" cultivator bolts, nor can we get any square heads. We send herewith a sample of what we can get. Let us know if they will do.

Lumber for N H R B will be shipped per "Lehua". Fertilizer from N Ohlandt & Co was shipped per "Hawaii" we hope it got to you all right.

Your Super-heaters are almost ready and the HIWCo wish to ship them. As you told us verbally that they could go up at any time we will ship them to you by the first opportunity.

Only one of your last lot of Japs was rejected, not 2 as we told you last week (May 23). You therefore got 34. 11477 was not rejected as we thought he was. Contracts go herewith.

Memo of Sugar received ex Kilauea Hou" May 23 is enclosed Receipt says 1573 bags more or less. We got less, viz, 1554.

Yours faithfully,
Theo H Davies Co

2

August 12, 1898, in Honolulu when the Hawaiian flag was lowered and the American flag was raised. Hawai'i was now the Territory of Hawai'i under the United States.

During the Private Contract Period (1894-1900), five immigration companies brought in most of the workers. It was a profitable business and the companies increased their earnings by bringing in as many workers as possible. The contract was between the immigration company and the immigrant. It included:

1. Compulsory deposits of $2.50 per month to the Keihin Bank in Honolulu for the duration of the contract. The funds were to be applied against outstanding loans and for passage back to Japan.
2. Delegation of power of attorney to the immigration company for access to the immigrant's account at the Keihin Bank.
3. Reimbursement to the immigration company in the amount of $35.00 per male and $30.00 for females to cover passage, should the worker terminate the agreement or leave his job. An additional $12.00 was collected for brokerage fees.

The contract was decidedly in favor of the companies. Besides receiving fees from the immigrants and the planters, the companies had banded together to organize the Keihin Bank to increase their profits. They were not concerned about the welfare of the workers, many of whom found themselves in debt for the first three years. The companies were often collecting on loans which the immigrants had not received at all. When the immigrants failed to make the payments on time, legal action was taken against them and their two guarantors in Japan.

The immigrants became incensed with the dishonest and unsympathetic tactics of the Keihin Bank and organized a Reform Association. In September, 1906, the Reform Association was successful in getting the Japanese government to force the Keihin Bank to cancel all agreements between itself and the immigrants and to restrain it from further activities. This eased the lot of the workers to some degree.

Chapter IV
TOO MANY JAPANESE?

Annexation brought stability to the political life of Hawai'i. As confidence in the government increased, confidence in the economy also grew. The sugar industry rode the crest and there was immediate expansion. The tonnage produced increased from 229,414 in 1898 to 360,038 in 1901, to 426,248 in 1905. Not only was more land needed, but more workers were needed to supply the growing industry.

In the two year period between Annexation and the passage of the Organic Act, the Constitution for the Territorial government, approximately 30,000 Japanese immigrants were hurriedly brought in. This was in anticipation of the abolition of the labor contract system by the Organic Act which not only forbade further importation of contract laborers, but also cancelled all existing contracts.

Japanese contract laborers at Honolulu awaiting a steamer to take them to the island of Hawai'i where an extensive new sugar plantation was recently opened, ca. 1899.
Hawaii State Archives

When the Organic Act was passed in 1900, the Japanese laborers were quick to recognize their new freedom. Several hundred of them on O'ahu marched to Honolulu a few days after passage of the Act and paraded with signs rejoicing in the abolition of the contract system and their new status as free people. They were delighted to be able to leave the plantations and to look for work elsewhere, should they choose to do so.

In the ensuing months there were also many small strikes as the workers recognized their right to collective bargaining. They struck for an increase in wages, better working conditions, reinstatement of discharged workers, and employment of Japanese lunas.

The Hawaiian Sugar Planters' Association (HSPA), which had been organized in 1895 to do agricultural research, to help with management, and to regulate wages, counseled planters to handle the Japanese with dignity. But, it was difficult for the planters and the lunas to change their thinking and their ways. Therefore, working conditions did not improve appreciably. Although profits to the planters increased, the laborers shared only in a small part of them.

Dissatisfied and unhappy, some left the plantations and became salesmen, carpenters, shopkeepers, and general laborers in the villages and towns. By 1907, over 40,000 had left for employment on the mainland U.S. where there also was a labor shortage. Employment brokers who represented employers on the West Coast solicited workers among the Hawaiian laborers. In the Seattle-Tacoma area, wages quoted were $1.25-$1.35 for work on the railroads, and $1.00-$1.25 with room and board in the salmon canneries for a day's work, while strawberry and tomato picking and domestic work in the San Francisco area promised wages of $1.50 a day. These wages were tempting since the Japanese laborers were receiving only sixty-nine cents for a ten hour work day.[1]

Compounding the problem was the outbreak of bubonic plague among the immigrants of Honolulu, most of whom lived in a section known as Chinatown. Many died. Others lost their homes and belongings in the "sanitary fire" of January, 1900. The health officials had determined that burning the infected area was the only way to curb the spread of the disease. Careful preparation had been made by the Board of Health to contain the fire to a portion of Chinatown. However, a sudden shift in the wind blew the fire out of control. The entire twenty blocks of the city known as China-

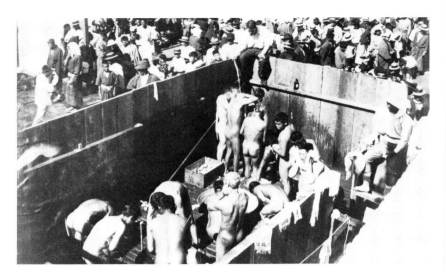

January 1900 during the bubonic plague.   *Hawaii State Archives*

THE PASSING OF CHINATOWN.

The burnt area now covers all the blocks except the ones marked in

Hawaii State Archives

Behind the Store-Front Scene in Chinatown. There was much interaction among the families in the area behind the store fronts. Mothers gossiped as they did their laundry while children devised ways to amuse themselves.

Hawaii State Archives

Chinatown Before Fire
Upon leaving the plantations, the Japanese congregated in the Chinatown area along with the Hawaiians and the Chinese. The family living quarters were above the shops which were on the street level.

Hawaii State Archives

town was demolished. About 6,000 residents, 3,500 of whom were Japanese, escaped with only the clothes on their backs. Merchants lost not only their residences but their businesses. Using bubonic plague as the reason, the Japanese government discouraged emigration. From the high of over 25,000 in 1899, the number of emigrants dropped to under 3,000 in 1900. Once again there was a critical labor shortage.

The planters petitioned in vain to Congress to modify the 1882 Chinese Exclusion Act which prohibited Chinese immigration to the United States. They suggested that Chinese laborers be allowed to come for five-year periods to work and then to be shipped home. This would not only aid the sugar industry but would lessen the threat of a "take-over" by the large Japanese population. Although the Issei were ineligible for citizenship, their second generation American-born children, Nisei, were citizens by birth and would be able to participate fully in the government regardless of their customs and beliefs. With a large enough Chinese labor supply and no employment, the Japanese would go home. However, Congress did not think it was a good idea to meet the danger of the Japanese by bringing in more Orientals of another kind.

President Theodore Roosevelt, in a message to Congress in December, 1905, said that:

> . . . the Territory has serious commercial and industrial problems to reckon with; but no measure of relief can be considered which looks to legislation admitting Chinese and restricting them by statute to field labor and domestic service . . . Hawaii shall never become a Territory in which a governing class of rich planters exists by means of coolie labor. Even if the rate of growth of the Territory is thereby rendered slower, the growth must only take place by the admission of immigrants fit in the end to assume the duties and burdens of full American citizenship.[2]

Failing in their attempts to bring in more Chinese, the planters brought in Portuguese and Spanish workers, but many of those who came also left Hawai'i for the Mainland. To solve their dilemma, the planters turned to the Philippines, an American protectorate since the Spanish-American War of 1898, as their source of cheap labor. Filipinos were classified as nationals, hence were free to enter Hawai'i, a U.S. Territory, to join the labor force. The 1900 census showed no Filipinos, but by 1910, 2,361, mostly males, were living in Hawai'i.

Emigration from Japan gradually increased again through 1906.

In 1907, because of the desire of the Hawaiian planters to curb migration of laborers to the mainland United States and because of the hostility against the Japanese in California, primarily caused by their willingness to work long hours at low wages, a new Immigration Act and the Gentlemen's Agreement came into being. Japan agreed to stop issuing passports to laborers bound for America – the Territory of Hawaii was a part of America. Only former residents, their immediate family members, and persons with established farming interests would be allowed to enter the United States. Laborers with passports to Mexico, Canada, and Hawai'i were excluded from the mainland U.S. In turn, America agreed not to openly discriminate against the Japanese. Japanese children were to be allowed in the public schools along with children of other races.

Continued pressure from West Coast anti-Japanese advocates resulted in the passage of the Japanese Exclusion Act of 1924 by Congress. Whereas the 1907 Immigration Act was a partial exclusion which allowed the entry of certain groups of immigrants, the 1924 Exclusion Act prohibited any Japanese from entering the U.S. to work or to live. It halted all Japanese immigration.

Chapter V
LIFE ON THE PLANTATIONS

Mother and child in front of their home in Japanese plantation village, ca. 1890.

Charles Furneaux – Bishop Museum

Life on the plantations even during the late 1890s was not easy. Living and working conditions were dependent on the manager's disposition and varied from plantation to plantation. In general, the Japanese, as it was true of other late arrival immigrant groups in other lands, were in the smallest and shabbiest houses and were paid the least. Like other immigrant groups, the Japanese were also segregated. They lived and worked among their own kind. Contact with persons of other racial groups was limited to a laborer-supervisor or a customer-merchant relationship. Planters deliberately kept the racial groups apart to keep each group in its place in the plantation hierarchy and to promote competition. In some ways, the Japanese were happy living and working amongst their own, for they were able to communicate in their own language and were able to carry on some of their Japanese customs and traditions.

There was a disproportionate ratio of men to women. Most of the men were bachelors who had come with the idea of making fast money and returning to Japan. After hours of work in the hot sun, they came home to barrack-type quarters which they shared with other lonesome men. They slept on multi-tiered bunks and kept their worldly possessions in the *kōri* (wicker baskets) in which they had brought their belongings. Some did their own cooking and laundry, but most of them paid part of their salaries to the wives of other workers for laundry services and meals, including a *bentō* lunch to take to the fields. Married couples received small rooms. There was little or no family life. All in all, everybody lacked privacy.

Women's Hanahana Outfit

I'm pictured here, second from the left in my *hanahana* (work) clothes at 'Ewa Plantation in the 1920s. Okā-san sewed my *shigoto gi* (working clothes) on her sewing machine, the type that you pumped back and forth with your feet. She also sewed men's working *tabis* (cloth footwear) to sell to single men. In dressing for work in the sugar cane fields, our biggest worry was to keep out the centipedes and other things from crawling inside. The clothes also had to protect us from the irritating fuzz on the sugar cane and the sharp edges of the leaves.

This is how I dressed for work: 1) I put on long tight cotton pants. 2) I put on my tabis and tightened the drawstring. 3) I firmly wound a *kyahan* (knee to ankle leg wrapping) and tied it to keep the centipedes from crawling between the pants bottom and the tabis. 4) I put on my long sleeved shirt, and 5) I put on my short striped cotton *hakama* (skirt) which was about an inch or two below the knee. 6) I wrapped an *obi* (cumberbund) firmly around my waist so that nothing could creep in between my shirt and skirt. Sometimes in unwrapping the *obi,* we found centipedes and other insects. 7) I tied on the *te oi* (arm cover which extended from my finger joints to the elbow) to keep bugs out of my sleeves and to prevent the back of the hands from getting cut. I did not wear gloves. 8) I then covered my head with a white muslin cloth, put on my *papale* (hat), and put a pin through the hat to hold everything down. The papale styles differed from plantation to plantation. Some had wide brims while others were like bonnets. Because we wanted to keep our complexion fair and our faces from being scratched by the sharp leaves, we covered our faces with a man's handkerchief when we worked. Only our eyes were exposed. Nowadays, they wear goggles.

I came from Japan at age ten in 1915. I started to work in the fields at age thirteen by faking my age because I was tall. I helped my father on the contract system with hāpai kō by piling up the heavy cane stalks and by helping to load the cane on Otō-san's shoulders. During certain months of the year, I also worked for the plantation as a "water boy." We filled the square cans with water at the upper end of the ditches where the water was cleaner. I also delivered the bentō at lunchtime because the men stacked them in a pile when they arrived in the morning. My job included getting the workers' bangos for the timekeeper. As I got older, I moved from "water boy" to *hoe hana.*

Haruno Nunogawa Sato
Interviewed on November 4, 1984

Bachelor Laborer's Life circa 1900

I first arrived in Honolulu on the *Lennox* on September 15, 1899, through the Morioka Imin Gaisha. Along with fifty others from

Niigata Ken, I was sent to Kealia, Kaua'i at $15.00 per month. . . . Seven of us stayed in one room in the *nagaya* (long house). At first we spread *goza* (straw mats) on the floor to sleep. Then I bought a straw bed for 50 cents at the company store. The cotton pants and *yukata* (cotton kimono) which I had brought with me were not suitable for the fields so I bought a pair of *tabis* (socks) at 25¢ and *ahina* (denim) pants and shirt at $1.50 on credit. The purchases were deducted from my pay. . . . By the way, we were paid in coins.

. . . In 1900 when we were free to break our contracts, I went to work for Chōkichi Ueyama, a contractor from Niigata. I worked at clearing fields and building a mill in the Kōloa area. I was paid $1.00 a day, which added up to more than the $18.00 a month that other employers were paying. The work day was from 6:00 a.m. to 2:30 p.m. with 30 minutes for lunch.

. . .One of the married women packed lunch for me in a stack of round metal containers about five inches in diameter. On one layer she packed rice and *ume* (pickled plum). In another she usually had *nimame* (cooked beans) and *nishime* (vegetables cooked in shōyu). Occasionally there was fish. She also provided a bottle of tea. I paid the woman $6.00 for meals, 30 cents for *furo* (bath), and 75 cents for laundry per month.

. . . There were only a few women. Only about two out of 100 men were married. Some of the women made *manjū* (bean cake) and sold them house to house on Sundays.

Tomonosuke Takahashi - Age 90.
Interviewed in 1974

The day started with blasts from the mill whistle at 4:30. The working day was from 6:00 a.m. to 4:30 p.m. with a half-hour for lunch. They wore layers of shirts and pants, arm guards, denim *tabis* (socks), and hats to protect themselves from the sharp-edged cane leaves. The workers carried their tools and their lunch cans over their shoulders in *ahina* (denim) bags as they rode on railway cars or walked to the fields in gangs of twenty to thirty. They planted (pula pula), weeded (hoe hana), fertilized, watered, stripped cane leaves (hole hole), harvested by cutting with a cane knife (kachi cane), and loaded (hāpai kō) the sugar cane, which had taken eighteen months to two years from planting to harvesting. The work was simple, but it was hard work made more difficult by the weather – be it the hot sun or the driving rain. Those in charge of the welfare of the laborers were generally unsympathetic. Each laborer was referred to by his assigned number, bango, and never by his name during working hours. The constant

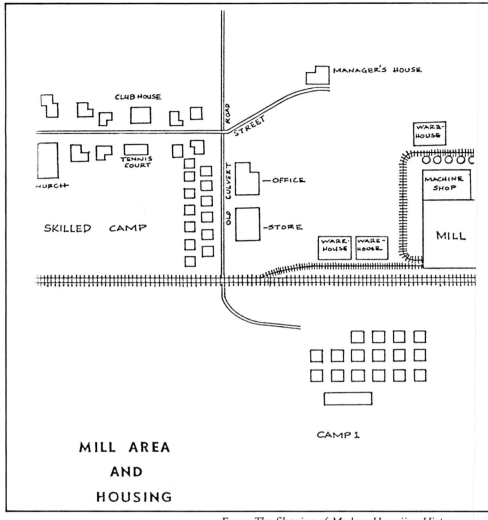

Text inside figure:

MANAGER'S HOUSE

CLUB HOUSE

STREET

ROAD

WARE-HOUSE

TENNIS COURT

CHURCH

OFFICE

OLD CULVERT

MACHINE SHOP

SKILLED CAMP

STORE

MILL

WARE-HOUSE WARE-HOUSE

CAMP 1

MILL AREA
AND
HOUSING

From *The Shaping of Modern Hawaiian History*

goading by the lunas to the tune of "hai-go, hai-go" (hurry up, hurry up) did not allow any moments of rest outside of lunch time (kau kau time). They were not allowed to talk or even to stretch their backs. Often the mules were given better care than the workers. One plantation manager on the Island of Hawai'i even said the death of one or two contract laborers did not concern him as much as the care needed by his mules, which cost $1,000 each.

The plantations paid wages to workers depending on their ethnic backgrounds. At the top were those in management and supervisory jobs – Americans, Englishmen, Scots, and Germans.

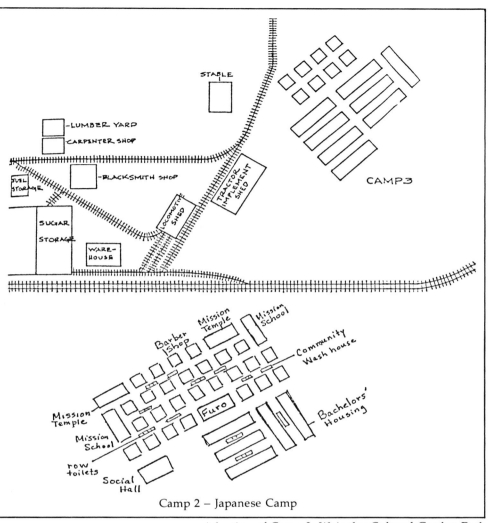

Camp 2 – Japanese Camp

Adaption of Camp 2. Waipahu Cultural Garden Park

The 1888-1890 report of the President of the Board of Immigration to the Governor of Hawai'i gave the following monthly wages for laborers:[1]

Ethnic Group	Contract Laborers	Free Laborers
Portuguese	$19.53	$22.25
Hawaiian	18.58	20.64
Chinese	17.61	17.41
South Sea Islanders	15.81	18.56
Japanese	15.58	18.84

Field work was hot and back breaking. Some of the laborers worked without the protection of gloves and tabis. *Women often sang the plaintive lyrics of the* **hole hole bushi** *to take their minds off the pain and hard work.* *Arakawas Collection*

Hole Hole Bushi

Hole hole bushi were songs which were developed and sung by the immigrant laborers in the fields. In the songs, the workers bared their hearts and described their working conditions, their frustrations, and their anxieties. The verses often incorporated Japanese, Hawaiian, and English words. They were sung to a melody from Hiroshima Prefecture.

Kane wa kachiken	My husband cuts the cane stalks,
Washa horehoreyo	And I trim the leaves,
Ase to namidano	With sweat and tears we both work,
Tomokasegi	For our means.
Ikkai Nikai de	Those who came on First and Second ships,
Kaeranu mono wa	And still don't go back home to Japan,
Sue wa Hawaii de	Will become fertilizer at the end
Poi no koe	For the poi plants.
"Okure okure" wa	"Send us money, send us money!"
Kuni kara no tegami	Is the usual note from home.

Nan de okuraryo	But how can I do it
Kono zama de	In this plight?
Honomu goku raku	Honomu is paradise,
Papaikou jigoku	Papaikou is hell,
Hilo no Waiakea	But Hilo's Waiakea
Hito goroshi	Is murdering me.
Ryokō-menjō no	Though I checked what's written
Uragaki mita ga	On my passport,
Mabu o suruna to	It doesn't say a word that I can't have
Kaicha nai	A secret lover.

The Horehore-Bushi. Social Process in Hawaii, 28:110-120
Yukuo Uyehara

Red Ants in My Lunch

Yeah, water. All most time water. The guy was job, see. Water and then lunch. They go bring 'em. So we go make *hoe hana* like that, all over they go, eh, and then they go take 'em down. Way down the other side, see. And then, about *kokoraga* lunch *ni naruyutoka,* the field *no* way down the other side, *ni oite oru,* eh (And then when they reach just about this spot, it will be lunch time, and the lunch is way down on the other side of the field). Sometime, you know, the lunch *ga no,* red ant, they go inside. Hoo, you look, hoo boy, all the lunch *dake de omottekara yorokonde akeru* (Hoo boy, you look, hoo boy, when you think about lunch, you open the lunch so eagerly). *Miru,* eh red kind – ant *ga minna haitoru* (Then you see red kind - ant; red ants are all over the food). You no can eat, eh. Hoo, boy, goddam, no can do nothing! All *kokoraga kaburareru,* eh (All this got bitten by ants). *Ana koto ga* three, four time *gurai attoruyo* (That kind of thing happened three, four times). Yeah, plenty guys *atta yo* (Yeah, that happened to a lot of guys).

Noriyu Koga
Waialua-Haleiwa Ethnic Studies
Oral History Project, p. 664

Frustrated, lonesome, and unhappy about their living and working conditions, men gambled, played *hanafuda* cards, drank, and fraternized with prostitutes. All night drinking and gambling sessions were common, especially after pay days. Fights erupted

Kau kau *time was a welcome break. The lunch tins were carried in* ahina *bags.*
R.J. Baker, Bishop Museum

when the men were drunk or when they could not pay off their gambling debts.

Because the work in the fields was boring and the conditions very poor, some feigned illness and did not report to work. Drinking shōyu to raise the body temperature was a common ploy. Plantation policemen came around to check on the absentees and often forcibly took even sick men out to work in the fields, for besides being unsympathetic, they often could not differentiate between a sick person and one who pretended to be sick. There were incidents where men collapsed and died while working. Shirkers were sometimes locked in rooms without food or water. When released, they were put to work at the most vigorous manual jobs.

Others attempted to run away from the plantation. Some of these made it to other plantations, especially those in Waimānalo on Oʻahu or Kona on Hawaiʻi where they could become "Free Laborers." Running away was not an easy task, as all of the plantations had policemen who were on the lookout for deserters. Travel usually had to be done at night. The deserter also had to find sympathetic people along the journey who would give him food and protection when needed. This was risky for the deserter and the person coming to his aid, since both would be severely punished should they be caught. When caught, the deserter was taken back to his plantation, whipped, fined, and imprisoned.

List of Deserters

Laupahoehoe, H. I. Jany 18th 1898
We hereby certify that the following Japanese laborers, under contract to us, have deserted service on the dates as set forth in the following:

No.	Name	Date of Desertion
964	Chikashige Chikaji	Nov. 26/97
978	Kawamura Nagojiro	Dec. 28/97
975	Sumidani Tsuyajiro	Nov. 1/97
985	Muraoka Masutaro	Dec. 28/97
989	Yoshida Tokutaro	Dec. 28/97
996	Yamasaki Seiichi	Dec. 28/97
1005	Nakamura Nadamatsu	Dec. 28/97
1012	Saiki Isaburo and wife Natsu	Dec. 2/97

Laupahoehoe Sugar Co.
Manager

Theo H. Davies Co. Plantation Records, Bishop Museum

Still others saved their money and purchased their freedom in order to escape the hard life on the plantations. As time went on, the managers realized that the Japanese, as a whole, were hard workers. The plantations needed them, but many had started to leave the fields. In order to entice the workers to remain, and to curb their desire to unionize and to strike, the planters offered incentive plans. Under the *ukupau* system, a group of workers was assigned a certain amount of work. No matter what time of day it was, they were free to go home as soon as they finished that amount. In some other arrangements, workers were paid for the amount of work they did. The more they worked, the greater was their pay.

By 1892, another system known as tenant cane growing was introduced. Under this "kompang" system, a group of men were assigned a certain acreage. The company supplied the equipment, water, and fertilizer. The workers lived in plantation houses and were paid basic wages. When the cane was harvested, the group received further monies, depending upon the tonnage produced and the price agreed upon. The Japanese worked even harder under the incentive plans, and they were paid more, but it was still a meager, hard life.

Contract System

All contract, see. One – I think I remember one big load, eh, fifty cents. That one train, train *no* one big load *itte hoo boy* (What they called one big train load, hooboy)! *Ame ga futtara* (When it rained), boy you stiff, eh. *Ippai naru ke* (The rain filled up the cane box cars). *Nani wo hapai shite ikunoyo,* see (You go and carry, see). *Kibi no uwe ni agatte, ano . . .* stepladder *wo* (Get up on that sugar cane train. . . . using stepladder). *Sore ga kondo suberuno yo* (The stepladder sometimes became slippery so) you go fall down. *Kibi ippai kakaeta* (While carrying an armful of sugar cane), fall down from the top. You watch out, you know, plenty guys injure *shita no ga aru* (get injured).

Noriyu Koga
Waialua-Haleiwa
Ethnic Studies Oral History Project, p. 665.

Annexation of Hawai'i to the United States in 1898 and the passage of the Organic Act, the basic constitution for the Territory of Hawaii in 1900, ushered in many changes including the abolition of the contract system and the gaining of the right to strike. Recognizing their rights, the Japanese staged many strikes for varied reasons. In 1900 alone, there were twenty labor strikes. All of these were spontaneous local strikes over specific incidents. The first organized and planned strike of Japanese laborers took place in Waipahu in May, 1904, when the workers were forced to buy lottery tickets from their lunas. The strike at Lahaina in 1905 was over mistreatment by the lunas, and the killing of one Japanese worker and the wounding of several others by plantation guards. In the four-day Waipahu strike, the lunas resigned, whereas in the Lahaina situation, the grievances were settled through negotiations.

The first major strike, that of 1909, was called after eight months of unsuccessful meetings and negotiations on higher wages and the discriminatory wage system. It involved most of the O'ahu plantations. In 1908, the Japanese were being paid $18.00 per month while the Portuguese and the Puerto Ricans were receiving $22.50 for the same type and amount of work. Besides, the latter groups were in better houses and were given the use of an acre of land each. The employers justified these differences on the basis that Orientals had a lower standard of living. Furthermore, they said that the wages being paid the Japanese were much better than those they would be getting in their native country.

Beginning in the fall of 1908, some of the Japanese newspapers such as the *Nippu Jiji* and the *Hawaii Nichi Nichi* carried articles suggesting an increase in wages. Writing in the *Nippu Jiji*, Motoyuki Negoro, an attorney, contended that the wages were exceedingly low, especially in light of the large profits that the planters were making. Negoro asked the Japanese government to intercede on behalf of its citizens who were being exploited. He further asked that the Japanese government seek a repeal of the Immigration Act of 1907, which prohibited the emigration of workers from Hawai'i to the mainland U.S. In order to spread the higher wage sentiment, a Higher Wage Association was formed in Honolulu and was followed by similar groups on the other islands. The Higher Wage Association submitted a demand for an increase in wages to the Hawaii Sugar Planters' Association. The *Pacific Commercial Advertiser* and the *Evening Bulletin*, the mouthpieces for the planters, called the demands "extraordinary and foolish."

Not all of the Japanese newspapers agreed with the Higher Wage Association. When the Planters' Association continuously ignored the demands, the workers at 'Aiea and Waipahu went out on strike on May 11 and 12, 1909. On May 16, 1909, they were given notices to return to work or to vacate the plantation houses by the 22nd. The strikers moved out, mostly to Honolulu where they were fed and housed by the members of the Higher Wage Association. Workers at Waialua, Kahuku, Wai'anae, and 'Ewa also went on strike. By June, 5,000 persons were in Honolulu under the Association's care. Laborers on the other islands did not strike. However, they formed sympathizers' clubs and assisted those on strike by sending words of encouragement, food, clothing, and money. The strike leaders including attorney Negoro and Yasu-taro Soga, editor of the *Nippu Jiji*, were imprisoned as dangerous persons.

The planters hired Chinese, Hawaiians, Koreans, Portuguese, and some Japanese as strike breakers at $1.50 per day. Some of the planters were willing to negotiate but could not do so as they were members of the HSPA, the Hawaii Sugar Planters' Association. The Association's stand was firm. It would make no concession for the demands called for paying higher wages to laborers who were not willing to do a substantial day's work. Nothing would be negotiated as long as the workers were on strike.

By the end of July, the strikers realized they could not continue

An early court interpreter. ca. 1900. Having arrived as a youngster in 1885 and being proficient in English and Japanese, George Mankichi Yamada had the qualifications for this highly regarded position. He is shown in the center with a hat next to a wagonload of newly arrived immigrants. When he served as the interpreter during the 1909 strike, he was viewed with suspicion by the Japanese laborers who did not understand his role.

Yamada Collection

to stay out much longer as their funds were low. After an emergency meeting of representatives from all the islands, the strike was called off on August 5, 1909. Even before that, small groups were forced to return to work due to lack of money. The strike had lasted about three months and cost the strikers and supporters $40,000. It had cost the planters over $2,000,000!

Soon after the termination of the strike, conditions did improve. Payments to workers were increased from $18.00 to $20.00 per month; a bonus system was introduced; the tenant farming system was improved; and housing and general sanitation conditions were upgraded. Plantation managers were also encouraged by the HSPA to provide recreational and amusement activities for the laborers and their families.

The planters increased their efforts to get more Caucasian workers, for they felt that maintaining a balance of races was the best insurance against strikes and labor troubles. They were successful only to the extent that they were able to get the Caucasians to come to Hawai'i. The Caucasian laborers were lured by better wages and more opportunities on the mainland U.S. More than 50 percent left for the continent, particularly the West Coast.

Non plantation leaders of the 1909 strike were imprisoned in the Honolulu Jail. All of the men except Attorney Negoro were newspaper men. Front row, left to right: Yokichi Tasaka, Yasutaro Soga. Back row, left to right: Genshi Negoro, Kinzaburō Makino.

Biography of Fred Makino

The assassination of Archduke Francis Ferdinand in Austria set off World War I during the summer of 1914. During the early days of the war, President Wilson declared America's neutrality. It was a difficult position to maintain because America was involved financially and commercially with the countries that were at war.

German submarines unlawfully attacked unarmed American commercial steamers continually and finally on April 6, 1917, the United States entered the war on the side of the Allies. The American people had watched the war and had known that their neutrality could not last. They, therefore, had begun preparations. The National Defense Act was passed on June 3, 1916.

When the Selective Service Act was passed, more than 27,000 men in Hawai'i signed up on the first day of registration. Of that number 11,000 were non-citizen Japanese and 596 were Nisei. A Japanese Company for the First Regiment of the National Guard was formed.

Other Japanese, aliens and citizens alike, participated fully in the war effort. They bought savings stamps and bonds, participated in Red Cross activities, and worked towards assuring a continuous food supply. The latter was a crucial problem for Hawai'i raised

45

very little of what it consumed. Most of the food, including the staples, needed to be imported.

With increased war activities, the economy improved and the cost of living rose. The sugar workers found it increasingly difficult

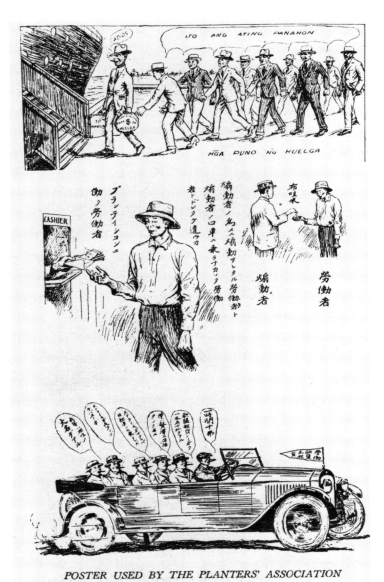

POSTER USED BY THE PLANTERS' ASSOCIATION

This propaganda poster was used by the planters during the 1920 strike. The Japanese and Filipino writing emphasize that it is not the workers who would benefit from the strike, but the outside agitators who would.

Hawaii State Archives

to meet the rising costs. During the summer and fall of 1917, the Higher Wages Society was organized and the plight of the workers was brought to the planters' attention. Besides higher wages and changes in the bonus system, they asked for the establishment of day care centers to enable more wives to work to supplement the family income.

However, the planters ignored the demands, declaring that it was not the workers who were asking but the newspapers and others in the community who were interfering. According to the planters, the complaint about the low wages came as a complete surprise. They felt that establishing nurseries was not their responsibility. Although these were significant problems, they were overshadowed by the war.

The workers were patriotic and believed that cooperation by all segments of the nation was important towards winning the war. Hence, it was not until after the victory that demands were renewed. A newly formed Japanese Federation of Labor presented the following demands:[2]

1. An increase in wages from 77 cents to $1.25 per day for men and 95 cents for women.
2. Retention of the bonus system with some changes.
3. An eight hour work day.
4. Leave with pay for two weeks prior to and six weeks after delivery for women.
5. Double wages for Sundays, holidays, and overtime.
6. Changes in the cane growing contract to 40 percent of market price to planters and 60 percent to workers after deducting marketing costs.
7. Proportionate increases in prices paid to cane growing contractors.
8. Improvement in health and recreational. facilities.

The recently organized Filipino Labor Union also prepared a demand for higher wages and presented it separately to the Planters' Association. While repeated efforts at negotiations were still being made, the Filipinos, under the leadership of Pablo Manlapit, went on strike on January 17, 1920. The Japanese called a general lay-off. Finally a strike was called by the Japanese Federation two weeks later, when once again their requests were turned down. The Secretary of the HSPA had even turned down a request for an interview. The workers at 'Aiea, Waialua, Waipahu, 'Ewa, and Waimānalo struck on February 1 of the same year.

Soup Kitchen

Taisho Gakkō, *asoko ga* before *no* strike *no* Waialua *no* main office *ni natta* (Taisho Gakkō became the headquarters of the strike in Waialua). *Ako de* cook *shitari, nanka shitari* (People cooked and also did other daily living activities there). *Soshite* all over *akora henni minna* striker *ga atsumattotan* (And that's where the strikers assembled). Twin Bridge *kara,* all outside *ni,* no more plantation house, eh (From Twin Bridge on, there were no plantation houses). No can go, stay inside there, 'as why all outside *ni,* Haleiwa *ni, itte soshite asoko made aruite kite,* and lunch *yara,* supper *yara, asoko kara moraiyottayo* (That's why we had to walk there for our supper and lunch).

Hode (So) young kids *wa,* you got to peel the potato and rice cook, and. . . . *yasai* (vegetables) – go buy the *yasai.* All truck *de kara, itte areraga* drive *narota no koro* (That's when some of them learned to drive a truck). Me *yori ka* one, two guys *ga hotondo arukiyota* (Me and a couple of other guys mostly walked). But me, *mada* young *dattake* (But I was still too young). I no more chance to drive.

Noriyu Koga
Waialua-Haleiwa Ethnic Studies Oral History Project
p. 666.

On February 18, two weeks after the strike was called by the Federation, the planters issued an eviction order for those not sick, who did not report to work within 48 hours. Over 10,000 men, women, and children left their homes after the plantations threw out their furniture and other household goods and nailed the doors. Under these circumstances even those who were sick with the flu carried their personal belongings and moved out.

To leave the plantation, however bad the conditions, was a tough decision; but the workers were determined. They were being treated too shabbily. Some moved to neighboring villages to be with independent and sympathetic fellow Japanese. Others went to Honolulu. Some 6,000 strikers and their families, including some Filipinos, were housed in various temples, churches, and a *sake* (rice wine) brewery. However, the brewery, which was home for 300 persons, was declared unfit by the Board of Health; and the people were moved to a tent city in Kalihi. It was at the height of the flu epidemic and over 20 percent were ill at one time or another. Many died.

The planters made every effort to crush the Japanese Federation and the strike. They did their best to fan an anti-Japanese feeling in the community by accusing the Japanese of trying to take over the sugar industry and even the Islands generally – both politically and industrially. At one point Pablo Manlapit was so influenced that he even called his Filipinos off the strike and joined the employers in decrying the selfishness of the Japanese movement. He said that the Japanese were interested only in promoting their own welfare and failed to support the Filipinos' requests. The Filipino workers, however, were not swayed by Manlapit's leadership and stayed out. Manlapit, five days later, retracted his statements. His union, however, had been weakened considerably.

Concerned, not only with the economic dilemma, but with the racial and social overtones and consequences of the strike, a group, consisting of six Japanese and Caucasians from the community at large and under the leadership of Dr. Albert W. Palmer of Central Union church, submitted a proposal to the HSPA and the Japanese Federation. It called upon the planters to establish a committee of representatives of labor to confer with the plantation managers. The group asked that voting for these committee members be by secret ballot. It also asked the Japanese Federation to call off the

Women laborers marched down Depot Road in Waipahu and boarded the train to A'ala Park to join the strikers' rally. April, 1920.   *Arakawas Collection*

strike and to work towards an organization of workers along inter-racial lines.

On February 27, 1920, the Japanese Federation agreed to accept the plan, but it was not until the end of June that John Waterhouse, President of HSPA, sat down with the representatives of the Hawaii Laborers' Association, the successor to the Japanese Federation of Labor. The planters, decrying the dangers of alien control of the sugar industry, refused to negotiate while the strike was on. It was costly, but they were able to withstand it. Although no terms were agreed upon, the workers, citing their belief in the planters' sincerity, surrendered and terminated the strike on June 30, 1920. The strike had cost the Japanese over $200,000. The planters had lost $12,000,000. This was the longest and costliest strike in the Territory thus far and the first strike in which more than one racial group participated. It was also the first time in which mediation was attempted in an effort to end a strike.[3]

Even with the end of the strike, the planters continued their efforts to seek changes in the law to allow them to bring in more Chinese laborers. They wanted to assure themselves of a large, cheap labor supply. However, they were not able to convince Congress that it was in the best interest of Hawai'i to do so.

The end of the strike saw the immediate rise in wages as well as improvements in working and living conditions for the laborers. In spite of these changes for the better, some of the Japanese chose to leave the plantations for other fields of endeavor. Others who remained worked even harder and in increasing numbers rose to become skilled laborers and management personnel.

Strike Aftermath

Soredake de Nihonjin ga, Japanese *ga* all most, *ano* strike *kara,* plantation *nimo dettemo, bakarashi.* (Well, from that strike, most of the Japanese thought it would be stupid to go back to the plantation). You know. Same amount you get. They no going pay 'em. "Ah, you striker, you," *ittekara,* plantation *kara,* kick 'em out, just like, eh ("Ah, you striker, you," they would say, and would kick the Japanese out from the plantation). 'As why, ah, more better go outside. He go inside pineapple and then contracts him. All down-town *no hō minna deta* (Everyone went downtown). *Hodake,* plenty Waialua *kara detoruyo,* downtown *ni,* plenty guys stay (So, a lot of guys went downtown from Waialua). 'As why *mo, arekara, jibun no* own job, eh, *jibun no* business *ni botsubotsu* old man *ra ga haiteita* (That's why even the old people went into their own businesses).

Hodake, my father *demo,* all same (Even my father was no exception). *Kondo* plantation *kara detari jibun no* own job, eh (Once he got out of the plantation, he had to do his own work). *Dake,* any kind, he go make *yasai ya shitari,* contracting, sub-contracting, *uketori* (Then he did all kinds of work; raised vegetables, did contracting work, took sub-contracts). Just only *dokashite kara, ma, kūte ittawakeyo* (One way or another, they earned enough to eat). *Hodake, nanika eraime ni otoru yo* (so they suffered a great deal).

Noriyu Koga
Waialua-Haleiwa, Ethnic Studies
Oral History Project, p. 666

Artifacts From Plantation Homes

Charcoal Iron   *Wooden Washboard*

Hair Clipper   *Ice Tongs*

Bentō Can in Two Tiers: one for rice and the other for the rest of the lunch.

Individual Water Can For Field Work

Waipahu Cultural Garden Park

51

Old Wood Burning Stove

Kerosene Stove

Pump Type Sewing Machine

Screened Seifu (safe)
kept food safe from insects.

Chapter VI
ESTABLISHMENT OF COMMUNITY

Most of the early workers had come with the intention of serving out their three-year contracts and returning to Japan. The objective was to earn quick money – enough to pay off family debts, to be able to purchase land in Japan, and to live comfortably for the rest of their lives. However, in spite of frugal living, not many were able to do so in the early years of immigration. Wages were low and the cost of living was unexpectedly high. Besides, the workers had to pay off their debts to the immigration companies first. It often took three years just to do so. Many made regular, small remittances to their poor families in Japan. Visualizing Hawai'i as a land of plenty and easy money, the families often asked for more and more money as they found their cost of living also rising in Japan. The workers were in a dilemma. They were not prepared to stay in Hawai'i for very long, but they had no alternative. They had to remain and endure. It was a matter of economics as well as pride. Traditionally, the Japanese were very concerned with the opinions of others. Unless they could return as prosperous and successful people, they felt they could not face their families and friends in Japan.

Because they had considered their stay in Hawai'i only temporary, the early immigrants did not bring their families with them. Without them, the men found it difficult and lonely. Besides having to adjust to very different housing and working conditions, they were unaccustomed to the daily chores of cooking, washing, and mending. They were tired after their day's work in the hot sun, and they struggled to feed and clothe themselves.

With additional arrivals, which included a few more families, the workers sought the services of the non-contract immigrants. The women cooked for the bachelors and charged $5.00 - $7.00 per month. Another arrangement was for the cook's family to eat without charge. The women also ran bath houses and did laundry. Having such a business became profitable as more and more workers arrived.

Observing the potential market for Japanese products, some,

Oppa *(carrying a child on the back)*
allowed the Japanese woman to care
for her baby while tending to her
many tasks. Pu'unē nē, Maui,
ca. 1910.   Hawaii State Archives

Shihyoe Ninomiya, a carpenter by trade, owned a blacksmith shop with living quarters
attached to it. ca. 1905 in Hale'iwa, O'ahu.   *Ninomiya Collection*

54

My Father's Furo Concession

"Rabbit" Yasui remembers helping his father who had the job of taking care of the large community *furos* (baths) in the plantation camps. It was a full-time job for his dad who had lost his arm in an accident. He had been a plantation carpenter. One afternoon at pau hana time as he jumped on the cane car which had slowed down for workers, he dropped his lunch pail. In trying to retrieve it, he fell and lost his arm. After the accident, he could no longer continue his work as a carpenter, so he got the job of running the furos.

"As kids we helped my father run the furos which were heated with firewood. Every Saturday and Sunday, we had to saw long keawe stumps for the week. Later, we switched to charcoal. The furo was open from 2 to 8 p.m. on a first come, first served basis. The cost was 35 cents for single people and 60 cents for a family. The furo was one big, huge bathtub, like a shallow swimming pool, which was partitioned to separate men from women, but the kids swam back and forth under it."

"To the Japanese a hot bath was a daily must because being clean was very important. Sitting on stools, people first scrubbed themselves with a long soapy washcloth and then rinsed themselves thoroughly before stepping into the steaming hot water to relax."

Robert "Rabbit" Yasui, Age 86
Interviewed on September 27, 1984

after fulfilling their three year contracts, started their own businesses such as importing food, clothing, hardware, and general notions, which they peddled in the plantation camps. Other workers went into vegetable and poultry farming, carpentry, and blacksmithing after working hours and on weekends to supplement their incomes to care for their growing families.

As the community grew, there was a need for even more services. The first manufacturing was of food products such as tōfu, noodles, fishcake, and confections. In time seamstresses, midwives, priests, and morticians were needed. Still later came the need for Japanese newspapers, language schools, and special instructors in "leisure" activities – *go* (chess), flower arrangement, and music. All of these needs were gradually met by the workers themselves, by their family members, and by those who came later specifically to provide these services.

These immigrants with higher levels of education and skills, such as priests and teachers, arrived with special green passports which differentiated them from the laborers who carried beige colored passports. In the hierarchically minded Japanese communities, these influential people were accorded a special status. Children were taught to know their place and to conduct themselves with dignity.

Gradually, the dreams of returning to Japan began to fade and there was a feeling of greater permanency. Life in Hawai'i was not easy, but the news from home indicated that life in Japan was getting even harder. The workers began to see and appreciate the more positive aspects of Hawaiian living, especially after the passage of the Organic Act of 1900 which cancelled the plantation labor contract system. One could remain as a sugar or pineapple worker – a company worker or an independent grower. One was free to move and to go into other occupations and businesses; and the immigrants saw many opportunities to do so in their pioneer communities.

My Father Was a Japanese School Principal

My younger sister, two older brothers, and I grew up in Onomea on the Big Island in the 20s and 30s where our father served as principal of the Japanese Language School. Our home was adjacent to the school campus. Unlike our friends, none of us had to do yard work and other heavy chores around the house as the plantation people did them for us. My sister and I did, however, help with the cooking and housework. My father felt that the boys needed to undergo what the other boys experienced, so they were sent to work in the fields during the summers. At the time, his attitude was considered liberal for a man in his position.

One of the things I remember vividly was our dining room with its chairs. We ate there daily, while our friends in the camp sat on benches in their kitchens for their meals. We were never allowed to bring the food in pots to the table. Everything had to be transferred to dishes before being taken to the table. Mother was also very careful not to have dirty dishes in the sink because it would not be "nice" when people came to our house. And we had many, many callers.

Because of our father's leadership position in the community, we were expected to serve as model children and were not to bring shame to him or to our family. Our lives and our behavior were centered around my father's role. We did not need daily oral reminders about this. We took our cues from the deferential treatment we received from all segments of the community. Even the teacher at the English school treated us differently from the others.

Mother was responsible for teaching us manners, while Father made sure that we had a Japanese cultural background. My sister and I had to take lessons in flower arrangement, tea ceremony, and *okoto* (Japanese zither). I wasn't too interested in them, but as a result of this early training, my sister is now a qualified tea ceremony instructor. Father also saw to it that we were exposed to many people, places, and events. Whenever anyone came to our house, we had to drop whatever we were doing to greet our guests. I am grateful for the varied experiences that were a part of my growing up years.

Elsie Koike Honda
Interviewed in October, 1984

Soyo Koike serving her guests at the Hatsugama, *the first ceremony of each year. Nisei Nancy Noriko Koike studied for fifteen years before receiving her special name. She then studied for three years in Kyoto, Japan, and is now known in Hawai'i and Japan's tea ceremony circles. She is shown serving Bishop Matsuura of the Soto Zen Temple first because of his status among the honored guests.* Koike Collection

Tokubei Yamagata's Legacy

This is the story of an Imin (immigrant) who was a part of the plantation system but did not work as a laborer. His legacy has been passed on to his descendants; and four generations later, he still has a strong influence on his family. A portrait of Tokubei and his wife is a cherished possession in their homes.

When Tokubei, who was born in 1860, arrived at Hakalau Plantation with his wife, he was selected by the manager as one of the first Japanese lunas. In this capacity he served as a liaison between the Japanese workers and management. For many generations, his family in Hiroshima had served their lord as archery masters who taught this martial art to the samurai warriors. One can only surmise whether this background may have been the reason why he was chosen to be a luna. As a perquisite, he was given a large homestead in Nīnole, and a roomy four bedroom house situated on a knoll. Many, many years later, when he parceled out his land equally to his three sons, one son's parcel alone was twenty-nine acres.

Dr. Bernice Hirai, Tokubei's granddaughter, in reminiscing about her childhood experience said: "I remember that the whole Yamagata clan gathered at his spacious house every weekend. There was a sizeable ofuro (bath) so that he did not have to go to the community ofuro. The ritual of elders first was always honored, and then the eight young cousins went in last. Such splashy, noisy laughter! He had a wooden replica of a samurai sword made specially for him – scabbard and all. It seemed to be a symbol of his past, a way for him to recall his childhood; and he used the token sword to remind his children of their heritage. After his untimely death, Grandmother Take presided for the clan in true matriarchical fashion; and Teso, the eldest son, and his family lived in that wonderful big house with her."

"Reio, my dad, was their second son; and was born in 1896. He was one of the few non-haoles in his class at Hilo Boarding School and at Hilo High School. Not even his older brother had graduated from high school. Upon graduation, John M. Ross, the manager, gave him a position in the Hakalau plantation office, a C. Brewer company. The Yamagatas were blessed with having had a rather innovative and benevolent employer."

Mother came from Japan at age eighteen and was a Japanese language teacher at Laupāhoehoe. She was chaperoned very carefully by the priest and his wife at the large Buddhist temple there. My father always accompanied his mother to the shrines at the temple, and that is how my parents first met. My dad was said to have been *haikara,* fashionable and stylish. He must have been quite a sight as he came calling on my mother in his dark green felt hat and green serge suit. When they were married in 1922, their wedding festivities lasted three days. The first day's celebration was for the members of the family and guests; the second was for the community. The third day's party was for all those who helped to prepare the food and other things."

"Our home was in what was considered 'haole row.' Every Friday, my father insisted upon T-bone steak for dinner, so that we would be comfortable using knives and forks. My parents brought us up very strictly. Everything had to be *kichinto* (just so). We were reared with a stringent unwritten code. I remember being told when I was naughty: *"Sodatta no dewa naku, sodaterareta!"* (You did not just grow up; you were brought up!). We were never allowed to intermix Japanese and English. We always had a 'live-in' girl; but we were expected to learn to do household chores because we were told: 'When you have your own home, you will have to know what is entailed in running a household.'"

"We were not allowed to go to the *Bon odori* (Bon dance) or to work in the field; but we had just as arduous a schedule which kept us busy with osaihō (sewing) and other pursuits. At age five and six, my sister and I were sent into Hilo town to take piano lessons. How I dreaded those lessons! My mother, who was an accomplished player of the *chikuzen biwa* (Japanese lute), understood my misery and allowed me to switch to the *okoto* (13 stringed zither) instead." In 1995, she was awarded the title of *Shihan*, Master Teacher, of *koto*, and in 1998, an Imperial Decoration by the Japanese Government.

"My family stressed education, and we were expected to be on the honor roll in English school as well as bring home the *ittōshō* (first place in Japanese school) through the years. As a child, I often thought that I'd rather be like the other kids and felt like I was missing out on the fun they were having. But now that I'm older, I feel that I've been fortunate in having assimilated so many of the Japanese traditions especially when I see my daughter showing a keen interest in learning about her Japanese heritage. I do appreciate much of what my parents and grandparents passed on to me."

Dr. Bernice Hirai
Interviewed in October, 1984

The unmarried men began to think of establishing families in Hawai'i. There were not many women that they knew, and those were already married. Because of their strong pride in being Japanese, only a few ventured to marry native women as did the early Gannen mono. Most longed for Japanese wives. As was the traditional procedure, many a worker asked his parents for help in

When Bernice Yamagata and Henry Hirai were married in 1950, anti-Japanese feelings were still high in postwar Hawai'i; however, the bridal party and the mothers of the bride and groom chose to wear kimonos for the wedding. When their daughter Anna Hirai (to the right) married Dr. Gunnar Gibson in January, 1982, at Central Union Church, she also wore the traditional Japanese wedding kimono ensemble to a special luncheon at the Honolulu Club two days before her wedding.

Hirai Collection

Vignettes of Picture Brides

I was thinking about nothing but coming to Hawaii; I didn't think about anything else. At the physical inspection in Nagasaki my eyes were fine, but I had hookworms. So I was suspended in Nagasaki for a week. My mother went home, leaving my father with me, saying she would be back when I got rid of the hookworms. She came back a few days later. At the inspection site, where we had our stool examined, a person gave me somebody else's stool, which didn't have hookworms. The person told me to keep it in my *obi* and switch it with my own stool. But a *haole,* a white person, was watching me when I was using the bathroom, so it was impossible to switch, you know? I couldn't even urinate. So I gave up and took my own to be inspected. A person who'd come back from America, who helped arrange my going to Hawaii, told me to eat a lot of nuts which apparently made it difficult for the microsocope to find worms. So I ate quite a lot of these nuts which my mother roasted for me. And I must have been lucky; I was told there weren't any hookworms, so I passed. My mother and father filled up a *shingenbukuro,* cloth pouch, with persimmons, pears, candies, and rice crackers, and so many other goodies. They said I would be on board for one week to ten days, would be lonely, and should eat all of the fruits and treats.

Osame Manago
Interviewed by Michiko Kodama-Nishimoto
Hanahana, p. 153.

I was working at *Nippu Jiji* when my future wife's uncle suggested that I take a bride. Uncle said: "Perhaps then you will quit going to geisha houses and will be able to save some money." He wrote to his niece's family who approved of the idea. We exchanged pictures and our marriage was performed in proxy.

Kakuji Inokuchi, Age 86
Interviewed on July 9, 1974

I was dressed in formal white kimono and had my hair done up in Shimada and rode in a jinricksha to Kakuji's sister's home since his parents were already deceased. His brother-in-law threw a large party for me and hired geisha and maiko. The next day, the

An early love match. Nisei Shigeyo Ninomiya was courted by two suitors. When she fell in love with Issei Giichi Ochiai from Hiroshima ken, her parents were greatly concerned at the possibility that Shigeyo might marry outside her ken. Her father traveled from Hale'iwa to Honolulu to consult a priestess who said: "Nowadays differences in ken do not matter. Besides, Yamaguchi and Hiroshima are neighboring kens." So, Shigeyo and Giichi were married in 1923 with her parents' blessings and the help of nakahodos.

Ochiai Collection

hairdresser redid my hair. Kakuji's sister said that she wished her brother could see his bride all dressed up.

Koisa Inokuchi
Interviewed on July 9, 1974

Life aboard *Shinyo Maru* was not too bad. The passengers slept on hammocks. The food was prepared by Chinese cooks, but the food was too greasy. Fried foods, you know; and it was served with rice and tea.

I brought one *kōri* (wicker basket) with me which contained my futon and kimono.

Matsu Takahama, Age 82
Interviewed on August 21, 1976

---

locating a suitable wife. In turn, the parents, resorting to a prevalent custom, asked a trusted friend to act as a *nakahodo* (go-between) to look for a bride. When a girl who was satisfactory to the family was located in the prefecture, pictures and sometimes letters were exchanged. A proxy marriage was held in Japan and the girl was officially entered as a member in the groom's family register, Koseki Tōhon. She then had to live for six months, as required by Japanese law, with the groom's family before sailing for Hawai'i in the company of other picture brides.

The many brides and grooms were naturally excited, anxious, and nervous as the ship docked. A few had seen each other in Japan, but many years had passed since. Others were meeting complete strangers as marriage partners. The grooms on the pier and the brides on the ship carried photographs of each other as they tried to locate their mates. Some met with difficulties because the pictures were old or had been re-touched. There were even a few instances where a prospective groom had sent a picture of a friend who was handsomer or younger.

Although the young couples were already married properly according to their laws and religion, the proxy Japan marriages were not recognized by the Hawaiian government. A Christian minister was brought to the Immigration Station to perform mass Christian marriages as soon as the brides were cleared, processed, and had found their husbands. Fred Makino, the fiery editor of the *Hawaii Hochi* newspaper, protested this practice vigorously. He argued that assembly line marriages were a violation of the Japanese immigrants' freedom to worship as they chose. Eventually, the mass Christian ceremonies were dropped.

A Young Picture Bride

In 1919, when I was an eighteen year old living in the Hiroshima countryside, a nakahodo came to ask my parents for my hand in marriage to a young man in far away Hawai'i. The nakahodo brought a picture of a young man standing in a dark American suit. I'll never forget walking very far with my mother to have my picture taken to send to Hawai'i. When we and our families had agreed on the marriage, it was recorded in the *Koseki Tōhon* in Hiroshima. I had no problem in accepting the arrangement because it was the Japanese custom for parents and the nakahodo to arrange the marriages.

After a simple *shashin kekkon,* picture marriage, I went to live with my in-laws for six months. This, too, was the custom; but I was so unhappy because I had to work very hard in my in-laws' home. I was like a servant; no, my life was worse than a servant's. So, I ran away to my family several times; but each time, my in-laws and the *nakahodo* came to plead with me to return to their household. Since I was the *chōnan's* (oldest son's) bride, they said I had to stay with them for six months. Some dejected picture brides refused to return to their in-laws' houses and were registered as divorced before they ever met their husbands.

After six months, my father-in-law accompanied me and a young sixteen year old picture bride for my husband's brother, to the port city of Yokohama. We traveled by *jinricksha,* a small carriage pulled by a man, and by train to the port city. It was my first train ride and my first view of the ocean! I was excited about the trip so I didn't worry about what my new husband would be like. The young girls in my village wanted to have the opportunity to travel.

The *funachin,* boat fare, was $53.00, and we had to pass an inspection to show that we were free of diseases. Once on board the *Shunyo Maru,* the brides showed off the photographs of their husbands. I was so ignorant about the trip that I had packed my clothes and my husband's picture in the trunk which was taken from me and stored in the hold. I was so embarrassed because the other brides teased me and wouldn't believe that I had packed his picture away.

Most of the trip on the *Shunyo Maru* was miserable. I was so seasick that I couldn't eat. The trip to Honolulu took eight days. I was too sick to get up so I lay on my bunk for six of those days. Just as I began to feel better, our ship reached Honolulu Harbor. By then I was suffering from the heat because I had to wear the heavy kimono which I had on when I boarded since my things were in storage.

As we docked, I looked down and recognized my husband from

the photograph; but we were not allowed to meet or talk together for about a week. We were taken straight to the immigration station for another inspection. We were all afraid of the inspector who was Japanese for he talked loudly, scolded everyone, and ordered us around. Once, he grabbed my hairdo and said: "Get rid of your *nezumi* (rat)." It was the style to wear a high hairdo with a cushion inside to give it body, so I had one of those in my hair.

When the day finally came for us to meet our husbands, we excitedly helped to dress each other in a *montsuki,* special kimono with a crest, and a fancy sash called a *maruobi.* Outside the immigration station, our husbands waited eagerly for a glimpse of us. We were nervous and shy. I thought my husband was tall and handsome. We rode in a two horse carriage to Onomichiya Hotel. The next day, my husband and his brother took us to see Waikīkī.

Two days later, we went by boat to Līhue, Kaua'i, to live on the plantation. We were already married in Japan, but we did have a party. The people in the camp prepared the food for the celebration which was held in the social hall.

One month after arriving in Hawai'i, I was expected to go out to the fields to work. A friend made me a shirt, skirt, an apron, and arm protectors; and I did hoe hana. Later, I had the job of putting foot long pieces of sugar cane into bags for planting. If the bags were not full enough, we were scolded and told to fill the bags again. Some luna were strict and shook the bags hard to make the stalks settle way down. Others were kind and gave the ladies a wink and went on. I was young so I was a pretty good worker. When I became pregnant, I went to Honolulu to learn a skill. I boarded there for six months while I learned to sew so that I wouldn't have to labor in the hot sun with my children.

Tatsuyo Hazama, Age 83
Interviewed in 1978 and 1984

Etsuo Comes To Hawai'i

I was born in Hiroshima, Japan, in 1895. When I was seven years old, my father and mother left us with our grandparents to go to Hawai'i because the family needed money. My grandparents had signed as witnesses when their friend borrowed some money. When he was unable to repay his debt, my grandparents had to sell their farmlands to honor that debt. They believed it was the honorable thing to do even if it meant hard times for their own family.

When my father became ill in Hawai'i, he sent for me and my younger brother to work on the plantation too. By then, I was sixteen; and since I was taller than many older men, I was hired to do

64

Etsuo and Tatsuyo Hazama at their fiftieth wedding anniversary celebration at a tea house in Honolulu, 1969. Hazama Collection

the work of grown men. I didn't complain for I earned 75 cents a day like the men while my smaller friends were paid only 25 cents a day as water boys. My only regret now is that I was too tired to attend the English night school run by the company. I had a ten hour workday from Monday through Saturday. I had to get up at 4:30 and work from 6:00 in the morning until 4:30 in the afternoon. Then I helped my parents after work. For extra income, my mother made tōfu, and my parents raised pigs.

While my brother and I ate dinner with Okā-san and Otō-san, we had to sleep in another building for single men. My parents often talked about how two or three married couples had to sleep in one room when they first came to Hawai'i. By the time we arrived, they at least had a small room to themselves although there was only a thin wall between families. They could hear everything that people were saying or doing next door.

My parents also talked about the earlier days – how mean the lunas were and how they had to work even when they were sick. While we still worked hard in my time, and the days were long, I was never mistreated and the German luna was not mean to me.

Later, I got a job in the sugar mill. It was heavy work *hāpai* (carrying) 100 pound bags of sugar. But, I was lucky because I could earn $1.00 a day!

When Okā-san and Otō-san returned to Japan, they took my

savings and my brother's with them too. They said they would look for suitable brides for the two of us. We continued to work hard and save money to send back to Japan. Our money was worth double in Japan. The price of a bag of rice here was $4.00 and that would last a month. Ahina pants, heavy blue jeans, cost $1.00. The plantation gave me a free sleeping place in the bachelor's bungalow, and the tax cost $5.00 a year. Some men drank heavily or gambled and couldn't save any money. They were the ones who often got into fights too.

At age 25, eleven years after I first arrived in Hawai'i, I went to the immigration station to meet my picture bride. I was so happy when I saw her because she was really lovely. I brought her back to Līhue, Kaua'i; and we were given a small, two room place. We shared the kitchen and toilet which were outside, away from the duplex.

After my brother and I had saved enough to buy a truck, we moved our families to Maunaloa, Moloka'i, when Libby Company just opened their pineapple plantation. We made money on contract as truckers. Eventually, we owned three trucks and employed four men because it took a driver and a loader to man each truck. As time went on, Libby Company bought our trucks, and we worked for Libby until we retired. When I left Japan as a teenager, I didn't think that Hawai'i would be home for the rest of my life, but I'm happy here. I have my children, grandchildren, and even great grandchildren.

Etsuo Hazama, Age 89
Interviewed in 1978 and 1984

Most couples adjusted to each other and had satisfactory and happy marriages that lasted for a long time. Others who were not as congenial just accepted their fates and endured as their families grew. A few brides ran away and sought refuge with other Japanese in the city. Still others were forced or lured into prostitution. The coming of the picture brides and the establishment of families among more workers helped to stabilize the plantation and the Japanese community. Beginning with 466 brides in 1907, more than 14,000 had come by 1924 when the Japanese Exclusion Act became law. [1]

Field work was a new experience for most of these picture brides. But, like their husbands, they also learned the different tasks required in the growing of sugar. After putting in a full day's field work, the women returned to their crowded living quarters to do their household tasks of cooking, washing, cleaning, and caring for their children. Later some found themselves unable to work in the fields as one child after another was born.

66

Childcare In The Fields

Nevertheless, I was the lucky one. A person of my father's age, you know, carried a two month old baby on his/her back while doing *hapai ko.* If the baby is two months, maybe you can't do that. Anywhere, from three, four months old, the baby can be carried on the back. Then in the field, see. Then there's a small tent, you know. It's just like an umbrella. You put that kind of cover. You know, the what-you-might-call-it of the sugar cane, on that burnt cane, they leave the baby so the baby won't be hot. When it came to a certain time, the girl used to go there to breast-feed the baby. There are so many red ants swarming there, biting the baby. Sometime, such a thing happened. In that way, my brothers grew up. My mother used to make *tōfu* so she had a profession. So she didn't have to take us to the field. Smitty didn't have to go to the field, but most of the fellows had to. Oh, when one gang of fifty to seventy guys worked to load the train cars, most of them were Japanese because they were the ones who did the dirty jobs. That's why even if you gave birth to a baby, you couldn't rest much. So you had to carry the baby, leave it because the husband and wife had to work together as one team.

Noriyu Koga
Waialua-Haleiwa, Ethnic Studies Oral History Project, p. 664

Women Washing Clothes at a Near-by Stream.
In the absence of scrubbing boards, the women apparently used rocks. The child in the foreground has a chawan (rice bowl) haircut.		*Hawaii State Archives*

The Courage And Determination
Of A Young Girl

I was six years old and my sister, Kinuko, was four when our grandfather took us to Japan. My father and mother worked on the sugar plantation and they wanted us to have a good Japanese education because they planned to return to Japan as soon as they had saved enough money. It was so hard leaving my father, and mother, and a baby brother, but *"shikata ga nai"* (it couldn't be helped). My parents were thinking of our own good.

Two years after we reached Japan, my grandfather died and my sister and I were sent to two different relatives to live. They were busy farmers so we were expected to work in their rice paddies until dark and then to help in cleaning up. Afterwards, late at night only after all the chores were done, I could get to my homework; and so I had little sleep. I was so tired and lonesome; I used to cry myself to sleep.

Then when I was twelve years old, my mother, who was getting ready to visit us in Japan, caught the flu and died suddenly one week before leaving Hawai'i. Her death left my father with four young brothers in Hawai'i. My youngest brother Shiro was only two years old. So, our father sent for the two of us girls to come home to help.

In Hawai'i, I had to get up at four o'clock in the morning to cook breakfast and to make bentō lunch for my father and brothers. I went to work with the other plantation women taking along my two younger brothers. I put them under a shady tree so that I could keep an eye on them while I worked. I felt so sorry for them.

Then my father died two years after my mother. I made up my mind to keep our familiy together no matter what, and I don't know how we managed. I was strict with my brothers, but I'm so happy that they turned out to be good people. I had to be a mother and a father to my younger brothers, and I had to work so hard from early morning until late at night; but you know, it was nothing compared to the hard life I experienced in Japan. I was happy to be back in Hawai'i with my family.

Sumiko Tanaka (pseudonym at request of interviewee)
Interviewed in 1984

Children, especially sons, were considered family treasures in Japan. In Hawai'i, they took on added significance, for having been born in Hawai'i, they were eligible for American citizenship and attendant rights such as voting. This was something the parents could not attain at this time.

As it was in Japan, the welfare of the family and nation took precedence over that of the individuals. This was a manifestation of the concept of *on* (a sense of obligation to family and country). Filial piety was preached and practiced. The family took great pride in being Japanese and in things Japanese. They often subjugated their personal dreams and desires so as not to bring disgrace and dishonor to their families. Their actions were controlled by concern over how others would perceive them. Therefore, it was better not to express a contrary opinion or to be shamed by an error.

There was a definite hierarchy in the family structure. The father, *Otō-san*, as head of the household made the major decisions and was not to be questioned or challenged. He was served first with the best portions at mealtimes and no one dared to take a bath before him. He was followed by sons from the eldest to the youngest, then by the daughters, and mother was last. The eldest son was particularly important, for it was through him that the

"*Otō-san had this family portrait taken inside our 'Ewa Plantation home in 1921 to send to my grandparents (portrait on wall). The other large photograph of Okā-san's brothers in Japanese army and navy uniforms was burned as soon as Pearl Harbor was attacked because my parents were afraid to reveal any connection with the Japanese military.*"

Haruno Nunogawa Sato

family line continued. It was his responsibility to care for his parents in their old age. A good son tended family graves, which assured the ancestors of regular prayers.

Okā-san or mother, on the other hand, held an important place in the day-to-day routine decisions of the family. It was she who saw to the training of her children and in the process instilled in them the values she had brought with her from Japan. It was the woman's total responsibility to see that the household chores were done.

The immigrants rapidly developed camaraderie and a real sense of community. They had no alternative but to do so, for their homes were often separated only by thin walls which were covered with newspapers to seal the cracks. They shared kitchen sinks, stoves, and washing facilities. They had only each other for they were thousands of miles from family and home. Because the planters had tried to form the work gangs and camps with workers from the same ken or prefecture, the immigrants' daily contacts were largely with people of similar backgrounds and customs. When there was a special occasion or a crisis, they helped each other. This was especially true at births, marriages, and funerals. Friends would go in to assist or even to completely take over. They

---

Community Bath

In the old days, the plantation camp had a bath. . . . women's side and men's side. They had two baths. In the middle, there was a partition. You were in the same water. Eh, you were dirty. If you did work like *hapai ko,* you were really filthy. After work when you go to the bath, there was no more hot water so you had no choice. Hot water, bath, Japanese style bath, you see. But a lot of people used that water. Even if you felt the water was dirty, you had no choice. You had to use that bath. A poor guy like me couldn't go early because I had a lot of work in the *tōfu* business. And I had a horse. I have to cut grass and feed that horse. Any kind. That's why every-time when I came late, the water was so dirty. And then the toilet was so far away. It was about a hundred feet from the house. The toilet was far away. There was a hole in the ground. You couldn't get there in time. If you had a stomach ache, there wasn't enough time. You had to run.

Noriyu Koga
Waialua-Haleiwa, Ethnic Studies Oral History Project, p. 678

70

Outhouse behind residence. Waine'e Village, Lahaina, Maui, ca 1920. The neighborhood communal toilets were arranged in a row of about five private compartments with doors. The deep hole in the ground was covered with stalls which contained elevated seats with cut out holes. Any cut up paper available from newspapers, mail order catalogs, and orange and apple wrappings from crates served as toilet paper.   *Photo by Leighton Liu*

formalized their help by forming *kumiai* (neighborhood clubs) and *kenjinkai* (prefectural clubs). The clubs also met some of their social needs.

The groups, especially in the early days, developed along ken or prefectural lines. The immigrants had come from various parts of Japan, bringing with them their different dialects, customs, and experiences. It was easier and safer to associate with the familiar.

People from other prefectures were often looked upon with suspicion or looked down on. They were also stereotyped. Those from Kumamoto Ken were considered rough and daring, from Yamaguchi Ken, shrewd and from Niigata Ken, boorish.

Those that received the greatest disdain and discrimination were the immigrants from Okinawa, the southernmost prefecture. Geographically, the Ryukyu Islands where the Okinawans came from are 275 miles from the southern tip of the Japanese mainland. Historically, the Ryukyus were an independent nation until 1871 when they were placed under Kagoshima Prefecture. In 1879, the Ryukyus were declared a separate prefecture – Okinawa Ken. Culturally, the Okinawans are closer to the Chinese as their early contacts were more with China than with Japan.

71

Okinawan Status Symbol

Kamadō Teruya, who lived to be 103 years of age, is shown here in 1960, slicing *nantu* or Okinawan *mochi.* The photograph reveals the tattoo marks on her hand. Upon their marriage, Okinawan women tattooed the backs of their hands. This status symbol was darkened and expanded as a sign of wealth especially around age 49. A woman with faded markings was considered to be unfortunate.

According to Uto Uehara, age 85, the Okinawan practice of tattooing was so important that if a woman were not tattooed, upon her death, her husband returned her remains to her own family. A tattoo session was accompanied by *ogochisō*, delicious and festive foods. As a young girl, Uto and her friends admired their tattooed elders so they decided to emulate them by piercing their fingers with needles in sewing class to make small imitations.

Unfortunately, when the Okinawan women arrived in Hawai'i, they became so ashamed of their once proud tattooed status symbols that they hid their hands when they were photographed. A practice similar to tattooing was followed by some Naichi women in Japan who blackened their teeth after marriage.

Teruya Collection
Uto Uehara
Interviewed on November 15, 1984

On Being Okinawan Among the Naichi

I spent my childhood years in the late 40s and 50s on the island of Maui. My parents ran a butcher shop. I always thought I was just plain Japanese. At least, this is what I assumed until I transferred from a parochial school to a public school at the beginning of my third grade year. The first inkling that I was "different" came on the playgound. One of the Naichi students, from her perch on the jungle gym, told the other girls that her father forbade her to play with me since I was Okinawa Ken. I don't recall what else she said, but I do remember her snide remark that all Okinawans were hairy.

I recollect feeling very hurt, confused, and for the first time, began to see my arms from her perspective and felt ashamed. I had assumed I was the same as they were and now I was singled out as being "different." I was not raised in an Okinawan community and had no sense of being Okinawan. I was confused and felt that somehow I was inferior. I realized many years later that I allowed the experiences of my third grade year to influence the way I subsequently thought of myself. I was ashamed of being Okinawan and wished many times that I were a regular Japanese girl.

I don't recall other specific incidents of harassment. But I do remember the times during my elementary school years when the girls would be mentioning their prefectural backgrounds and my being Okinawa Ken would be stated with negative undertones. I carried my inferiority complex with me into my early adult life.

My next encounter with Naichi-Okinawan prejudice came when my Naichi husband-to-be and I were seriously thinking about marriage. He warned me that not all of his relatives might accept me into the family because I was Okinawan. He had been taught that the Okinawans were inferior to the Japanese and had "bad blood." He had not been allowed to date Okinawan girls during his high school years. He claimed that my being Okinawan did not matter to him. He wanted to marry me. We were married in 1964.

Over the years, attitudes have changed, not only of the Naichi toward the Okinawans, but also of the Okinawans toward themselves. I was warmly accepted into my husband's family, and my parents have rediscovered their Okinawan heritage. They look forward to their weekly Okinawan *samisen* and language lessons, though they are in their sixties and seventies. I feel good and at peace with who I am and my two sons are proud of their Okinawan heritage.

Jane Miyahira Kinoshita
October, 1984

In the discrimination against the Okinawans the *Naichi,* or those from the four main islands of Japan, were united. The Okinawans, or the *Uchinanchu,* had come to Hawai'i beginning in 1900, by which time many of the Naichi were well settled. They filled the labor positions on the plantations that the Naichi had left. Those who were not field hands went into hog-raising, a familiar occupation, as their diet, unlike that of the Naichi, included much pork. The hog raisers collected slop from households and restaurants in the community to feed their animals. Understandably the slop cans and trucks smelled. This was associated with uncleanliness and the Okinawans were considered to be primitive and dirty. This was also a transfer of feeling, for in Japan anyone who raised, slaughtered, or handled animals was called *Eta* and shunned. The Naichi, especially the children, taunted the Okinawans with "Okinawa ken ken, buta kau kau" meaning Okinawans eat pig. Another way to insult them was to call them "Big Rope," which was a play on the word Okinawa, for when pronounced Ōkii nawa, it translates to big rope.

It was difficult for the Uchinanchu and the Naichi to converse as Okinawan is a separate language and not a dialect of standard Japanese. This further limited interaction and prevented understanding.

Physically the Uchinanchu tended to be darker, more hairy, and had larger, rounder eyes than the Naichi. Their clothing was often brighter and worn more loosely. Upon marriage, the women tattooed their hands and arms.

Just as the Naichi felt superior, the Uchinanchu felt inferior. To non-Japanese, both the Naichi and the Uchinanchu were Japanese. However, in the Japanese community, a clear distinction was made. Many Okinawans tried to hide their backgrounds or to pass as Naichi. They did not invite their Naichi friends home. Some went as far as to change their surnames to Naichi sounding names, for example Gibu to Yoshitake and Kiyan to Kiyabu.

Okinawan parents often advised their children to marry Okinawans to escape degradation from Naichi in-laws. Naichi parents, on the other hand, forbade dating and courtship of Okinawans by their children. When a defiant son or daughter married an Okinawan, he or she was disowned by the family and laughed at by the community. This discrimination continued until World War II. As a result, the Okinawans have developed very strong and close ties to their families and community.

Other groups called *tanomoshi,* or mutual financing groups, were

Performers dressed in their traditional dance outfits for an Okinawan celebration in Waipahu. Waipahu has a large Okinawan population. ca. 1980s.

Cherishing The Okinawan Heritage

Throughout my early life, I did not particularly feel the personal "sting" of discrimination by the Naichi, although it definitely existed. Perhaps it was because we did not reside in the plantation camp where other Okinawan families lived.

In the late 40s, my brother-in-law became active in organizing the Okinawan Club in Hilo. My first reaction was very negative. I felt that the action was one of segregation, whereas we should have been thinking of working together.

When I came to Honolulu to attend the University in the early 50s, I met my future husband-to-be. He is Okinawan and had been attending functions of his sonjinkai. I soon became involved too and began to see that the Okinawan club was not one of segregation but one of lending support to each other. The picnics, New Year parties, and other sonjinkai functions produced such warm feelings of comradeship and concern, that till today, our own two children can still relate to that "Okinawan connection."

The awareness of my cultural heritage increased when I became involved with *Hui O Laulima* in the early 70s. *Hui O Laulima* is an organization of women interested in the promotion, preservation and perpetuation of the Okinawan culture. We have presented a cultural exhibit to the public every year since 1971, sharing the arts of music, dance, costume, cooking, and other artifacts. Along with the United Okinawan Association of Hawaii, we host different groups coming from Okinawa, participate in the Okinawan Festival, Medical Group project and many other activities. We also plan luncheon speakers and workshops to learn more about the language, religion, and geography of Okinawa. Through *Hui O Laulima,* I have developed a greater understanding and appreciation of my cultural heritage.

1980 is truly remembered as a highlight of my life. In August of that year, my husband and another active member of Nago Club were invited by the Mayor and City Council of Nago in Okinawa to attend their 10th anniversary (since becoming a city) celebration. It had been 31 years since my husband last visited Okinawa, and it would be my first. Meeting the families that our parents talked so often about was a thrill of a lifetime! Here were the people of my family; here was the land of my people. As we visited and shared our lives with each other, the bonds strengthened.

I am truly proud of my Uchinanchu heritage!

Betty Higa
October, 1984

---

organized among friends. Each of these groups was made up of ten or twenty persons or families who put a specified amount of money into the pot each month. The first month's pot automatically went to the "house" or person in charge. Beginning with the second month, the members bid for the pot. The highest bidder took the pot and paid each remaining member a portion of his bid. Once a person took a pot, he was not eligible to receive ensuing dividends. The members, therefore, tried very hard to be one of the last to take the pot. They received more by doing so. However, their incomes being limited, they often found it necessary to get additional funds to meet a crisis or to start a business. Bank loans

Rev. Kanichi Miyama, a samurai who had been converted to Christianity in San Francisco, was sent originally to Hawai'i for two months by his San Francisco congregation. His evangelical meetings in Honolulu and on the Big Island attracted many. On a second trip in March, 1888, he organized the Japanese Methodist Church on the outskirts of Chinatown. This church became a part of the Hawaiian Evangelical Association in 1892 and is the forerunner of the Nu'uanu Congregational Church. Insisting on a Japanese Methodist fellowship, Rev. Kanichi Miyama relocated the Japanese Methodist congregation to the River Street Church. The River Street Church has grown over the years to become the Harris United Methodist Church.
Harris United Methodist Church Collection

A Christian funeral procession at the Nu'uanu Congregational Church in Honolulu, ca. 1918.
Yamaguchi Collection

were available, but they were not as convenient. Besides, the tanomoshi also provided opportunities for socialization.

By the mid 1880s, Christian missionaries were hard at work spreading the Lord's gospel among the Japanese immigrants. In 1887, a Japanese Methodist minister, Kanichi Miyama, arrived in Hawai'i and it was largely through his evangelism that eighty-four Japanese were baptized in two years. This was an important milestone in the Hawaiian Christian community, for Christianity was a totally new experience for the immigrants. Their background had been Buddhism and Shintoism. Among the coverts was Japanese Consul General Tarō Andō, who also worked tirelessly to get the Japanese interested in Christianity and temperance. When Consul Ando returned to Japan, the evangelistic work was continued by other Caucasian and Japanese ministers who operated through the Hawaiian Board of Missions. Missions were established throughout the islands, and members contributed towards the construction of churches. However, growth of the Japanese Christian community was rather slow. In 1894, only 400 out of the 25,000 immigrants were Christians.

Most of immigrants had come from small rural communities and adhered to the beliefs and customs they had brought with them. As they did in Japan, they practiced Shintoism and Buddhism at the same time. Both were based partly on ancestor worship, one of the Imperial family and the other of their own families.

In Shintoism, the Japanese native religion, the worshipers revere various *Kami,* or supernatural beings. There are gods and goddesses of the sea, river, wind, fire, and mountains. Amaterasu-ō-Mikami, the sun goddess and principal deity, is an ancestor of the Japanse Imperial Family. Shintoism stresses purification and purity of mind and body in all of its rites.

Buddhism teaches that man is born in a state of ignorance and by shedding egoism attains Enlightenment to become one with the Universe, the External, and the Real. To reach this state of Nirvana, one must practice selfless love and compassion and live the Noble Eightfold Path – Right Viewpoint, Right Mindedness, Right Speech, Right Action, Right Living, Right Effort, Right Attentiveness, and Right Concentration. It is important to honor one's ancestors, both living and dead. It is also important to practice filial piety for the living soon die, and the dead can become Buddhas with the help of prayers by the living. At the same time, the well-being and happiness of the living are dependent upon the fulfillment of one's obligations to the dead.

There were no Buddhist clergymen among the early immigrants. Therefore, when the need for one arose, such as with a death, one of the men took the lead and chanted a few sutras. Recognizing the need for Buddhist priests, some of the immigrants got together and sent petitions to the temples in Japan asking for help. Their requests became especially urgent when imposter priests collected large sums of money and absconded.

Reverend Gakuō Okabe of the Jōdo Sect was the first official Buddhist priest to come to Hawai'i in 1894. He was supported by immigrants of both the Christian and Buddhist faiths in Hāmākua, Hawai'i. The first official Buddhist priests from Honpa Hongwanji, the True Pure Land Sect, came in October, 1897. Priests from other sects followed. The True Pure Land Sect was the leading sect in southwestern Japan from where most of the immigrants had come.

The lives of the priests were often made complicated and hard by Christians as well as by some of the immigrant workers. The Christians resented the large Buddhist following and accused the priests of being agents of the Japanese government. The Christians believed that Buddhism was a heathen religion that should not exist in an American community. Frustrated by their unsatisfactory living and working conditions and angered and ashamed for having been fooled by imposter priests, many workers drank

Because the immigrants had earlier been cheated by imposters, the officials thought that it was imperative to send a priest who was known to the people on the plantation. Rev. Gakuō Okabe was selected from a temple in Yamaguchi Ken. Until 1896 when a temple was dedicated, he traveled through five camps on the Hāmākua Coast on horseback while carrying the Buddha image on his back.

Hawaii Jōdo Shū Collection

79

Ola'a Cemetery. Neighbors and friends joined the widowed husband at the installation of a tombstone for his wife. The deceased's Buddhist name is inscribed on the face of the monument. ca. 1905.   Okamoto Collection

excessively and lived amoral and unruly lives. They treated the priests with scorn and contempt.

Other devout followers, however, welcomed the priests and shared a part of their meager wages and food with them. The devout were happy, for now there were people qualified and able to officiate at temple rites. Proper services could be held for the newly dead, for their ancestors, and for established events on the Buddhist calendar such as *Obon,* the festival welcoming the spirits of the departed.

The priests also performed other personal and social services. They often wrote and read letters for the illiterate immigrants, made the necessary contacts with the Japanese Consulate, interceded in family, as well as labor-management disputes, organized women and youth groups, and taught the Japanese language and the martial arts. In time, the immigrants fully accepted the priests, who then came to hold special places of honor in the community.

Although the planters were Christians, they welcomed the Buddhist priests and often donated land and materials toward the construction of temples, much to the dismay of the other Christians. The planters recognized that the priests emphasized patience and endurance of adversity, non-violence, resignation, and peaceful cooperation. They praised manual labor, thrift, and industry. The coming of the priests tended to calm the unruly and brought order to the life of the plantation.

One of the outstanding priests was Bishop Yemyō Imamura of the Honpa Hongwanji who served from 1899 to his death in 1932.

During his term, he helped to establish congregations on all the major plantations, participated in settling labor disputes, went out into the larger Hawaiian community to explain Buddhism, established Japanese language schools, and worked towards providing English-speaking priests to accommodate the Nisei.

The immigrant workers saw education as the means of getting their children away from the meager, hard life of the plantations. They were willing to work hard and to make tremendous sacrifices to educate their children. Fortunately for them, the Christian missionaries had earlier brought with them their zeal for universal education. Firm in the belief that education was for everyone, rich and poor, they had established a public school system by 1840. Attendance to age fourteen was compulsory. A subsequent law in 1865 made school attendance compulsory for all children between six and fifteen years of age.

With the appointment in 1896 of Henry S. Townsend as Inspector General of Hawai'i's schools, a Normal School was started to train local teachers. Townsend believed in democracy in the classroom, student initiative, and the need for higher education. He was responsible for bringing outstanding leaders of progressive education, such as John Dewey, as instructors at the

Classroom Scene – 1890
With the establishment of public education, English became the predominant means of instruction rather than Hawaiian, a change which was objected to by the missionaries.
"Haru Nakamura, Japanese," appears with the composition on sugar on the blackboard.
Bishop Museum

Normal School. With his urging, tuition fees in public schools were abolished in 1899, making it easier for more children to continue their education.

The children, in compliance with the Compulsory School Law, were sent to the public schools. On the one hand, the parents were happy that their children were learning the English language and American customs. This would enable the young people to train for jobs available off the plantations. At the same time, many immigrants still had hopes, however faint, of returning to Japan "in glory." They became aware of the fact that their children were wanting in Japanese traits and customs as they became Americanized. They also found it increasingly difficult to communicate with them. Because the parents knew Japanese and the children English, the only means of communication was the use of pidgin, a mixture of English, Hawaiian, Japanese, and other languages. Pidgin English allowed only simple conversations between parent and child and was not satisfactory when more serious matters were discussed. Therefore, when circumstances and finances permitted, the children were often sent to Japan for a more formal education. When these Hawai'i-born students returned with a Japanese education, they were known as *Kibei*.

A Game Of Marbles

Students played games while waiting for their Japanese language classes. Marbles was a favorite. Any youngster with a large collection of marbles won in games was greatly admired. The *kini* was a favorite "good luck" marble used as the shooter, and the *bumbucho* was an extra large marble used to knock other marbles out of the ring. There were several variations of marble games, but all were played on a hard dirt surface which was carefully dusted off frequently by the players who cleared their marbles' pathway before shooting.

In one game, accuracy was the skill needed as players vied with each other to return "Home" by shooting the kini into five tiny holes marked in the pattern of a cross. Once "Home," the kini became a killer and could knock opponents out of the game until only one winner was left.

In another variation, power and accuracy with the Big Bumbucho were crucial. The players placed their marbles in a triangle in the center. Then they shot from outside the circular boundary and won for keeps any marbles which were knocked out of the boundary.

See Appendix: Games and Recreation in the Early 1900s.

These Issei immigrants journeyed back to Japan to leave their two children in the care of their grandmother so that they could receive a Japanese education. Upon graduation, their daughter returned to Hawai'i just before World War II began. The son remained to finish his schooling. When the war started, he was inducted into the Japanese army and was never permitted to return to Hawai'i. Since his last request was to have his ashes brought back to his family, soon after his death, his mother made a pilgrimage to bring his remains back to the land of his birth.   *Hazama Collection*

Others sent their children to language schools which they helped to establish or to schools operated by the churches and temples. Classes were held for an hour or an hour and a half either before or after the public school classes and all day on Saturdays.

Reverend Takie Okumura, a Japanese Protestant minister, established one of the first Japanese language schools in Honolulu in 1896. His objectives were to teach the Japanese language and to convert the children to Christianity, thus enabling them to become good American citizens. Other Christian language schools were also started on the different islands by the Hawaiian Board of Missions. In 1899, when the Christian leaders realized that the Buddhists could also start language schools to promote their faith, all religious connections were removed from the schools. This was done to protect their own faith, for if the Buddhists were to promote their religion through the schools, they would gain even more in membership. They already had a much larger following among the immigrants.

Soon in 1902, Hongwanji opened its first language school. It, too, was followed by many other schools which were all patterned after the schools in Japan. Language, etiquette, filial piety, patience, courtesy, obligation, and other virtues thought to be distinctly Japanese were taught. The textbooks and other materials used were those approved by the Japanese Ministry of Education.

By 1916, there were over 14,000 students enrolled in the 140 Japanese language schools throughout the Territory. The 360 teachers who had received their training in Japan included many Buddhist priests. The schools were sustained by tuition, donations from Japan and from the Hawaiian-Japanese community, and monetary subsidies, land and material donations from the plantations.

At first, there was very little concern about the existence of the Japanese language schools. As long as the schools were preparing the students for eventual life in Japan, there was nothing to be worried about. However, with the rapid growth of the Japanese population in the Islands and the realization that the Japanese were in the Islands to stay, more and more looked upon the schools with questions. In 1910, out of the total Territorial population of 191,909, some 79,675 were Japanese. Of this number 59,675 were non-citizens and 20,000 were citizens. By 1920, the Territorial population had grown to 255,912. The number of Japanese jumped to 109,274 – 60,258 of whom were aliens and 49,016 were citizens. Many felt that the Hawaiian-born children as citizens of the United States should be taught loyalty to the United States. True, they were exposed to U.S. history, government, and American customs in the public schools, but was the teaching in the language schools geared toward loyalty to Japan?

Increasingly, questions were asked about the schools. From as early as 1906, Territorial Governor George R. Carter refused to grant a charter to Hongwanji Mission on the basis that it was more

Kōkun (School Motto)

Every Japanese language school had a *kōkun* which was designed to instill values in the students. The *kōkun* of the Buddhist schools were more detailed and elaborate. This version was less complex and was recited in independent language schools. When the leader said, *"Kiritsu!"* (attention) at the start of each class, everyone stood up and recited the kōkun in unison.

Lippa na hito ni narimashō.
(Let us become worthy individuals.)
Nakayoku benkyō itashimashō.
(Let us study together in a friendly atmosphere.)
Shokumotsu ni ki o tsuke, karada o taisetsu ni itashimashō.
(Let us take care of our health by eating properly.)
Oya ni kōkō itashimashō.
(Let us be good to our parents.)

---

a patriotic entity than a religious one. Public school personnel as well as members of the larger Hawaiian community questioned the absence of Japanese children from the public schools on Japanese holidays such as the Emperor's birthday. The children were kept out of school to participate in the ceremonies and festivities at the language schools.

Some members of the Japanese educational community sensed these concerns and organized the Hawaii Japanese Educational Association in 1915 to work towards improving language school instruction and to make it more adaptable to Hawai'i. A textbook revision was undertaken and the new Hawai'i series was used beginning in the fall of 1917.

After World War I, when the entire nation was carried by a wave of patriotism, the existence of the language schools, be they German, Chinese, or Japanese, was seriously questioned by communities across the nation. Americans, they reasoned, should only speak English. The popular motto was, "One language under one flag."

At the 1919 session of the Territorial Legislature, a Foreign Language School Supervision Bill, popularly known as the Judd Proposal, was introduced. Although it was defeated, the Legislature did authorize a survey of the language schools by the U.S. Commissioner of Education. The survey recommended that foreign language schools be abolished except for those serving

Hawai'i Chūō Gakuin students at a Tenchōsetsu celebration commemorating the Emperor's birthday. The blank spot on the right shows where the Japanese flag had originally been displayed. When World War II began, someone fearful of being incriminated, obliterated that portion. Yamada Collection

students ineligible for citizenship. When there was sufficient need, classes for citizen-students should be held after school hours by teachers regularly employed by the Department of Public Instruction.

The Japanese community leaders were alarmed by the recommendations for, if enacted, it would mean the death of the language schools. They quickly met and presented a proposal to the American Chamber of Commerce which was eventually passed by the Legislature and signed into law during the 1920 session. Act 30 prescribed the time and hours of school, required the licensing of schools and teachers, and authorized the Department to prescribe the courses of study and the textbooks.

The relief that the Japanese felt at the passage of Act 30, or the Irwin Bill, was short-lived, however, when a supplementary regulation called for a $1.00 per pupil assessment. Gradual elimination of the lower grades was proposed by a special committee of the Department. Part of the community, led by Frederick Kinzaburō Makino, editor of the Japanese daily *Hawaii Hōchi,* felt that the time had come to stand up and challenge the proposal. In December 1922, the Palama Japanese Language

School filed a petition for injunction in the Territorial Circuit Court. A temporary injunction was granted. Other court and legislative actions followed. When the Territorial Legislature passed Act 15.2, which among other provisions, prohibited the language schools from filing petitions of injunction against regulations relating to language schools, Makino took the matter to the U.S. District Court.

Following a series of court cases, the U.S. Supreme Court on February 21, 1927, declared that:

> the enforcement of the Act (Act 152) certainly would deprive the parents of fair opportunity to procure for their children instruction which they think is important and we cannot say is harmful. The Japanese parent has the right to direct his own child without unreasonable restrictions. The Constitution protects him as well as those who speak another tongue . . .[2]

The Japanese protest group had won the case and the language schools were able to continue. At a mass meeting on March 29, 1927, Editor Makino said:

> Individuals and organizations alike must never forget to stand up for their rights and freedom. But we must not become selfish or irresponsible in our actions because of our victory. We ask that the Japanese schools cooperate with the Territorial government officials to strive to raise good Americans capable of understanding both the English and Japanese languages.[3]

Makino, with his sincere belief in the fairness of the American people and the Constitution, had led the Japanese community to victory in a seemingly hopeless cause.

With a strong desire to succeed and to provide their children with job opportunities and life away from the plantation, increasing numbers of families left for urban areas. The exodus that had started earlier accelerated after the 1920 strike. By 1930 only about 9,000 or 18 percent of the Japanese work force of 50,000 was in sugar, whereas that percentage was 44 percent in 1920. However, the Depression forced many families back to the plantation so that by 1935 the figure had again risen to 25 percent.

In the 20s and 30s most of the older workers who remained accepted their places in the plantation hierarchy economically and socially. The work remained hard and strenuous for the field laborers as there was very little mechanization; but by the early 30s, many were in skilled, supervisory, and even professional jobs on the plantations.

Laborers considered it an advancement to work in the mill for it brought higher wages. An additional bonus was not having to work in the hot sun. The women workers are stamping the burlap bags with the name of the plantation while the men are bagging the sugar as it comes down the chute.

Ethnic Studies Oral History Project
University of Hawaii

Hawaii Importing Co.
Hilo, Hawaii
Circa 1910
This dry goods store handled merchandise from Japan and America. Sliding stairs enabled
the clerks to take down merchandise from the higher shelves.   Nakamoto Collection

Lasting expression of appreciation on
Kaua'i. The monument to Plantation Manager

Benjamin D. Baldwin stands in a remote
clearing. The Japanese laborers in Makaweli
saved $2,000 from their hard earned wages
to erect this monument of granite from
Japan in 1938. The Japanese had a strong
sense of on *(obligation to those in authority)*
and believe in giri *(returning of an*
obligation) to those who have been helpful
or kind to them.

Photo by Cathy Hazama

Changes In Plantation Housing

Many of the architectural features in housing for the masses in modern Hawai'i can be traced to the influence of plantation houses which were simple, low cost, box-like residences which made efficient uses of available materials. After key strikes in 1909 and 1920, plantation management gradually became more enlightened and provided for workers' needs. The single-wall houses of pine and redwood were remarkably efficient, economical

Houses in Transition. Stable Camp, ca. 1910, shows changes in materials of walls and roof. Houses were built with no apparent conscious design or plan.   Hawaii State Archives

Although their pay was low, the laborers were relatively comfortable and carefree as many of their needs were assured through the perquisite system. Homes were provided for and maintained by the plantations. There was no need to worry about repair costs and rents. Medical services and recreational facilities were also the plantations' responsibilities. Workers were able to purchase their food, clothing, and other needs from the plantation and village stores and from traveling salesmen who took orders and delivered the merchandise. The companies also donated land for houses of worship and for language schools.

District public schools were available through the eighth grade. In the early years, although political activity was limited and monitored, it did not matter much as the Issei were not eligible to vote.

and appropriate to Hawai'i's mild climate. Single walls provided added sanitary benefit of eliminating cavities where disease carrying vermin could live. Formerly maintenance was a perquisite provided by the plantations, but residents now take care of their own homes particularly in areas where employees have been allowed to purchase their houses from the company. Consultant, Leighton Liu, Department of Architecture, University of Hawaii Manoa

Gardens were important and utilitarian. Most Japanese families raised their own vegetables, chickens for special occasions, and some flowers for the altar in their yards.
Waipahu Cultural Garden Park

More than one-half of those who were still connected with sugar in the 20s and 30s, however, were either independent cane growers or long or short-term contract workers. The independents leased their land and grew their own cane which they sold to the plantations. The long-term contract workers, share croppers who used plantation facilities and supplies for living and working, were paid the minimum wages of $1.00 per day plus a monthly bonus of $2.30 if they had worked for more than 23 days that month. They were given additional bonuses based on the tonnage of clean cane delivered to the mill at the end of the growing season. These workers organized into "kompangs," cultivating gangs, and worked 50 to 280 acres per crop. The work was the same hard work, but they were freed of the lunas' goading and were paid according to the tonnage produced.

The short-term contract workers were paid according to the amount of work completed during the day, for example, the number of rows of cane worked. Some left the sugar plantations and became independent farmers in other endeavors, such as truck farming, dairying, poultry and pig raising, as well as coffee and pineapple growing. There were about 9,000 Japanese workers in these jobs by 1930. Of that number about 1,300 families had leased 5-15 acres and grew coffee in the Kona area. By 1938, the growing pineapple industry claimed over 5,000 workers as growers, laborers, and cannery workers.

Those who moved into the urban areas congregated in different localities. In Honolulu, Japanese communities were found in the 'A'ala, Kalihi, Pālama, Kaka'ako, and Mō'ili'ili areas. Many of the men went into facets of the construction industry as independent contractors, carpenters, painters, plumbers, electricians, masons, and general laborers. Others went into aspects of land transportation and became railroad, trucking, and auto workers. Still others worked as fishermen. The Japanese were hired as domestic servants, the men as gardeners and chauffeurs and the women as maids and cooks. Both men and women became sales clerks, office workers, and bank personnel. Many started small businesses in retailing, wholesaling, food processing, and in manufacturing, which they operated with the help of family members and other hired Japanese workers. By 1930, 49 percent of the retail stores in Hawai'i were operated by the Japanese.

They worked hard, lived frugally, sent money back to their families in Japan, but also managed to send their children to school, to begin investing in real estate, and to have savings accounts. According to the government reports, their assets rose from $2⅓ million in 1910 to over $28 million in 1930.[4]

Outside of the schools and their jobs, the Japanese kept pretty much to themselves. Because they lived close together, neighbors became extended families in practice. They worked side by side at weddings and funerals where it became a time to exchange feelings as well as gossip.

It is thought that the fear of being talked about and losing face kept Japanese close to their own communities and caused them to abide by their group's standards. People did not want to bring shame upon their families, their community, and their race by crime, delinquency, bizarre behavior, or interracial marriage. Displaying any one of these negative behaviors would certainly result in one's becoming the subject of much gossiping.

Two Women Visiting on River Street
Japanese families lived and marketed in the
River Street/A'ala area in great numbers
during the late 20s and 30s. Shopping
provided a time for socialization.
                              Hawaii State Archives

Barber shops were found in the towns as well as in the plantation camps. They were readily
identified by the spiraling candy stripe barbers' poles located at the entrance.
                                                        Bishop Museum

Besides their many temples, shrines, and language schools, the Japanese organized their own banks such as the Hawaii Sumitomo Bank and the Pacific Bank. The Japanese Hospital, now known as the Kuakini Medical Center, moved to its present site in 1918 upon completion of its facilities which cost $130,000. By 1930, there were about 60 Nisei doctors, 50 dentists, and 20 attorneys.

Japanese newspapers including the *Nippu Jiji* and the *Hawaii Hochi* continued to be published on all of the major islands. By the mid 1930s, there were even Japanese radio programs. Both the newspapers and the radio kept the community informed of local events as well as news from Japan. Japanese theaters such as Nippon Kan and Honolulu Za, which showed the latest films from Japan, were very popular, especially on Japanese holidays. Before talkies, a narrator or *benshi* stood on stage to emote and verbalize for the characters on the screen.

The latest Japanese popular songs were sung by Issei and Nisei alike. They learned these through the radio and from records which were available locally. Also popular were other forms of Japanese music such as *buyō* (classical dancing), instruments such as *samisen* (three stringed banjo-like instrument) and *koto* (thirteen stringed elongated zither), and traditional Japanese songs called *nagauta*. The community enjoyed these both as spectators and as performers. Many Nisei, especially girls, spent their Saturday afternoons and Sundays at music lessons of one kind or another. A few whose families could afford a piano took piano lessons.

Other girls spent some of their leisure hours studying the tea ceremony, flower arrangement, and calligraphy. Still others were sent to sewing schools, where they learned to draft and to sew Western clothing. Boys who were not fishing or playing in organized sports activities could often be found at lessons in the martial arts such as *kendō* or *jūdō*.

At community-wide celebrations such as the festivities held on February 17, 1935, commemorating the Fiftieth Anniversary of the arrival of the first contract immigrants, there were jūdō, kendō, tea ceremony, and dancing and singing exhibitions after the formal ceremonies.

In Honolulu, Wesak Day ceremonies were held, and continue to be held, under the auspices of the Council of Buddhist Temples. This event, also known as *Hanamatsuri* or Flower Festival, commemorates the birth of the Buddha in a flower garden. Sutras are chanted, hymns are sung, and sweet tea is poured by all the

Honolulu Theatre, popularly known as Honolulu Za, located near A'ala Park, showed Japanese films until World War II. The A'ala Park area was the center for business and amusement for the Japanese people.　　　　　　　　　　　　　*Hawaii State Archives*

The Japanese brought their love of sumō (wrestling) with them to Hawai'i. They staged tournaments on special holidays.　　　　　　　　　　　　　*Hawaii State Archives*

The Haleiwa *Jōdo* Mission conducts a Floating Lantern Festival at the end of the Obon season. *After a service in the temple, a skiff three to four feet in length laden with offerings of food, flowers, incense, and scrolls inscribed with the names of the dead is released into the ocean. Hexagonal lanterns with candles are also launched to escort the souls on their trip back to the Western Shores.*   Hawaii *Jōdo Shū*

participants over the small statue of the Buddha. There are similar services on all the other islands.

Another major event in the Buddhist calendar is *Obon* or *Bon* during which time the belief is that the souls of the departed return to their families. Paper lanterns are hung on porches and at the family and temple altars to welcome the spirits back. After the recitation of the sutras, a Bon dance takes place in the temple court-yard where a *yagura* or tower is set up. On the *yagura* are the drummers and singers who provide the music for the dancers who move in concentric circles around it. After the third day, the spirits are guided back to the other world. The Jōdo sect commemorates this event by sending hundreds of lighted lanterns adrift from nearby beaches.

Another large public celebration was held on *Tenchōsetsu,* the Emperor's birthday. The students took a holiday from their English school classes to participate in the programs at their respective Japanese language schools. No longer a major celebration, formal ceremonies are still held at the Japanese Consulate to which community leaders, Japanese and non-Japanese, are invited.

Girls' Day, with the dolls and pink *mochi* (rice cakes), is celebrated on March 3, while Boys' Day, at which cloth carps are flown, comes on May 5. To honor the child on her/his first Girls' or

96

In addition to flying carps, families set up displays of dolls and martial implements for Boys'
Day. The all male dolls include warriors, knights, courtiers, and martial arts figures. They
symbolize courage, strength, and perseverance which are desirable male qualities for the
Japanese. A portrait of a son's first Boys' Day was usually taken before the display. Many of
the dolls were given by relatives and friends.   *Maeda Collection*

Boys' Day, friends and family send appropriate dolls and banners. In return, the parents of the child give boxes of mochi, pink hexagonal ones for Girls' Day and bamboo and oak leaf wrapped ones for Boys' Day.

The most important family and neighborhood celebration of the year, however, was New Year's. Quarrels were settled, debts were paid, and the homes and business premises were cleaned thoroughly. By the stroke of midnight on December 31, enough food to last for three or four days had been readied, baths had been taken, and new clothes had been put on. Then the family went to the Shintō shrine to ask for a blessing for the coming year.

97

The Gradual Americanization of the Japanese Immigrants

Cultural transitions in an early day care center. The tatami *(straw mat) floor, kimono, chopsticks and tiered lunch boxes show the Japanese influence. Low chairs, hats, and the presence of a haole woman and some haole children indicate an intermingling of cultures.*
Hawaii State Archives

New Year's Day, 1910. On this most important holiday, children were given brand new outfits, special gifts, and money. The boys are riding their new tricycles which had no rubber tires. Gift giving at Christmas became a practice in most families in the late 1930s.
Ninomiya Collection

The car, a much admired possession, ca. 1916. Men friends gathered around to "check out" a new car.

Hazama Collection

A day at the beach. ca. 1929. The ocean provided moments of relaxation from work for an Issei family who donned American style bathing suits for swimming.

Hazama Collection

New Year's Day was a fun-filled and relaxing day of visiting for everyone except Mother who stayed at home and served all the traditional Japanese New Year's foods that she had prepared for her family and guests. Father visited friends in the neighborhood and camps and was served drinks and food wherever he went. The children also visited their friends and exploded firecrackers. For some families that had moved off the plantations into small towns in the country, it was a time for a break from the busy routines of running small businesses with a picnic or a trip into exciting Honolulu. Although some of the customs are no longer observed, New Year's Day continues to be a festive and significant day of the year for the entire family. Families also gather for American holidays such as Thanksgiving and Christmas.

Although they lived largely in their own ethnic communities, the Japanese were slowly integrated into the larger Hawaiian community. Many worked for and with peoples of other racial groups. The Japanese women (mama-sans) were much sought as domestic servants by the Caucasians. Larger businesses in towns hired Japanese workers, first in entry positions and later in middle supervisory positions as a result of promotions. However, like other Asians, they were paid less than others as many firms maintained a dual pay scale. They were paid less for the same jobs because they were thought to have a lower standard of living, hence required less.

The social agencies such as the Ys, Boy Scouts, Girl Reserves and the churches brought the Japanese into contact with others of the larger community. Japanese businesses began dealing with non-Japanese as a result of relocating outside of the Japanese districts and by expanding to provide goods and services desired by non-Japanese.

However, the greatest factor towards integration was the public schools. They were organized according to districts, which encompassed different racial groups. This was especially true of high schools as only one per major island existed in 1920. The four high schools were Līhu'e High School on Kaua'i, McKinley High School on O'ahu, Hāmākuapoko High School on Maui, and Hilo High School on the Big Island. Students from all over the island had to journey to one of the schools on each island for a high school education. For example, a student in Waipahu caught the train to the Dillingham Depot in 'A'ala and then paid a nickel's fare to ride the trolley to McKinley or walked the distance in order to save the fare for lunch money. The ride home was just as long for the weary student who still had homework to do at night. A number of neighbor island students worked for room and board in Honolulu or lived with relatives in town in order to attend high school. Families made great sacrifices to send their children to public or private boarding schools.

A 1920 federal survey reported that the Hawai'i students were well-behaved, neat, and attentive. The report reiterated the need for an agricultural education, but students were also encouraged to develop along the lines of law, medicine, and other professions. It further designated that teacher-pupil ratios be lowered, teacher salaries be raised, better and more physical facilities be provided, free transportation be made available to students living at a distance, kindergartens be started, and more secondary schools be built.

It was reported that many capable students were not able to go beyond the eighth grade because of the distances and the additional attendant costs. As a result of the team's findings, new high schools were added, enrollments increased, and junior high schools were established for the first time on all of the islands. The team also suggested that pupils be separated according to their ability to speak and write English. This recommendation coincided with the mounting pressure coming from non-private school haoles and Hawaiian parents who felt that the pidgin spoken by the Asian children slowed the progress of their children.

In 1924, the first English Standard grammar school was established at Lincoln School in Honolulu. That year only nineteen Japanese and twenty-seven Chinese students passed the test to enroll with the 572 haole and 126 part-Hawaiian pupils. The children went on to Stevenson Junior High and finally to Roosevelt High, which opened its doors in 1930.

The English Standard School System tended to segregrate the public school population by race and brought on many negative reactions. It was argued that the system caused those enrolled there to feel superior to the other public school students. Not only was their English superior, but because they tended to come from the more affluent families, they wore better clothes and had more spending money. This elitist attitude permeated to the teachers and some of the teachers even felt superior to those assigned elsewhere. In the Asian community, many viewed the English Standard Schools as an opportunity to get a prestigious education, to mingle with the haoles, and to learn "American ways." Many Asian families aspired to send their children there and the percentage of Asians at these continued to increase.

I Didn't Think We Were Poor

According to today's standards, we were poor. But I didn't think so then. After all, most of my friends in Nishi Camp in Waipahu during the 20s and 30s lived in the same kind of company house that we lived in. The things they had, the clothes they wore, and the food they ate were similar to ours. We knew about each other for our houses were so close. Besides, we were always in and out of each other's homes.

True, there was the Miyagi family that lived in a bigger house like the lunas'. But Mr. Miyagi was special! Unlike other fathers, he wore a white shirt and tie to his job at Waiahole Water Supply's office. As long time President of the Japanese Social Club, he frequently lectured us on Japanese values before the monthly movies. At school, there were a few students who seemed to have better things than most of us. Their families were in business in Waipahu town.

But most of my friends were like me. In fact I thought I was luckier than others. We always had enough to eat. We had milk daily, something many other families didn't have. My father, who worked for the Plantation, was convinced of the benefits of milk for growing children. He made sure that we had some every day. Then there were the two holidays, New Year's and Obon, when we had soda water. Hanaoka Soda Water Company used to deliver the case of soda. We could hardly wait to get a sip.

One summer I went to Kokubun Sewing School where I learned to draft patterns and to sew dresses. Other summers were spent at Japanese sewing and craft classes. After graduating from Waipahu School, I went to ninth grade at Central Intermediate School in Honolulu and on to McKinley High School. During these four years I boarded with relatives in Honolulu, returning to Waipahu on the weekends and during the summers. After high school, I went on to Cannon's School of Business which enabled me to get an office job at O'ahu Sugar Company.

My parents believed strongly in giving even their daughters as much education as they could afford. My older sister was sent to Japan to study while my younger sister graduated from the University of Hawaii. One brother went to Mid Pacific Institute and the University of Hawaii while the other went to St. Louis College in Honolulu before studying electronics on the mainland.

To finance these endeavors, Mother did her share to bring in additional income. She was one of the few in Waipahu who could sew Japanese clothing. She also custom made khaki pants at 50 cents per pair. Her customers liked her pants because they fit well and were comfortable. She sewed late into the night to meet her customers' deadlines for kimonos and pants. Later she added the sewing of dresses to her list. Because she couldn't draft dress patterns, it was my job to do that on the weekends at home from school in Honolulu. A completed outfit brought 35 cents.

There were fun times also. Father used to take us clamming at Pearl Harbor in his second-hand Model T Ford. He fashioned nets out of chicken wire which we used to drag the bottom and to sift out the clams. We also went to the adjacent Honouliuli area for crabs. The sea delicacies were so plentiful then. We took home only what we needed. We never "hogged," for we knew we could come back for more.

Tomoe Inokuchi Yamaguchi
Interviewed on November 4, 1984

Tomoe Yamaguchi graduated as Valedictorian of her 8th grade Waipahu School class. Because 8th grade was the terminal grade for most, graduation was a big event. Friends and family showered the graduates with bouquets of flowers as well as flower, silk and paper leis.
Yamaguchi Collection

The teachers in the public schools in the 1920s were primarily mainland haoles and locally trained part-Hawaiians. With the expansion of the Territorial Normal School under the principalship of Dr. Benjamin Wist, the proportion of locally trained teachers increased. For the Asian, it was an opportunity to join a much respected profession without having to complete an expensive Mainland education. In the late 1920s about one-third of the Normal School students were of Japanese ancestry. By 1935, there were over 400 Nisei teachers in the public schools. Not only did the Normal School grow in size during this period, but its training standards and teacher salaries were raised. A change in policy made high school graduation a prerequisite to admission. The training period was lengthened from one year to two years. Further improvements were made when Teachers College was organized as part of the University of Hawaii in 1931. Wist became the Dean of Teachers College and continued to exert his philosophy of "progressive" education. He sincerely believed that one of the main objectives of education was good citizenship.

The locally trained teachers joined the Mainland teachers who had been helping the eager public school students not only to read and to write, but to value democracy and patriotism. They taught them that all men were created equal and that the U.S. Constitution guaranteed each person the right to liberty and the pursuit of

Waialua Elementary School Faculty, 1940

Educators greatly influenced the Nisei during their impressionable years. Five locally trained Nisei teachers have taken their place on the predominantly Caucasian and Hawaiian faculty. They were respected by the community, and children aspired to be like them. Their number grew in the years to come.

Ninomiya Collection

happiness. America, it was said, was a place of opportunity where, with hard work, one could succeed in any field of his choice. American history and government, with frequent references to heroes such as Thomas Jefferson, Abraham Lincoln, Thomas Edison, and Henry Ford, were taught. Student governments and clubs were encouraged to give the youngsters the opportunity to practice self-government, decision-making, and self-responsibility.

This "progressive" trend in education did not sit well with the ruling haole business community as the principles advocated ran contrary to their paternalistic business practices. Many of them believed that schooling for the Asian children should be limited and that education beyond the sixth grade was not necessary for plantation laborers. When educated, the young people tended to leave the plantations, thus depriving the industry of much needed laborers. They also argued that too much of the tax money was being spent on public education. They resented the fact that the Asians, the Japanese in particular, had the largest percentage of children in the public schools, but paid only a small percentage of the taxes.

Then there were other haoles led by Governor Wallace Farrington (1921-1929) who felt that the expanded educational opportunities would help the students to become better American citizens who could contribute to the growth of the Hawaiian economy and community. He told the business community that, among other values, the dignity of manual labor would continue to be taught. He believed that young people would then see the benefits and choose to remain in agriculture. He had the help of able Superintendents of Instruction to implement his philosophy.

Still another group followed the principles advocated by Miles Cary, principal of McKinley High, who hoped some day to see a change in the Hawaiian social and business structure from a paternalistic one to a democratic one. The way to this was through educating the students to become independent thinkers who could utilize their creativity and talents to the maximum.

Under the leadership of educators such as Superintendents of Public Instruction Vaughn MacCaughy and Will C. Crawford and Principal Miles Cary, the schools continued to expand the students' horizons. They began to question the paternalistic economic and social systems and wanted to work toward changing them. It was not the menial work that the students resented most. They remembered the indignities and limitations that they and their parents had encountered. They wanted out and education was one of the keys to a better life. The students dreamed of and worked towards not only completing high school in increasing numbers, but of going to colleges and professional schools both locally and on the Mainland. Even those who could not or did not complete high school learned a trade, as they did not want to remain laborers.

Black and Gold Annual

"Dr. Cary made a difference in my life. Through words and through actions he taught me that I was a worthy individual. I was one of 3000 students, but I knew he cared for me just as he cared for every other student. We had an assembly on Friday mornings. Dr. Cary was there in his white suit singing McKinley's Creed of Honor along with us. He always had a message and a challenge to us to dare to dream big dreams," recalled a former student.

Miles E. Cary who served as principal of McKinley High School from 1924 to 1948 not only believed in democracy but practiced it. For him, student government and other extracurricular activities were laboratories for citizenship and necessary to an education. He fanned the hopes and aspirations of the students and encouraged them to work toward a better Hawai'i. During his twenty-four year tenure, he influenced thousands of students who took his message to heart. Many of them have become the builders of the New Hawai'i.

Former McKinley Student
Interviewed 1984

Also lending his talents and efforts toward Americanization of the Nisei was the Reverend Takie Okumura, who in 1927 helped found the New Americans, a student organization. It brought together Nisei delegates from the different islands for meetings in Honolulu. At these conferences, the group listened to leaders from government and business. They also discussed such topics as the problems between the other Americans and the Japanese, how the Japanese could mingle more freely with those of other races, and which Japanese customs hindered their occupational and cultural Americanization.

Reverend and Mrs. Takie Okumura
Ninomiya Collection

Okumura Sensei, as the students addressed him, was remembered as a warm person. A widow who asked to remain anonymous said that her husband from Kaua'i lived with the Okumuras from the time he was nine years old and until he finished his schooling. Sensei was an avid collector of Abraham Lincoln memorabilia of all kinds and displayed them in his home which was adjacent to the boarding home. Although he was strict, he never raised his voice.

Instead, when the students did not mind him, he sat on the porch and prayed. Mrs. Okumura would then explain to the children that Sensei felt very badly because of their poor behavior. The students in turn felt badly and tried to remember not to disappoint him again. Boarding with the Okumuras enabled many Nisei to go to high school in Honolulu in the early years when there were none in their home communities. It also introduced them to Christianity. Makiki Christian Church in Honolulu stands as a testament to Rev. Okumura's ministry among the Japanese.

Reverend Okumura advised the Nisei to be grateful for and to accept their positions in the existing community. He suggested that they reevaluate the benefits of agricultural work and that they get back to the land, not necessarily on the plantations but as independent farmers. The Reverend Okumura was supported in his efforts by the Japanese daily, the *Nippu Jiji.*

Fred Kinzaburō Makino and the *Hawaii Hōchi,* on the other hand, advised the Nisei to take to heart the American concepts of equality, justice, and freedom. The Nisei were admonished against feeling inferior to the whites and were told to fight any injustice. Only when Nisei incorporated these American ideals would they be respected as Americans.

The Public And The Private Glimpses Of Fred Makino

The public knew Frederick Kinzaburō Makino as the daring defender of the Japanese people, and this view was eloquently affirmed in this testimonial by Governor John A. Burns:

> Makino was fearless in expressing his opinions and in calling attention to the gross injustices that were then being perpetuated against the immigrant laborers. No cause was too small for Makino to champion when justice was the issue. No obstacle was too challenging when a matter of principle was involved.

Born of an English father and a Japanese mother in Yokohama, Japan, in August, 1877, he was a tall and imposing figure. He arrived in Hawai'i in 1899. His wife, Michiye, recalled that life with him was "one of continued turbulence" as he took a leadership role in the first plantation workers' strike and was subsequently imprisoned, and pressured by government authorities. At various

108

times, Makino also operated a drug store and raised pigs. In 1912, he ventured into publishing a newspaper, *Hawaii Hōchi*, in order to protect the rights of the local residents. "My husband," she wrote, "often had to sell pigs in order to pay for the newsprint used in his newspaper. He used to joke, 'The newsprint looks like pigs.'"

Sadasuke Terasaki, who had worked with Makino at the *Hōchi* for over fifty years as writer and editor, described Makino as having:

> . . . characteristics of the old-type bosses of the Edo period in Japan. He did not stand by and look on when the others were in trouble. . . . He had full faith in the American Constitution which stated that those living within the boundaries of the United States of America were equally protected and had equal rights.

Those who knew him also describe a human and compassionate side to this educated and articulate man. Makino, who had no children of his own, loved them, and was able to establish rapport readily. When he lived in Mānoa, he was much sought after as a speaker at the Mānoa Language School. The students loved his stories and American jokes. A neighbor, Mrs. Toyo Fujise, recalled how happy Mr. Makino was "when her first born was a son. He took over the task of naming the child . . ." Kinsuke Kaneshiro, who lived in Wai'alae as a youngster, reminisced, "I had to walk to and from the Kaimuki Public School those days . . . The streetcar terminal was then on Twelfth Avenue. There were no buses . . . Mr. Makino usually passed by in his car, in the morning just as I was about to climb the hill in Kaimuki. He'd stop and say, Boy let me give you a ride.' . . . He used to tell us jokes and interesting stories."

from *Life of Kinzaburō Makino*

The Japanese wanted to be fully accepted by the island community and the Nisei wanted to be accepted as Americans! But they were regarded with suspicion and antagonism by many. For one thing, the Nisei had been brought up with Japanese values, customs, traditions, and language at home and at the language school. In public school they studied the English language and American values, customs, and traditions. Many values such as honesty, hard work, and the desire for success were the same in the two cultures. However, there were other values that differed or were contradictory. The Nisei's family celebrations and customs differed from those of the larger community. The Nisei had to make choices and adjustments which sometimes resulted in conflicts at home. Secondly, the Nisei were faced with the question of how and to what degree they needed to make changes in their lifestyles to be accepted as Americans. One group was preaching acquiescence, while the other was advocating a more aggressive path.

Even while the Nisei were trying to work through their dilemma, prejudice continued to grow. The number of Japanese had increased during the twenties and thirties. According to government statistics, the Japanese steadily increased from a population of 109,274 in 1920 to 157,905 in 1940.

In terms of the total population of the Islands, however, their percentage had actually dropped from a high of 42.7 percent in 1920 to 37.3 percent twenty years later. Although their percentage was decreasing, their numbers were increasing and they had become more visible as more and more of them left the tight plantation communities for the urban areas.

The Japanese were thus feared and looked on with suspicion because of their numbers. This fear was not a new phenomenon, for, as far back as the 1880s, segments of the community had feared that the Japanese had been placed in the Islands in large numbers for an eventual takeover by the Japanese government. They had

A simple Shinto ceremony witnessed by family members and two sets of nakahodo united this couple in marriage. After a purification rite, the bridal couple sealed their marriage when each took three sips of sake (wine). The strip of fabric covering the hair, which is done in a special style, is called a tsunokakushi *or horn concealer. Circa 1930.*

Nakamoto Collection

remained clannish, and, unlike the Chinese, had not intermarried to any degree. They had continued to live by the customs and traditions of the old country. Were they biding time until a takeover? This fear was one of the major reasons given by those advocating annexation to the United States. Even after annexation, these suspicions continued as the Japanese laborers organized themselves and struck against the plantations. Their insistence on continuing the language schools added fuel to the negative feelings.

The thought of the large Japanese population was trouble enough, but when the proportion of U.S. citizens among the Japanese increased, the fear of political control of the Islands by these Nisei grew. A 1920 federal survey had predicted that by 1940, 47 percent of the electorate would be of Japanese descent. Was Hawai'i to become an extension of Japan?

The Nisei, by being born on American territory, were citizens and had all the attendant rights, including the franchise to vote. Their numbers had grown from 39,127 in 1920 to 113,189 in 1937. This phenomenal growth was attributed to an especially high birth rate during this period due to the coming of the picture brides. The birth rate reached a peak in 1925 when the 6,186 Japanese births were responsible for almost one-half of the total registered that year. By 1940, because of the increasing ages of the picture brides and the desire for a higher standard of living, the number of Japanese births decreased to about one-half of the 1925 figure.

In reality, although the Japanese had the largest population, only a small percentage was eligible to vote in the twenties and early thirties. The Issei, alien Japanese, did not have the franchise. There were many Nisei citizens, but they were not of voting age. In 1920, the Japanese constituted only 2.5 percent of the total registered to vote. This figure rose to 7.6 percent in 1926 and by 1936 to 25 percent. Through the thirties, the Republicans were concerned about bloc voting by the Japanese as their number of eligible voters increased. Analyses of the voting, however, proved this concern to be unfounded. Even in districts where Japanese dominated, Japanese candidates were not elected.

Those Nisei who ran for office, beginning with James T. Hamada, candidate for the House of Representatives from Kaua'i in 1920, were generally Republicans. It was easier in the twenties and thirties to run as a Republican, for the party was in control and was able to give liberal financial and campaign aid to its candidates. Only Republicans were allowed to campaign on the plantations, as most, if not all of the planters and managers were Republicans. In general, the Democratic party was powerless as it lacked leadership and was factionalized.

Dr. Harry Kurisaki, who was the first Japanese to be elected to the Republican County Committee in the twenties, ran for the House in 1928 and lost. However, in 1930, Republicans Noboru Miyake and Tasaku Oka were elected to the Kaua'i Board of Supervisors and to the House of Representatives from East Hawai'i respectively. Andy Yamashiro, a Democrat, was also elected to the House from Honolulu that year.

In the following years, others ran. Only a few such as Republican Thomas T. Sakakihara, Toshio Anzai, and Benjamin Tashiro were elected. In 1936, of the twenty-four Japanese who ran, only nine were elected. Of these, eight were Republicans and one was a Democrat. In 1940, there were twenty-nine Japanese candidates, only four of whom were Democrats. Of the twenty-nine, twelve Republicans and one Democrat were elected.

Nisei Wilfred C. Tsukiyama, who had graduated from the University of Chicago Law School in 1924, was the first Japanese to be appointed to a high position in government. He became Deputy Attorney for the City and County of Honolulu in 1929 and City and County Attorney four years later. He held that post until 1940 when he resigned his position because of growing tension between the United States and Japan. He felt it unwise for a Nisei to be in the foreground at such a time. Another prominent Nisei, Steere G. Noda, worked with the Internal Revenue Service and held the position of district court clerk and interpreter. Still another, Tomekichi Okino of Hilo was the first Nisei to be appointed to a judicial position in the Territorial government. While there were these individual cases of acceptance by the community and growing understanding and friendship on a one-to-one basis through increasing interracial contact, such was not the situation for the Japanese as a group. Not only were the Japanese, both Issei and Nisei, still looked upon with antagonism and suspicion, they were also discriminated against.

During a three-year period in the late twenties and early thirties, two tragic incidents rocked the island community, disrupted race relations, and glaringly revealed the lack of racial equality under the law. On September 18, 1928, a frail Nisei youth, Myles Fukunaga, distraught over the threat of his family's eviction from their home by the Hawaiian Trust Co., kidnapped and brutally murdered ten-year-old Gill Jamieson, the only child of a vice president of the company. He wrote a wordy, rambling ransom note and managed to collect $4,000 of the $10,000 that he had demanded. Japanese groups were the first to volunteer for the all-out search for Myles, a bright student and one who was considered trustworthy, gentle, but moody by those who had known him. Upon apprehension, he readily confessed. His parents publicly apologized and expressed their deep shame over their son's actions. The entire Japanese community felt that the murder was a reflection upon their reputation as well.

MR. AND MRS. JUSUKE FUKUNAGA

parents of Myles Yutaka, want to express their profound regret for the terrible thing that has happened, and their sorrow for the trouble and anxiety their son has caused the entire community. And to Mr. and Mrs. Frederick Jamieson, they offer their deepest sympathy.

An apology to the people of Hawaii from Myles' parents.
Honolulu Star Bulletin
September 24, 1928

The court system moved swiftly. By October 3, Myles was brought to trial and by October 8 he was sentenced to be hanged. Myles courteously thanked the court and the jury for their kindness and for the swift justice. However, some members of the Japanese community felt differently. Under the leadership of Fred Makino, outspoken editor of the *Hawaii Hochi*, they demanded a retrial on the basis of insanity, citing the ransom letter and the way in which Myles had placed the boy's body when it was found. University of Hawaii psychologists and a medical doctor agreed that Myles Fukunaga was indeed insane. The *Hochi* cited the fact that recently a politically influential haole who had murdered a Japanese taxi driver was charged only with second degree murder. In another case, a haole mechanic who had doused a Japanese worker with gasoline was tried for manslaughter and acquitted. The *Hochi* argued that these incidents clearly demonstrated that there was one law for the white man and another for the non-whites. The United States Supreme Court refused to reopen the case, and Myles Fukunaga was hanged a year and two months after the murder. [5]

Almost three years later, yet another case, the Massie case, shook not only the Hawaiian community, but also had repercussions on race relations on the Mainland and beyond. Just before 2 a.m. on September 13, 1931, Navy Lt. Thomas Massie telephoned the police that his wife, Thalia, had been beaten and raped at Ala Moana Park, near Waikīkī, by five or six Hawaiian boys. At about the same time a group of local boys were reported for being in a brawl after an automobile accident in another section of Honolulu. The driver was a young Japanese named Horace Ida and the passengers included two Hawaiians, another Japanese, and a Chinese-Hawaiian. Based on Mrs. Massie's descriptions, the boys in the accident were picked up and questioned about the assault and rape. At separate interrogations, each indicated that they had been driving around and partying in Waikīkī and in Nu'uanu Valley before the accident. They contended that they had nothing to do with the attack on Mrs. Massie.

When the case was tried, the jury, composed of six white men, one Portuguese, two Chinese, and a Hawaiian, could not agree on a verdict, and a mistrial was proclaimed. Five of the jurors felt strongly that the evidence did not indicate rape and that the timing could not have placed the suspects concurrently at the scene of the alleged rape and at the spot of the accident. A subsequent report by the Pinkerton Detective Agency to the Governor agreed that the acquittal was justified.

Six days later, driver Ida was abducted by some sailors from the submarine base, beaten with leather belts, and kicked unconscious. Thalia Massie's mother, Mrs. Fortescue, and her son-in-law, with the help of two other Navy men, kidnapped one of the Hawaiians and shot him, but they were caught with the victim's body still in the car. They were found guilty of manslaughter after a sensational trial and sentenced to ten years at hard labor. Angered by the verdict, the Commandant of the Fourteenth Naval District sent word to Washington condemning the administration of justice in Hawai'i. Congress as well as the general public on the Mainland were incensed for no one had been punished for the alleged rape, while a jury of people of mixed blood had convicted white persons for taking revenge. Within a day of the conviction, Governor Lawrence M. Judd, under instructions from Washington, commuted the sentence to one hour, after which the four guilty parties were freed.

The Massie case also aroused questions about Hawai'i's Territorial status and its ability to govern itself. The U.S. Attorney

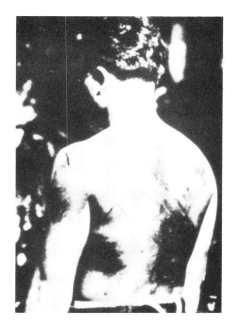

Ida's back.
World Wide photo
Wright, Theon
Rape in Paradise

General's office in 1932 reported to the Senate that the Territory's law enforcement system was "impotent, undisciplined, neglectful, and unintelligent." The Navy Commandant further reported that the Territory's racially mixed population included sinister people of low moral character amongst whom white women were not safe, as well as a group of disloyal Japanese. The Navy, therefore, strongly recommended that Hawai'i be placed under its control and be given a commission form of government. Hawai'i's sugar interests fought the recommendation, for with Territorial status they had almost complete economic and political benefits. There was much discussion in Congress, but none of the bills advocating changes passed.

Although they had been satisfied with Territorial status since annexation and had fought both the commission and statehood forms of government, the planters abruptly changed their stand in 1934 when the Jones-Costigan Act passed Congress. The Act not only decreased Hawai'i's quota of sugar to the Mainland by eight to ten percent, but altered Hawai'i's status from that of an integral part of the United States to that of a "foreign" place. The Territory's businessmen were made fully aware that they were being governed by laws made by a congress in which they had no vote. Therefore in May, 1935, when Congressional Delegate Samuel

Wilder King introduced a new version of a statehood bill in the House of Representatives, he had the support of Hawai'i's sugar interests. The very first statehood bill had been introduced as early as 1919.

In the Congressional hearings that followed, anti-Japanese feelings surfaced and the Japanese menace became a major issue used against statehood by Congressional leaders and by many of those who testified. In the 1937 hearing, one of the distinguished speakers was John F. G. Stokes, former curator of Polynesian ethnology at the Bishop Museum, who claimed that Japan had been plotting world domination. To support his argument that Hawai'i was but a step towards the attainment of this objective, he traced the history of Japanese involvement in Hawai'i since 1880. He explained the devious plot in this way:

> Unperceived by ourselves, the white population of Hawaii has become Japanese-minded, and this fact constitutes a strong argument against statehood. The technique has been that of the Japanese "Gentle Divine Spirit," to which white people yield very readily – especially those of wealth and importance. It appeals to the white man's conceit, and feeds his superiority complex to aid "his little brown brother." [6]

In responding to questions by a U.S. Senator, he further expanded on this insidious plot, asserting that "Highly educated and intelligent Japanese are put as servants in the homes of our most influential people," by the Japanese government so that they can reach positions of trust.

There were, however, others, such as Frank Midkiff, a highly respected educator, who refuted statements made by Stokes. Having involved himself in the community with various ethnic groups, Frank Midkiff testified for the loyalty of the Japanese Americans and further spoke out in favor of the retention of Japanese customs as a way to enrich American culture. He declared, "One thing we do know: They are good members of our community. They are industrious, law abiding, polite, self-dependent; they have excellent family life and they contribute their full share to the wealth and development of our Territory." In his testimony, Frank Midkiff advocated a positive philosophy which would have much meaning in the years to come: "To secure cooperation and loyalty, citizens must be treated as cooperative and their rights respected, otherwise suspicion and overt offense will engender resentment and noncooperation."[7]

At the conclusion of the hearings, the Joint Congressional

Committee recommended that the Territory hold a plebiscite on statehood. However, questions that had been raised about the loyalty of the Japanese remained in the minds of many people. How could a group of people that included 35,000 who were ineligible for citizenship, and whose children, the Nisei, held dual citizenship, be trusted as loyal Americans? Weren't the Nisei still under the domination of their Issei parents?

Dual citizenship had resulted when the two countries, Japan and America, claimed citizens on different criteria. America based its citizenship on Jus Soli, or citizenship by place of birth. Japan, on the other hand, operated on the principle of Jus Sanguinis, citizenship through that of the child's father. Hence, a child born to an Issei in Hawai'i was an American citizen by Jus Soli and a Japanese citizen by Jus Sanguinis. In 1924, the Japanese government moved towards alleviating this problem for the Nisei by providing methods of expatriation and by decreeing that any child born of Japanese parents in the United States after December 1, 1924, would not be a Japanese citizen unless his birth was reported to the Japanese Consulate within fourteen days.

Attitude Of Japanese Government Toward Expatriation

Our government does not have the least desire to retain, or make any claim on children born in Hawaii or America. Our earnest desire is that they shall grow up into strong, trustworthy American citizens, without any string tied to the old country. . . . *To expatriate oneself is not an act of disloyalty. It is a duty which every young man must perform to the country of his birth, and the performance of that duty is earnestly desired by Japan.* Go back and tell the Japanese in Hawaii that Wakatsuki said so, and urge them to speed up the expatriation of their children.

> Baron Reijiro Wakatsuki
> Minister of the Interior
> Summer, 1925

Quoted in Wakukawa (p. 321-322) from *The New Americans,* March, 1933, p. 4-5.

Penalized For Dual Citizenship

Excerpts from the minutes of the University of Hawaii Board of Regents' meetings:

July 26, 1940

Pursuant to a recommendation by the President, it was moved by Mrs. Frear, seconded by Mr. Collins and

Voted: to award the 1940 territorial scholarships to the following individuals, subject to the completion of expatriation in the case of any dual citizens:

Wai King Tong - First District
Tsugita Uehara - Second District
Toshikazu Shigezawa - Third District
Agnes Poindexter - Fourth District
Wilfred Lee - Fifth District
George Hyane - Sixth District

September 20, 1940

With reference to a previous action of the Board, the President reported that George Hyane, to whom a territorial scholarship had been tentatively awarded, had not been able to clear himself of citizenship obligations to the Japanese government. Accordingly, it was moved by Mr. Keppeler, seconded by Mrs. Frear and

Voted: that the tentative award should be withdrawn and the scholarship awarded to Miss Louise Samson who was next in order of merit on the list of applicants from the 6th Representative District.

April 28, 1941

With reference to the provision that applicants for the Territorial Scholarships must have effected expatriation from foreign allegiance before any award is made by the Board, the President called attention to the fact that some applicants of Japanese ancestry might have difficulty in meeting this requirement, citing as an example one prospective applicant, a girl, both of whose parents were American born; as they were not expatriated from Japanese allegiance the Japanese government would still have a technical claim on her, even though her birth had not been registered in the Japanese Consulate. After some discussion, it was generally agreed that in cases such as this an affidavit either from the Japanese Consulate or from the mother or father of the applicant declaring that the individual concerned had not been registered as a Japanese subject would be equivalent to expatriation for the present purposes.

Of the 40,000 births of Japanese Americans from 1925 through 1933, approximately two-thirds were not registered with the Japanese Consulate. The proportion of non-dual citizens continued to rise so that by the time Wilfred Tsukiyama testified before the 1937 Statehood Commitee hearings, only one of every ten young children was a dual citizen.

Also decreasing the number of dual citizens was the expatriation drive conducted by the Hawaiian Japanese Civic Association in 1938. Other organizations, including the Hawaii Congress of Parents and Teachers, aided in educating the Nisei about the importance of relinquishing Japanese citizenship and facilitated the process of expatriation. This movement was given major impetus by the questions raised during the 1935 and 1937 Congressional Statehood hearings.

Another major factor of suspicion was the continued enrollment of the Nisei in the language schools. In 1940, there were about 175 such schools where 40,000 youngsters studied after the regular public school hours. Many of the teachers were Buddhist priests, born and trained in Japan. Others were Kibei, Japanese who were born in the Islands but educated in Japan. It was often remarked that the Kibei were more "Japanesey" than the Issei. Also many of them had lived in Japan during the period of military control of the government. Therefore, there continued to be the question of whether things Japanese were being taught to prepare for an eventual takeover by imperialistic Japan.

The international situation did not help to allay the suspicions, as Japan became more and more aggressive beginning in 1931 with the Manchurian Incident. Then, in 1937, Japan's government was taken over by the military with territorial conquests as its goal.

During this period, the Japanese in Hawai'i, primarily the Issei, followed the battles and victories of the Japanese military forces and government through radio broadcasts, newspapers, and newsreels at the theatres. They responded to Japan's call for war relief contributions by sending money as well as goods. Japanese women, both Issei and Nisei, helped sew *sennin-bari*, waistbands of a thousand stitches which were intended to guard the Japanese soldiers from enemy bullets.

Concerned leaders in the Japanese community launched a drive to petition the U.S. government to seek the help of the Japanese government to simplify the expatriation procedure. Seated: Wilfred C. Tsukiyama. Standing left to right: Katsuro Miho, Masa Katagiri, Shigeo Yoshida, and Shunzo Sakamaki.

Sakamaki File
University of Hawaii

The prospects of a confrontation between the United States and Japan increased as Japan continued its war activities in China and Southeast Asia. To protect itself and to prepare for war, the U.S. took many steps. In May of 1939, the U.S. declared Pearl Harbor and its surrounding waters as a restricted zone, and stationed the Pacific Navy fleet permanently there in early 1940. In the latter part of 1939, the Selective Service Act was instituted requiring registration of all young men for possible military service. Many Nisei were thus inducted into the Army. Those selected considered it an honor to serve their country, and the proud families gave them memorable sendoffs with parties, speeches, leis, and gifts of money.

Throughout 1941, the mounting tension between Japan and the United States had an impact on Hawai'i as the American military worked towards building up its forces and defenses in the Pacific. By the fall of 1941, the Army had soldiers, not only on O'ahu, but on Hawai'i, Maui, Kaua'i, and Moloka'i. The Navy had about 80,000 men in Hawaiian waters. Both groups were very much involved in maneuvers. The civilian worker population, especially at Pearl Harbor, increased as the military prepared additional housing and built supply and repair facilities. Improvements were made on ships, and more and better planes were brought in.

Military intelligence activities also increased. The Federal Bureau of Investigation and the Honolulu Police Department were also working on the problem of internal security and the possibility of sabotage by the Japanese community in the event of war. Although studies indicated that the Nisei were loyal, there were questions about the Kibei, the Buddhist and Shintō priests, the language school teachers, and the Consular personnel. Lists of the suspects were made and revised as more information was gathered by the military and civilian intelligence. The Red Cross was placed on virtual wartime alert.

The civilian population also geared itself for war. The Governor named committees on such matters as increasing local food production and storage, transportation, handling of civilian casualties, and additional police. He even made evacuation plans in the event of an emergency. The Major Disaster Council created in 1941 consisted of twenty subcommittes whose responsibility was to prepare for the possibility of war. In October, 1941, a special session of the Territorial Legislature passed the M-D Act often referred to as the civilian martial law, which gave the governor additional powers in the event of an emergency.

The Japanese community was also very involved in preparations. Some leaders cooperated with Robert Shivers, agent in charge of the F.B.I. in Honolulu, on the Committee for Inter-Racial Unity in Hawai'i. This committee served in an advisory capacity to the F.B.I. on how to maintain racial harmony in the event of war.

Another group, the Oahu Citizens for Home Defense, focused on the Japanese community to promote loyalty to the United States and to prepare the people psychologically for war. The group sponsored a large patriotic rally at McKinley High School in June, 1941. A resolution reaffirming the AJA's loyalty and willingness to serve the country was adopted and copies were sent to government officials in Hawai'i, and in Washington, D.C. The several thousand AJAs present were reassured that in the event of war, they would be protected by U.S. laws. The Army said it would deal fairly with the Japanese as long as they remained loyal to the United States.

These were but two of the many organizations which worked to meet the needs of the Japanese in Hawai'i during these troubled times. But, the question of loyalty remained and became more urgent as relations between the two countries worsened. What stand would the Japanese in Hawai'i take in the event of war between the two countries?

Chapter VII
THE WAR YEARS, 1941-45

7:57 a.m., Sunday morning, December 7, 1941. Japanese fighter planes swooped out of the skies and attacked Pearl Harbor and other military installations on O'ahu. The Japanese had launched 360 planes in three waves from six aircraft carriers stationed 200 miles north of O'ahu. The first U.S. anti-aircraft batteries were in action within seven to ten minutes of the attack, but the Japanese inflicted much damage, most of it within the first half hour. Eighteen naval vessels were either totally destroyed or severely damaged while 188 planes were demolished. Hangars, machine shops, guard houses, and barracks were also hit; and 2,335 U.S. servicemen, mostly Navy personnel, perished in the holocaust. When the injured were included, the casualty list totaled 3,478. Japan and the United States were at war, and Hawai'i's people from Japan faced the most trying and challenging period in their history.

Hawai'i's residents were in a state of disbelief at first. But low-flying planes with the rising sun insignia on their wingtips, fires, accidents, and injuries in the military and civilian communities on O'ahu caused by bombs, shrapnel, machine gun bullets, and other projectiles, coupled with repeated radio bulletins recalling all military personnel to duty and medical workers and truck drivers to the hospitals, brought the reality of the war into focus. Other emergency units were also activated and citizens were asked to report to the Territorial Guard, the Red Cross, and the school cafeterias. American citizens of Japanese ancestry reported to their stations, military and civilian, along with the others. Subsequent announcements instructed civilians to keep off the streets, to fill buckets and tubs with water, and to listen to the radio for further instructions.

At 11:15 a.m., just hours after the attack on Pearl Harbor, Governor Joseph B. Poindexter issued a proclamation invoking the powers delegated to him by the M-Day Act. However, by 3:30 p.m. of the same day, the Governor, at the insistence of Lt. General Walter C. Short and, after a telephone conversation with President Franklin D. Roosevelt, proclaimed martial law. The Governor had

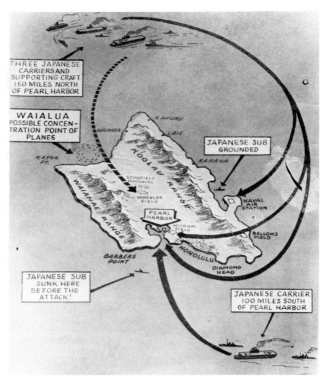

This drawing shows the routes that the enemy took in attacking the various O'ahu military establishments on December 7, 1941.

Hawaii State Archives

been reluctant to accede to military rule, but did so because of the imminent possibility of an invasion and attendant dangers from the large Japanese population in the Islands. He hoped that civilian rule could be restored in a short while. However, such was not to be. Although subsequently declared unconstitutional by the U.S. Supreme Court, martial law was continued in the Islands for about three years until October 24, 1944.

Under martial law, Lt. General Short, Commanding General of the Hawaiian Department, became the military governor and moved into 'Iolani Palace. He assumed charge of all facets of the Territorial and City governments including the judiciary. The writ of habeas corpus, which provides protection against unjust imprisonment, was suspended. Within three hours of declaration of martial law, about 200 members of the Japanese community,

124

"You Dirty Japs!"

Dan Inouye, a senior at McKinley High School, got on his bicycle to go to the aid station at Lunalilo School. He saw frightened people out on the streets and wondered what would become of them.

> They had worked so hard. They had wanted so desperately to be accepted, to be good Americans. And now, in a few cataclysmic minutes, it was all undone, . . . And then, pedalling along, it came to me at last that I would face that trouble, too, for my eyes were shaped just like those of that poor old man in the street, and my people were only a generation removed from the land that had spawned those bombers, the land that sent them to rain destruction on America, death on Americans. And choking with emotion, I looked up into the sky and called out, "You dirty Japs!"
>
> Why had they done it? Why couldn't they let us live in peace? My mind reeled with tormented, confused, unanswerable questions. Once, with the sharp pain of a fresh wound being freshly plucked, it came to me that any one of the men in that armada of planes flaunting the rising sun could be my cousin, and to this day I do not know but what it might have been so, for I have never wanted to find out.

Inouye, Daniel K.
Journey to Washington, p. 56-57

both aliens and citizens, were taken into custody by the F.B.I. and the Military Intelligence. The names and addresses of these Japanese who were considered most dangerous to the security of the Islands had already been compiled prior to the attack.

By nightfall, a curfew and a blackout were ordered. All cars, except military patrols, were to be off the streets by 6 p.m. Buses were to also stop running at 6. Everybody, except for an authorized few, was to be off the streets by 6:30 p.m. No civilian lights, including cigarette glows, were to show after 6. Until they learned to cover their windows with tar paper or black cloth, the Hawaiian community had early dinners and huddled around radios or went to bed.

Army gas masks were distributed to all Hawai'i residents. Masks were padded to fit children's faces while special "bunny masks" were made for infants. Everyone was encouraged to have his mask readily available at all times. Gas mask drills were held regularly in the schools.

Subsequent orders from the military governor's office covered every aspect of governmental regulations which determined the day-to-day activities of the civilian community. All schools, public and private, were closed, and teachers reported for emergency tasks such as the registration of aliens, fingerprinting of all residents, and the distribution of gas masks. Military tribunals were set up for the trial of civilians. Regulations were issued for traffic, firearms, gasoline, liquor, and foodstuffs. There was censorship of the mail as well as of the press, radio, and wireless. Wages and employment were frozen; and there were regulations for rents, restaurants, speed limits, and chlorination of water. Local Japanese fishermen were prohibited from sailing in Hawaiian waters, and their fishing fleet was impounded.

The Office of Food Supply was set up to take monthly inven-

SERVE IN SILENCE

Posters placed everywhere cautioned people against providing vital information. The admonition created an atmosphere of mistrust and suspicion. The enemy is portrayed as Hitler and Tojo combined.

War Records Depository
University of Hawaii

tories of food, to estimate the Islands' needs, and to maintain sufficient reserve supplies. Vegetable production, especially on O'ahu, was encouraged as locally produced vegetables were in short supply. Prior to December 7, most of the truck farmers had been Japanese aliens. Because of wartime restrictions such as no traveling before sunrise and no driving of trucks, fear of being interned, and loss of or fear of losing land to the military, the farmers drastically curtailed or stopped planting. The sugar and pineapple plantations were called on to help. They participated by making large tracts of land and labor available for farming. Victory gardens in backyards and vacant lots were encouraged. Because feed for poultry and livestock came primarily from the mainland U.S., the supplies had to be monitored and distribution regulated.

Through all of this, however, there was no territory-wide food rationing, only short periods of restrictions on the neighbor islands. There were periodic shortages of certain items such as fresh fruits, vegetables, and butter. Prices, however, were fixed and monitored by the Office of Price Control. Gasoline was an item strictly regulated by the government. Gas rationing cards were issued. Throughout the war, the basic ration was generally for ten gallons per month. Those in jobs important to the community or to the war effort received additional amounts.

Communiques issued in the ensuing days instructed all Japanese aliens to turn in any weapons, short wave radios, binoculars, and cameras in their possession to the nearest police station. Furthermore, households were cautioned against the use of short wave radios where Japanese propaganda could be heard by aliens. Confused and frightened, Japanese families, on their own, either turned in or merely threw away their precious heirlooms, such as samurai swords, kimonos, and artifacts without regard for their value. Buddhist and Shinto shrines were taken down. Pictures of the Emperor as well as those of relatives in Japan, books, letters, and family records that might cast suspicion on their ties to Japan were burned, for they feared a search by the military. In areas of Japanese concentration, the Army Signal Corps, assisted by volunteers, did make house-to-house searches to pick up contraband goods.

Contributing to the anxieties of the entire Hawaiian community and the Japanese in particular was the uncertain danger of further attacks by Japan, especially an invasion. Fears of espionage and

During the early days of the war, trenches were dug all over the Island. At the sound of the air raid siren, people jumped into the trenches with their heads down until the all clear signal. Drills were held at the schools to familiarize students with the correct procedure. Shown is a group of students in a drill at McKinley High School.

Honolulu Star Bulletin Photo
War Records Depository
University of Hawaii

128

sabotage were on everyone's mind. Rumors were reported and circulated about the role that the Japanese in Hawai'i had in supporting the sneak attack. There was talk about arrows having been cut in the cane fields by plantation workers to direct the Japanese flyers to Pearl Harbor and of cane fires that were set as signals. A Japanese dry goods store's advertisement on December 3, 1941, was interpreted as giving instructions to the enemy about the best time to attack and the names of the ships in Pearl Harbor.

Suspicion Without Grounds

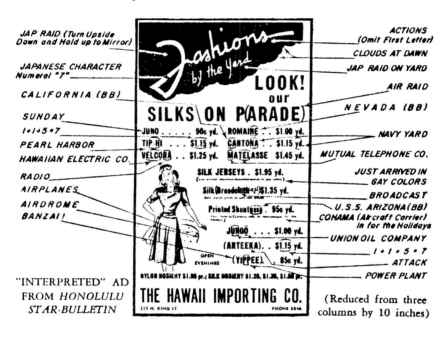

Ad for the store that Jane Komeiji's mother managed.

War Records Depository
University of Hawaii

Noboru Hino, who worked at Hawaii Importing for many years, had designed the advertisement. He recalled:

I had no idea about the furor that the ad was causing until about a week after December 7 when a Japanese newspaper man told me about it. It was such a surprise! I was taken aback, for the store had run an ad with the same over-all design the year before. Because I thought that the cloud-like heading and the phrase, "Fashions by the Yard," were clever and attractive, I used them again for the December 3, 1941 ad. The names of the fabrics were those registered by the mainland manufacturers. I couldn't see anything remotely suspicious about the ad! How in the world did anyone make such connections as the man was telling me? I just couldn't believe it.

Apparently the rumor was spreading because more and more people began coming in to ask for the fabrics by name. However, they didn't buy any. To this day I don't understand or know how the rumor started.

. . . No, I was not interned. Neither was I ever questioned by the authorities. I was not scared because I knew that the ad was not a means of communicating with the Japanese officials.

Kame Okamoto, who managed Hawaii Importing at that time, recalled that soon after December 7, two or three men stormed upstairs to her living quarters and searched it and left. Nothing was really said to her. She only surmised much later that she and the store were suspected because of the ad.

Interviewed on November 4, 1984

Rumors circulated about McKinley High School and University of Hawaii rings being found on Japanese pilots who were shot down, implying that they were former residents from Hawai'i. Word spread that the water supply was poisoned and that large caches of ammunition were found hidden on property owned by local Japanese. Each one of these rumors was investigated by the military and found to be false.

It was a time of extreme tension. Although persons of varying ethnic backgrounds had lived and worked side by side for many years, there was an undercurrent of anti-Japanese feeling even before December 7. The Japanese attack caused these latent feelings to surface. The Koreans disliked the Japanese because Japan had subjugated Korea, and the Filipinos were angered by the Japanese invasion of their homeland. Others had doubts about the loyalty of the Japanese Americans because they followed Japanese customs, went to language schools, and were generally clannish. "Once a Jap, always a Jap," was a phrase often heard. Should Japan land forces in the Islands, would Hawai'i's Japanese go to the aid of the enemy because of their ancestral ties?

130

On December 7, a Japanese pilot, unable to return to his aircraft carrier, landed his crippled plane on a field on the tiny isolated island of Niʻihau, inhabited by Hawaiians and owned by the Robinson family. Hawila Kaleohano took away the flyer's papers and firearm. While waiting for Robinson's boat to arrive to take him off the island, the pilot asked Ishimatsu Shintani, an alien Issei, and Yoshio Harada, a Japanese American Nisei, who acted as interpreter, for help in getting a gun and his papers. The alien Shintani became frightened and went into hiding, but the pilot was able to persuade American citizen Harada to get him some firearms. Together the pilot and Harada terrorized the Niʻihau islanders for several days.

Benehakaka Kanahele and his wife were captured by the two men. Held at gun point, they were threatened with death when the pilot was not able to retrieve his papers. According to Allan Beekman, who had researched the incident in depth, the Kanaheles simultaneously took charge when their two captors momentarily turned away from the couple:

Japanese Naval Airman 1st Class Shigenori Nishikaichi, crack fighter pilot from the carrier Kiryū. After attacking Oʻahu on December 7, 1941, he was to meet with a bizarre misadventure on Niʻihau.

Allan Beekman,
The Niihau Incident

131

. . . Ben and Ella leaped at him.

The pilot jerked the pistol from his boot top. Ella grabbed his arm and brought it down. The pilot shouted an order to Harada. Harada pried Ella loose. The pilot fired three times, wounding Ben in the left chest, left hip and penis.

Using the same grip he used in handling sheep, Ben picked up the pilot by the neck and leg and dashed him against the stone wall. The pilot fell stunned. Ella leaped at him and beat in his head with a rock. Drawing his hunting knife, the wounded Ben cut Nishikaichi's throat.

"I was so mad!" he explained later, "I was so mad!" [1]

Harada then killed himself with the shotgun. Later Kanahele and Kaleohano each received medals and honors for their courageous and heroic actions. Harada's actions, however, in the "Battle of Ni'ihau" added to the doubt about the loyalty of the 157,000 Japanese in Hawai'i.

In this atmosphere of distrust and suspicion, several thousand Japanese leaders and others who were thought to be sympathetic to Japan were arrested and investigated. Upon arrest, they were interrogated about their past activities, especially their relationship with Japan and their roles in the local Japanese community. They were incarcerated after hearings which were often conducted by untrained persons. Families, especially of Japanese aliens, lived in continuous fear wondering whether their fathers would be the next to be taken away. Some, aware of others who had been arrested before them, had suitcases packed to take with them in the event of an arrest. Families of the arrested were not informed for weeks as to their whereabouts. They were not sure whether the arrested were on the island or even alive. Eventually, 1,444 Japanese, 979 aliens and 525 American citizens, mostly Kibei, were interned. From a population of 157,000 persons of Japanese ancestry, the interned numbered slightly less than 1 percent. Nine hundred and eighty-one internees were sent to Mainland relocation camps. The rest spent the early years at Sand Island Detention Camp and were later moved to Honouliuli Internment Station outside of 'Ewa on O'ahu.

Internees, whether in Hawai'i or on the Mainland, were housed in very spare, crowded wooden barracks surrounded by barbed wire. Those on Sand Island lived in tents until wooden barracks were constructed. Until books and other materials were allowed, the internees found too much time to think and to worry. To pass the time away, they smoothed sea shells for necklaces by rolling

Arrest and Then a Hearing

Well, on April 15, a fellow from the FBI came and said they would like to further investigate me, so they say I should come along. And I ask him, "How long you going to. . . ." He said, "Oh couple days." So I wasn't prepared. I didn't bring anything. But when they took me to immigration station, I was put in the immigration station. And when I went there, there were thirty, forty people in there already. And they told me, "Did you bring anything for sleeping?" I say, "No. But they told me only about one, two days, you see." "No, I think you going to be detained here. So you might as well write a letter home." And I wrote letter to my wife saying that I would like to have my pajamas and my living clothes and what not. So it reached quite fast. My brother-in-law brought all the suitcase to the immigration station. About a week later, I had a hearing at the immigration station. At that immigration station, their court was composed of Army, Navy, and civilians. They were the judges there, and they were there for the hearing. And for witnesses, I had Mr. John Midkiff, the manager of Waialua Plantation, and Mr. Andrew Anderson, manager of the Waialua Bank of Hawaii. They came in as my character witness, because I knew them prior to the War quite well. They were good enough to come to my hearing and testify for my case.

Samuel Nishimura
Waialua - Haleiwa
Ethnic Studies Oral History Project, p. 101

---

them on the concrete floors and fashioned toothbrushes into rings and packing crates into small pieces of furniture. However, some could not cope and became mentally ill. At Honouliuli, 25 families per week were allowed one hour visits. Families took turns visiting, and bringing flowers, clothing, musical instruments, and magazines. Those sent to the Mainland were joined by their families in 1942 and 1943. They lived in crowded family quarters with little privacy. Everyone ate in mess halls. The food was often unfamiliar and of poor quality. Barbed wire fences and guards with guns and bayonets manning the watch towers were ever present at all internment facilities.

It was an extremely traumatic time, especially for the families of the men who were interned. The families were often shunned by others in the Japanese community who feared that contact with

Behind Barbed Wires at Honouliuli

Well, the camp was all barb-wired. I don't know how big it was. Pretty big compound. And had about, let's see. Four . . . buildings there. Dormitories, just like. Up and down. You can live up and down. And there were a good hundred fifty at that time when I was in there. The place was run just like an army. They had a captain and

Wooden barracks in the foreground served as home for the interned at Honouliuli on O'ahu. The oblong building at the foot of the hill was the mess hall. A barbed wire fence surrounded the compound.

Honolulu Star Bulletin photo

sergeant like fellow for all different barracks. And they used to take care of our every day needs. They used to go to the office. And whatever request we put to them, they went to get the request from the office.

Well, you want to borrow this and you want to do that and all kind. Because at that time, nothing was there in our barracks. Even for shaving, you had to go and borrow through the office. They give you the razor blades, otherwise, you cannot shave. Because nothing in there. When you want to write a letter, no papers, no pencil. That has to be borrowed from the office. All kinds of needs. And then, the family sent some money through the mail; it's censored, so you cannot get money, anyway. Because all our mail was censored. So whenever if there is a money in there, well, they've been confiscated and then, put in your account. You had your own accounts.

. . . There were guards there. Your wife would sit in the front and you stay opposite way. They didn't care where you sat. They were not very fussy about it; but only latter part of the meetings, I've noticed that that they were getting very strict. The rule was that you must speak in English – not in Japanese. So, all these Isseis who cannot speak English well, cannot just converse with their wife. 'Course, what we did was Niseis used to group in one place and told them the guard is away now. You speak in Japanese and we speak in English, so they won't notice. That's what we used to do. We used to let them talk. Otherwise, all the time wasted, coming there to see their husband. Yeah, for a time, it was rough but that was eliminated afterwards.

. . . They used to have a minister who come on weekdays. English minister come to give a lecture – in Japanese. Haole fellow used to come in, give a seminar in English and Japanese in Christianity. They used to, but we rather stay back and sleep. (Laughs) Because, well there was no hope, anyway. Just stay in there. Just wasting your time. Because you get no future. You don't know whether you are going to be released. What you're going to do is you have to make the most of yourself to keep yourself healthy. Just don't lose your mind. That's all to it. So we were telling to ourself, "Try and do something so that you won't get stale and you won't lose your mind." That's the main thing. You don't know how long you going to be in here, so you might as well make the best of it, so when we went to Honouliuli, that's where we started to make lot of things.

Samuel Nishimura
Waialua-Haleiwa, Ethnic Studies Oral History Project,
p. 373, 375, 378.

I Remember

The movie "Farewell to Manzanar" brought back memories that had been buried for over 30 years. You see, I, too, spent nearly three years in a concentration camp – first in Jerome, Arkansas, and later in Gila River, Arizona.

I was seven years old when I left our home in Maui and ten years old when I returned. My father was a minister of a Buddhist church in a plantation community. People ask me, "Do you remember much? You were so young then."

I don't remember as much as the grownups do. Just yesterday I asked my father whether he was paid wages for being a cook, mailman, and block manager at camp. He replied he was paid $18.00 a month plus $3.00 clothing allowance for each member of the family. Food and housing were free.

I'm sure there would be 100,000 different stories about life in a concentration camp – as many stories as the number of people interned in 10 different camps.

I REMEMBER:

The military police knocking on our door in the middle of the night on December 7 and taking my father away.

The rough voyages on boats from Maui to Oahu and from Oahu to California; being so seasick I could eat no food for five days except sucking on oranges.

The canned green beans which I disliked at the Immigration Center.

The long train ride from California to Arkansas and my little sister and I playing on the Pullman bed.

Looking out of our barrack window and seeing snow for the first time.

Wearing galoshes, woolen mittens, snow caps, earmuffs that my mother had knitted.

The big stove in the middle of our room to keep us warm.

The men going out into the forest to gather firewood and their stories of all the snakes they encountered.

The tall, handsome teacher who daily read aloud to us *Tales of King Arthur and His Knights of the Round Table* and who also held math speed contests.

Moving to dry, hot Arizona which was in sharp contrast to Arkansas in terrain and climate. Cooling the room with an electric fan placed in a frame with wire and grass and trickling water – a homemade air conditioner.

Sitting on our blankets under the stars on rocky buttes to watch movies such as "I'll Be Seeing You" starring Ginger Rogers.

After the war, standing on the deck of our boat in the calm Pacific Ocean in November, 1945, and seeing the island of Oahu and feeling so happy to be back in Hawaii again!

Sitting on our comfortable bed at home on Maui that first night back, munching milk nickel ice cream which our neighbor had brought from her store and bakery next door.

Feeling so good to be home again. . . .

I REMEMBER.

Gladys Miura Sodetani
March 19, 1976

---

them might jeopardize their own positions. Mothers were often left with young children and by necessity assumed the role of the head of the family and of breadwinner for the first time. Some found themselves in charge of a family business, the running of which was unfamiliar and was further complicated by the regulations issued by the military government. Others took outside jobs as clerks, seamstresses, and restaurant workers. Finding their bank accounts frozen, they often sold some of their precious possessions in order to make ends meet. Sometimes the older children left school to help support their families. Other families received financial assistance from the Department of Public Welfare. Still others received counsel from the American Friends Service Committee and the Swedish vice-consul who transacted the affairs of the Japanese government in Hawai'i.

Family patterns were drastically changed, especially in families where fathers had been taken into custody. Even in other families, however, anxious and confused Issei parents, although they were present, relinquished authority to their American children, many of whom were young and inexperienced. However, in recalling history, it appears miraculous, indeed, that less than one percent of the Japanese population, living on the spot where World War II began, would be interned, when far away on the west coast of the Mainland, the Japanese suffered mass evacuations with tremendous loss of property and belongings.

There were in the Hawaiian community as well as in Washington, people who continued to distrust the Japanese and who believed that the Japanese in Hawai'i were a threat to national security. Secretary of the Navy Frank Knox advocated mass evacuation of the Japanese, aliens and citizens alike, to a neighbor

137

Life As An Internee's Wife

. . . Grace Nishikawa was left with a seven-year-old son to support, a frozen bank account, and was forced to leave her job when her husband Dan was taken away for internment at Sand Island. She had no income and so went to the International Red Cross for help. The workers at first asked if her house had any furniture. As her household was still intact, they told her to sell everything and use the money to buy food. When there was nothing left, then come back and see them for help. Since they had to vacate the house because of financial reasons, much of the Nishikawa's furniture and appliances were either given away to friends or sold at ridiculously low prices. Their hothouse containing nearly 500 pots of orchids of varying sizes, some costing about $125 a plant, could not find any buyers. As a result, the entire hothouse was "given away" for $25.00 to a neighbor. Nishikawa explains, "Nobody like orchid wartime. Nobody like buy whole hothouse. But she gotta move."

The strain of her husband's internment took its toll on Grace's health. "I became very ill," she recalls. "There wasn't any real trouble, but the nerve affects the stomach. I went from one doctor to another, but they say there's nothing wrong. It's just nerves. I couldn't eat . . . it lasted for how many weeks, I don't remember. Even if I didn't eat for a few days, I just didn't get hungry. It was just like morning sickness; when you look at the food, you just don't feel like eating."

"Day of Remembrance"
From *The Hawaii Herald*
February 19, 1982
with permission from Dan Nishikawa.

---

island such as Moloka'i. John Balch, a Hawaiian Telephone official, proposed that at least 100,000 Japanese should be relocated to the mid-western states. What then made the difference for Hawai'i's people from Japan?

A few understanding non-Japanese leaders seemed to have played a major role in deciding the fate of the Japanese in Hawai'i. One of the key individuals was Honolulu Police Captain John A. Burns. This Montana born policeman, who had grown up in Honolulu with Japanese neighbors and friends, was the liaison between the police and the F.B.I. He was convinced of the loyalty of the Japanese and publicly and repeatedly vouched for them.

FBI Agent Robert L. Shivers is credited by persons who were in leadership positions during the war as being one of the key people who saved the Hawai'i Japanese from mass internment. According to Hung Wai Ching, Shivers studied the Japanese community and concluded that the overwhelming majority of the 160,000 Japanese (120,000 citizens and 40,000 aliens) were loyal. When war broke out, he used his powers to intern only those he thought might support the Japanese invasion of Hawai'i. He didn't believe in ruining the lives of thousands of loyal Japanese by interning them.

Hung Wai Ching
Interviewed on November 25, 1984
Photo from Rademaker, These Are Americans

His tenacious support of the Japanese influenced the Special Agent in Charge of the F.B.I. in Honolulu, Robert L. Shivers. Shivers' office had, in conjunction with the Army and Navy intelligence staffs, compiled a list of anti-American suspects since 1939. This was the list from which persons were taken into custody on December 7. Special Agent Shivers later testified at a Congressional hearing that his investigations indicated that the large majority of the Japanese were loyal to the U.S. and that "There was not one single act of sabotage committed against the war effort in the Hawaiian Islands during the course of the entire war."[2]

The intelligence work of Colonel (later Brigadier General) M.W. Marston and Colonel (later Brigadier General) Kendall J. Fielder also supported Shivers' findings. In fact, on December 11, 1941, Col. Fielder in a radio message reassured everyone that "There is no desire on the part of the authorities to organize mass concentration camps." [3] He went on to caution against believing in unfounded stories and the spreading of wild rumors.

There were others such as Waialua Plantation Manager John H. Midkiff, who vouched for the loyalty of the Japanese on the plantation. He was the brother of Frank Midkiff, who had earlier testified before a Congressional hearing in support of the Japanese. Members of the Committee for Interracial Unity in Hawai'i continued to support the Japanese.

It also was apparent that the Japanese, who constituted one-third of the population, were an important part of the labor force. A mass evacuation of the Japanese from Hawai'i and O'ahu, specifically, would hamper the war effort. Besides, there were logistical problems in transporting over 100,000 people with the existing shipping shortage. The problem eventually solved itself with the continued demonstrated loyalty of the Japanese in Hawai'i and the favorable turn of the war in the Pacific at the Battle of Midway in June, 1942.

The Sunday morning attack accelerated the changes in the manpower picture that had already started with the preparations for war. All efforts were concentrated towards protecting the Islands and their people and towards rebuilding the military strength of the United States. Everyone needed to make adjustments and to pitch in. With the shortage, increasing numbers of local persons entered the labor market. After martial law, those in "essential work," which included those activities directly related to the war effort, and in "locally needed" jobs in the laundries, restaurants, hotels, and fuel distribution facilities, were frozen to

... we here highly resolve that these dead shall not have died in vain ...

REMEMBER DEC. 7th!

their jobs. They could not terminate their employment unless they were granted releases from the proper authorities. Such releases did not come easily. There were regulations on work hours, absenteeism, and on wages. An unexcused absence or an unauthorized job change called for a $200.00 fine or two months imprisonment. Still others worked in stores, banks, theaters and on farms.

Workers were also recruited from the Mainland, and the Hawaiian community saw blue collar workers and laborers of the white race in great numbers for the first time. Laborers who had been paid $1.00 per day prior to the war were now given $4.00 per day and higher for the same jobs. Many women entered the job market for the first time, necessitating the opening of day care centers for children. More than one-half of the male university students and 14 percent of the women students worked more than 40 hours a week. Even children as young as twelve were encouraged to take summer jobs as warehouse workers and as laborers. Many upper elementary, intermediate, and high school students worked in the sugar, pineapple, or vegetable fields one day of the school week.

Although they were citizens, most of the Japanese Americans were barred from working at Navy establishments, particularly those situated at Pearl Harbor. The Army, however, was more lenient and hired the Japanese, including aliens, at construction jobs. The Japanese carpenters, masons, plumbers, concrete workers, and road construction crews helped build army piers and hangars and even did "Top Secret" work on underground oil

Students in the field bagging potatoes, their contribution to the war effort.
Waipahu Cultural Garden Park

142

The Keawe Corps
Under the leadership of the Army and the Emergency Service Committee, thousands of AJA men and women, along with workers of all other ethnic groups, spent Sunday after Sunday clearing keawe brush and setting up barbed wire in preparation for a possible invasion.
U.S. Army Signal Corps Photo
from Rademaker, We Are Americans

Japanese women of the Sheridan YWCA Service Club met weekly in the sanctuary of a Buddhist temple to knit for the Red Cross. For many of the women this was their first attempt at knitting. Similarly twenty-one other YWCA sponsored groups met in different parts of the city. Some of these women wore kimonos daily until the start of World War II.
War Records Depository
University of Hawaii

143

storage tanks at Red Hill. Their supervisors stated that citizens and alien Japanese alike were good and productive workers motivated to do their best for the war effort. However, most of the Japanese were involved in non-military and non-regulated jobs which paid lower wages than military jobs.

As it was with persons of other ethnic groups, the Japanese, too, volunteered. Along with going to work, oftentimes at more than one job, they served as block wardens, Red Cross workers, fire-fighters, medical workers, and as laborers. They responded to the urgent pleas for blood. As block wardens, they were responsible for patrolling their areas, investigating fire hazards, and for seeing that families abided by the 6:00 p.m. curfew and blackout regulations. Volunteers also manned first aid stations, the blood bank, and provided emergency ambulance services. In fact, 800 volunteers who had received emergency medical care training under the sponsorship of the United Japanese Society of Honolulu went directly from their December 7 certification ceremonies to the aid of their wounded.As members of the Kiawe Corps on O'ahu and Kaua'i and the Menehune Minute Men on the Big Island, they cleared kiawe thickets for evacuation and military camps, built trails, and strung barbed wire along the coast lines on Sundays. The women, both Issei and Nisei, devoted their free time to Red Cross activities such as folding bandages and knitting woolen socks. Others joined the Women's Division of the OCD (Office of Civilian Defense) and studied safety measures, disseminated necessary information, and worked on special projects such as Christmas gifts for service men.

The lives of the Japanese in Hawai'i were drastically disrupted, far more than that of any other group. The Japanese newspapers were ordered to stop their presses. Although no orders were issued, the Japanese schools, Buddhist temples, and the Shinto shrines became inactive as most of the teachers and priests were interned on December 7. Prior to the war, 84 percent of all Japanese children in the public schools attended language schools for an hour or so after their regular school day. The Shinto shrines had an estimated membership of 50,000, and the Buddhist temples had twice that number. Thus, the people were without the counsel of their leaders and deprived of the major institutions around which their social, educational, and religious lives were centered.

Nisei and non-Japanese leaders who had the foresight to begin planning even before the war began provided crucial direction during these traumatic times. They channeled the desire of the

144

Hung Wai Ching,
a Member of the Morale Committee

Liaison directors of the Morale Committee and Emergency Service Committees, from left to right, Shigeo Yoshida, Hung Wai Ching, and Charles Loomis received Meritorious Citations for Civilian Service to the United States from Lieutenant General Robert C. Richardson, Jr. after the war. These directors were key figures in helping to convince the military of the loyalty of the Japanese as well as in channeling the Japanese into positive and active participation. In an interview on November 25, 1984, Hung Wai Ching said:

Just before the war, I was appointed as the first Asian Executive Secretary of the University of Hawaii YMCA at Atherton House. Those four years there were the happiest times I ever had. I was in a position to get to know the boys and to help them. I was able to get scholarships for many of my boys. In 1940, I got a call from FBI Agent in Charge Mr. Shivers and he said: "Come on down to the Pacific Club." That was exactly one year before the Pearl Harbor attack. He wanted me to help organize a committee to work toward preserving racial harmony among the Chinese, Korean, Filipino, and Japanese people in the event of war. We became the Committee for Interracial Unity.

After the attack, Shigeo Yoshida, Charles Loomis, and I were appointed as co-directors to head the Morale Committee of the Office of the Military Governor. We had the confidence of Mr. Shivers and Colonel Fielder and were in touch with them. I just happened to be at the right place at the right moment to help people. I said to my A-House boys, "Go the second mile; go show the people in authority that you are good Americans!" They became Varsity Victory Volunteers and later 442nd soldiers and interpreters.

Through contacts that I had with Quaker groups, I was sent from Hawai'i to Washington to meet with Mrs. Eleanor Roosevelt at the White House to report on Hawai'i's racial problems. I said to Mrs. Roosevelt: "My mission is to tell you that everything is under control in Hawai'i under the leadership of Mr. Shivers." She later took me upstairs to have a private meeting with the President, and I met with him for forty minutes. I assured him that things were being handled well in the Islands. I also praised the President for his decisions to avoid mass internment in Hawai'i and for allowing AJAs to fight for their country.

Basically, Hawai'i wouldn't be where it is without our idealistic American educational beliefs and our public school system which were brought to Hawai'i by the New England missionaries. We were taught that America is a place where everyone has a chance. When I was honored by the VVV after the war, I told my boys, "You don't owe me anything . . . We still have lots of work to do. You have come a long way, and now it is your turn to help others. We need stimulating leaders and teachers who have not lost their idealism. I look forward to the day when we can have a society of "New Hawaiians."

Japanese in the community to actively demonstrate their loyalty to the United States. The groundwork laid by the prewar Committee for Interracial Unity in Hawaii, a multi-ethnic group of civic and military leaders brought together by Hung Wai Ching, led to the appointment of a Public Morale Section, first with the Office of Civilian Defense and a month later under the Office of the Military Governor. The appointees were Hung Wai Ching, a Chinese; Charles Loomis, a Caucasian; and Shigeo Yoshida, a Japanese. The advisory committee included many of the members of the original Committee for Interracial Unity in Hawaii.

One method devised by the Morale Section was the use of various racial morale committees. The Emergency Service Committee organized to work with the Japanese community originally included Y. Baron Goto, Masa Katagiri, Mitsuyuki Kido, Dr. Katsumi Kometani, Masaji Marumoto, Dr. Ernest Murai, and Shigeo Yoshida with Hung Wai Ching and Charles Loomis as ex-officio members. Later appointees were Ernest Furukawa, Tadashi Haga, Shigeru Hirotsu, Robert Ishikawa, Dr. Masao Kanemaru, Dr. Robert Komenaka, Yoshito Matsusaka, Walter Mihata, Katsuro Miho, Shigeo Mikami, Iwao Miyake, Stanley Miyamoto, Robert Murakami, Shizuo Onishi, Kaji Suzuki, and Masao Watanabe. These Nisei leaders, with the support of military authorities, prominent local business leaders, and the Honolulu Police Contact Group led by Captain John A. Burns, who later became Governor of Hawai'i, achieved major accomplishments. They served as a liaison with the military on matters affecting the Japanese community and assured the military of its complete loyalty to the United States. They suggested ways in which the Japanese could help the war effort and intervened in instances of unjustified arrests. They disseminated information through 209 meetings, contacting approximately 10,000 people during February through December 1942. With the suspension of Japanese radio broadcasts and newspapers, these meetings helped greatly with the morale at the time when many people were frightened and confused.

The Emergency Service Committee urged Hawai'i's Japanese to make an all out effort to concretely demonstrate their loyalty. The highly successful war bond drives netted millions of dollars and the $2.4 million dollars of frozen bank assets were converted into war bond purchases. Throughout the war, campaigns resulted in donations of blood to the Blood Bank. Volunteers turned out for the Kiawe Corps to clear underbrush along shorelines. The committee also conducted campaigns to reduce those factors that created distrust and suspicion against the Japanese by other racial groups.

The United States government distributed "Speak American" posters, leaflets, and even stamps. People were discouraged from following obvious Japanese customs and traditions such as the wearing of kimonos and zoris in public. The Japanese Americans withdrew their candidacies from political offices. It was pointed out that critics could use elected officials as proof of a "Japanese takeover." Wilfred Tsukiyama resigned from the Selective Service Board.

To implement the "Speak American" campaign, adult English classes were held in different parts of the community. This class of Japanese non-English speaking students at the Kaimuki YMCA go over a riddle.

War Records Depository
University of Hawaii

148

The efforts of the Emergency Service Committee were not always understood or appreciated by their own people. They were frequently referred to as "inu," or "dog," which was a derogatory remark meaning "informer." However, it is now known that the members of the committee were never asked to implicate any Japanese. Furthermore, the committee played a major role in the establishment of the Varsity Victory Volunteers (VVV) and the recruitment of men for military service, which brought the loyalty of the Japanese Americans into the limelight.

Hours after the attack on Pearl Harbor, the University R.O.T.C. unit with members of various ethnic backgrounds was mobilized to meet the enemy. They were sent to investigate reports of Japanese paratroopers landing on St. Louis Heights in Honolulu. The University of Hawaii students were the first and only R.O.T.C. unit in the United States to enter active service in World War II.

At the war's outset, classified as 4-C enemy aliens, Japanese Americans were not accepted as volunteers or draftees. Therefore, they joined the Hawaii Territorial Guard, which was organized to guard vital civilian installations such as public utilities, 'Iolani

No job was too low or too big for the boys of the VVV. The work was new and foreign to most of the boys, but they "gave it their all."

Photo by Ted Tsukiyama

Palace, and the waterfront. Many of the Guards were Nisei, but each was given six rounds of ammunition. Although they performed their jobs dutifully, the Japanese members of the Territorial Guard were divested of their firearms and ammunition and abruptly discharged six weeks later without any explanations. Although discouraged and disappointed by this obvious rejection, the men were determined to do their part as loyal Americans. They turned to members of the Morale Section, who encouraged them to take action in an organized and positive manner. In a petition to the Military Governor drafted by Shigeo Yoshida, a member of the Morale Section and the Emergency Service Committee, and signed by the young men who were former Hawaii Territorial Guard members, they declared their loyalty to the United States and offered themselves "for whatever service you may see fit to use us."[4]

On February 25, 1942, the Military Governor granted their request; and the group of 169 young men became the VVV, the Varsity Victory Volunteers. These volunteers were mostly young University of Hawaii students who were willing to sacrifice their college careers to work as laborers for their country. They were stationed at Schofield, O'ahu, and for eleven months worked six days a week quarrying, building roads and fences, stringing barbed wire, constructing warehouses, and repairing military buildings. They worked tirelessly, always trying to live up to their motto, "We do the difficult immediately. The impossible takes a little longer." The VVVs also rallied together to donate 350 to 500 c.c. of blood three times during that period and purchased nearly $28,000 worth of war bonds. Although the VVV lasted for only a year, the example they set made a significant impact on the attitude of the military officials.

Meanwhile on December 7, there were 1,432 Nisei volunteers and draftees in the U.S. Army. About 200 were members of the 1399th Engineering Construction Battalion and handled the construction of airfields, bridges, water systems, pill boxes, and training fields. The rest who were with the 298th and 299th Infantry Regiments guarded the shorelines during the early days of the war. Six months later on June 5, 1942, the War Department quietly withdrew the Nisei soldiers except those from the Engineers and transferred them to Camp McCoy in Wisconsin. Some said that the Army distrusted their loyalty in the event of an invasion. Others thought that the concern was because they would be difficult to distinguish from the men in the Japanese army,

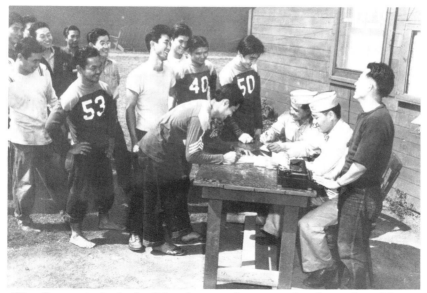

When the opportunity for the AJAs to bear arms became a reality, the members of the VVV signed up at once. Many of them later became leaders in the 442nd and in the Hawaiian community.

U.S. Army Signal Corps Photo
War Records Depository
University of Hawaii

should they be engaged in combat. The unit was officially named the 100th Infantry Battalion, and the soldiers nicknamed themselves, "One puka puka," "puka" meaning hole in Hawaiian. After six months of rigorous training at Camp McCoy, they were moved to Camp Shelby, Mississippi, for advanced training and then shipped to the European Theater in August of 1943.

The 100th Battalion, the first combat unit composed of Americans of Japanese Ancestry, embarked from Oran, North Africa, and landed at Salerno Beach in southern Italy on September 22, 1943. They amazed the Army and the enemy alike with their drive and dedication as they fought northward, participating in the capturing of Benevento, and fought at fortified crossings along the Volturno River on their way to a bloody attack on Cassino. They advanced in rain-soaked clothing and suffered frost bite and swollen feet. In the short time from September 22, 1943, to February 18, 1944, the 100th Battalion received much recognition for their bravery, but it was at a very high price. At one time, less than sixty riflemen remained from the entire Battalion of over 1,400 men. Some had been killed but others had been wounded. However, the wounded were quickly sent back into combat after recovery. The Nisei soldiers, having been distrusted, were determined to prove their loyalty. They earned the name of the "Purple Heart Battalion." But more fighting and honor were to come to them as their depleted ranks were replenished with 202 men and officers from the 442nd Combat Team. With added reinforcements, the 100th Battalion was sent against the Nazis at Anzio Beachhead against dropping bombs and strafing machine gun fire from planes, artillery, and tank attacks. With more men killed and wounded, they received more medals and honors. Finally at Civitavecchia, the 100th Battalion joined up and became a part of the 442nd Regimental Combat Team. The men of the 100th Battalion were honored with over 4,000 combat medals including three Presidential Unit Citations, one Medal of Honor, and 1,700 Purple Hearts for combat wounds.

In January, 1943, the War Department demonstrated a change of

---

The First AJA to Die
for His Country in WWII

In the first action in which the 100th Battalion took part, Sergeant Joe Takata of Waialua, Oahu, volunteered to silence an enemy machine gun which had held up the advance. With a squad he worked his way around the enemy. While his men covered him, he fired his tommy-gun and drove the Germans back. He kept after them, but the German artillery started dropping shells near him. One shell burst too close, and he went down. Even then he was able, before he died, to give the location of the enemy gunners, who were soon killed, and the Battalion was able to go forward again. Joe Takata was the first Japanese American to die in battle for his country in World War II, and the first to get the Distinguished Service Cross. Like so many others who were decorated, however, he received it posthumously – after he had given his life to advance the Stars and Stripes on the battlefields.

John Rademaker
in *These Are Americans*, p. 62.

War Records Depository
University of Hawaii

attitude and issued a call for 1,500 AJA volunteers. This was an attempt to officially show confidence in the loyalty of the Japanese, which, by this time, had been tested and proven by the VVV, the 100th Infantry Battalion, and FBI, military, and police intelligence reports. Hung Wai Ching spoke for the Japanese and used his contacts in Washington, including President and Mrs. Roosevelt, to further the cause. Within a month, 9,507 Island Niseis volunteered, 2,645 of whom were inducted into the Army to form the nucleus of the 442nd Regimental Combat Team. Among these were members of the VVV, who had asked to disband immediately upon notification that they could volunteer. Thus, after over a year of waiting, the door was open for these young Japanese to enter combat duty.

These volunteer AJAs became the core of the 442nd Infantry Battalion. They assembled en masse at the 'Iolani Palace grounds for the aloha ceremonies prior to their departure for training on the Mainland in March, 1943. With tears in their eyes, families watched with pride yet also wondered if they would ever see their sons and brothers again.
Hawaii State Archives

Fifteen thousand mothers and fathers, sisters and brothers, and friends watched with pride as the 2,645 local Japanese American volunteers marched into the grounds of 'Iolani Palace for an impressive induction ceremony on March 28, 1943. In April, 1943, twenty-five officers and 2,855 enlisted men were sent to Camp Shelby, Mississippi, for training along with 2,000 men from various parts of the mainland United States. The men of the 442nd joined the men of the 100th Battalion who had already been at

Camp Shelby receiving advanced training but who were on maneuvers when they arrived. They were together until August when the 100th embarked for the European battle front.

When they arrived at Shelby, the 442nd soldiers purchased $101,500 worth of war bonds with money they had earned earlier and from the customary *senbetsu,* or going away gifts, from friends and relatives. They excelled in their training with 97 percent of the men and officers qualifying on the small arms range. They even showed their prowess by winning the Southern AAU Swimming-team Championship and the Combat Team Baseball Championship.

While in Mississippi, they found a staunch friend in Earl M. Finch, a rancher and businessman of Hattiesburg. After a chance encounter with a lonesome Nisei soldier, Finch devoted his time, energy, and resources on behalf of the AJAs. He helped to organize the first Japanese American U.S.O. and bussed in Nisei girls from relocation centers to serve as hostesses at the dances. He also entertained hundreds of 442nd soldiers at his ranch, at

GIs on the Town. ca. 1943
"We're at the famous Latin Quarter in New Orleans. When we got weekend passes, four or five guys would rent a taxi and go from Camp Shelby to New Orleans and stay there for the weekend. The taxi driver spent the weekend there too, and we'd hop back in the taxi and come back to camp for basic training at the end of the weekend."

Eddie Ochiai
Interviewed on November 24, 1984
E. Ochiai Collection

Returning the aloha. Years after the war, grateful family members of 442nd boys whom he had entertained showered Earl Finch with leis and honored him with parties.

U.S. Army Museum of Hawaii Photo

watermelon busts and rodeos, as well as held parties at hotels for them. Later, as they returned wounded, he traveled 65,000 miles around the country to arrange programs and to visit his 442nd boys at Army hospitals. As relocation centers closed, Earl Finch helped to resettle families of the men from the 442nd.

After eight weeks of basic training, the 442nd Regimental Combat Team trained as a unit for a year before being shipped to Europe where they caught up with the combat tried 100th. In Europe, they distinguished themselves in seven major campaigns with the now famous motto, "Go for Broke!" They were faced with enemy artillery, mortars, self-propelled guns, and platoons of tanks as they fought against the battle wise Afrika Korp, SS Troops, Panzer Brigades, and Soldaten from the Hermann Goering Division and the Machine Gun Battalion, Kesselring. The 442nd fought in two beachhead assaults, attacked hill after fortified hill, captured a submarine, and were there to see the gates opened at Dachau to release the starving Jews.

The 442nd debarked in Naples, Italy, on June 2, 1944. They were sent to Anzio Beachhead on landing crafts. At Civitavecchia, the 100th Battalion, with heavy losses of men, became attached to the 442nd, but retained its separate designation in recognition of the

Survival

"Survival, that's what we were thinking about. We were fighting a war and every day we wondered if this was going to be our last day. We were Baka Bomb. We had that typical Japanese spirit of going all out and doing our best, so we fought fearlessly. Each time we ducked and dusted ourselves off, we were surprised that we were still alive. I left home thinking that I'd never get back. We had no time during the fighting to think of the future."

Dan Aoki
Interviewed on November 18, 1984
U.S. Army Museum of Hawaii Photo

outstanding battle record it had amassed. Of the 1,300 Japanese Americans from Hawai'i, over 900 had suffered casualties. Among the ranks were many mainlanders called "Kotonks" because, as the story goes, "when they fall their heads go 'Kotonk'." The boys from Hawai'i were referred to as "Buddha Heads." They learned to get along as they fought side by side under intense fire. The Combat Team battled its way northward through Italy taking the towns of Belvedere, Sasseta, and Castagneto, which dominated a vital highway and was, therefore, heavily defended. In the fighting, they killed 178 Germans, wounded 20, and captured 73. The 442nd then fought continuously for two weeks to take the town of Luciana, which controlled the seaport of Livorno.

A Bugler's Farewell

Bugler Pfc. Charles Mimura continued his interest in music in civilian life. He operated a music store and a music studio.

The names of the fallen were called; three volleys were fired, and then it was my turn to blow taps. It was a "choke-up" time regardless of whom I was playing for, but when the names called were of those I had known, the feeling of sadness and loss was indescribable. A kaleidoscope of common experiences flashed through my mind in the short while before I actually began my part. Sad as it was, I considered it an honor to blow this last taps for my friends and I really tried my best. It was my good-bye to those friends, some of whom I had grown up with, and others whom I had trained with. Ceremonies like this took place after each battle. The remaining members of the company were also in attendance. It was always a solemn occasion.

Charles Mimura
Interviewed on November 15, 1984
War Records Depository Photo
University of Hawaii

100th Rests in Livorno, Italy

Sakae Takahashi, who was captain for B Company at the time that the 100th Battalion entered Livorno, recalls:

It was so good to get into Livorno. For one thing, the Allied Forces needed the port city to bring in supplies. Secondly, the Germans left without too much opposition for this was no longer a strategic area for them. Therefore, our casualty list was low. Thirdly, the place was almost empty as the people had evacuated and the buildings were available to us. We had been on the road for about two months and welcomed this opportunity to sleep in buildings. And the food we got was much better than the C and K rations we got on the road. To top it all, we discovered some German beer in vats in the basement of an Italian brewery. The guys used to go down to get beer in their water cans. The beer was cold and so good! This good life lasted for about two weeks before we moved on to the area east of Pisa.

Sakae Takahashi
Interviewed on November 15, 1984
War Records Depository Photo
University of Hawaii

By the time the 442nd reached France, they faced Germans who were more determined than ever. The battlegrounds were closer to the German border, and the Germans had more intensive and extensive fortifications. In the Rhineland Campaign, the 442nd faced minefields, boobytraps, heavy artillery, rockets, and mortar fire. The Combat Team attacked hill after hill entrenched with Germans in the Vosges Forests in chilly, rainy weather to capture the town of Bruyeres, "the most viciously fought for town" encountered so far.[5] The Germans suffered approximately 130 casualties and 134 prisoners of war.

After two days of rest, the 442nd was summoned to rescue the 275 men of the "Lost Battalion" of the 141st Regiment of the 36th (Texas) Division. The "Lost Battalion" had been cut off near Bruyeres, and rescue attacks had been beaten back by the Germans. The 442nd, supported by artillery from the 36th Division, did not give up until they rescued the "Lost Battalion." To effect the rescue, the 442nd suffered 800 casualties in less than a week. This became one of their best known exploits. The grateful men of the "Lost Battalion" gave the 442nd Combat Team a plaque which read: "With Deep Sincerity and Utmost Appreciation For

"Otō-san and Okā-san, don't worry. I'm fine." Wherever they were and whenever they could, soldiers wrote home to their families. They tried not to worry their parents so they wrote about their illnesses or injuries only after they had recovered. In most cases, the GIs wrote letters home in English which were translated by sisters and brothers for their Issei parents.

U.S. Army Signal Corps Photo
from Rademaker, These Are Americans

Bruyeres: The People Who Never Forgot

This photo was taken in October, 1974, when our chartered group of two hundred 442nd veterans and wives journeyed 10,000 miles on a pilgrimage to France for the 30th anniversary of the liberation of the town in Bruyeres by the 442nd Infantry. The townspeople had planned two days of celebration – services in the town square, church, and at the monument, parades as well as banquets. Former President Walter Matsumoto and I are placing a wreath during the ceremony in the town square. The monument itself is in the Vosges Forest up in the hills and we went there later by bus.

I really found out that those people have a very sincere aloha for the 442 and Hawai'i. They weren't trying to make headlines when they built that monument. I thought the most impressive part of the event was when the little French elementary school children sang "Hawai'i Pono'i" in perfect Hawaiian. Bruyeres is now officially a "Sister City" of Honolulu.

Eddie Ochiai
Former President, The 442nd Veterans Club
Interviewed on November 24, 1984
Photo from John Tsukano

John Tsukano interviewed fourteen people who had been living in Bruyeres at the time when it was liberated by the 442nd. He wanted to know why the people continued to remember the men of the 442nd year after year with memorial services. Some of the most commonly expressed sentiments were:

"They were generous. They shared their food with us."

"They loved children."

"They never took advantage of us."

"They had respect for the elderly."

"They treated old people with dignity."

"They never mistreated our womenfolks."

"They never asked for anything in return."

Tsukano described the simple monument as a slab of granite less than six feet tall on a concrete base which, ". . . resting in the wilds of a forest thousands of miles from the birthplaces of those for whom it is dedicated, the mere sight is enough to bring tears to all who are familiar with its story."

The bronze plaque on the monument has this touching tribute in French and English:

> To the men of the 442nd Regimental Combat Team, U.S. Army, who re-affirmed an historic truth here – that loyalty to one's country is not modified by racial origin.
>
> These Americans, whose ancestors were Japanese, on October 30, 1944, during the battle of Bruyeres broke the backbone of the German defenses and rescued the 141st Infantry Battalion which had been surrounded by the enemy for four days."

Tsukano, John
Bruyeres Booklet

---

the Gallant Fight to Effect Our Rescue After We Had Been Isolated for Seven Days . . ." By the time of the unconditional surrender of the German armies and government on V-E Day (Victory in Europe Day) in May, 1945, the 442nd had received seven Distinguished Unit Citations, two Meritorious Service Unit Plaques, an Army Commendation, and 3,915 individual awards.[6] The press covered their activities closely, for the men with an average height of 5'4" and an average weight of 125 pounds had earned the 442nd and 100th the distinction of being "the most decorated unit in United States military history."

In some instances, this press coverage backfired as it irritated

Decorations
100th Infantry Battalion and the
442d Regimental Combat Team

    7 Major campaigns in Europe
    7 Presidential Unit Citations
9,486 Casualties (Purple Hearts)
18,143 Individual decorations, including:
    1 Congressional Medal of Honor
   52 Distinguished Service Crosses
    1 Distinguished Service Medal
  560 Silver Stars, with 28 Oak Leaf Clusters in lieu of second
       Silver Star awards
   22 Legion of Merit Medals
4,000 Bronze Stars, 1,200 Oak Leaf Clusters
       representing second Bronze Stars
   15 Soldier's Medals
   12 French Croix de Guerre, with two Palms representing
       second awards
    2 Italian Crosses for Military Merit
    2 Italian Medals for Military Valor

In addition to the individual awards earned, the Combat Team as a unit, won 36 Army Commendations, 87 Division Commendations, Meritorious Service Plaques for the Medical Detachment and Service Company, and 7 Presidential Unit Citations. Five of these were earned in a one-month period during the fighting for Bruyeres and the "Lost Battalion." (The Presidential Unit Citation for a unit is deemed the equivalent of the Distinguished Service Cross for the individual.) Additional postwar honors included a tribute from Gen. George C. Marshall, Chief of Staff, U.S. Army, in his report to Congress; a further tribute from Winston Churchill, Prime Minister of England, in his report to Parliament; and presidential invitation to march down Pennsylvania Avenue and attend a reception at the White House to receive the Presidential Unit Citation.

Tanaka, Chester
Go For Broke, p. 144

other military personnel, especially those non-Japanese from Hawai'i who had also fought bravely and who misconstrued the attention to mean that these Nisei were better than they. The Army issued a special statement:

> Many stories circulated by overenthusiastic correspondents have given rise to a popular fiction that these were supermen. They were not. They could die and be wounded as easily as other men were. They had the same weaknesses and shortcomings that other soldiers were heir to. Above all, however, they had the fire, the courage, and the will to press forward that make crack infantry on the line. They would, and often did, drive until they fell from wounds or exhaustion. They were never driven a backward step in many months of battle against an enemy who counterattacked skillfully and often. More than one commander acclaimed them as the finest assault troops he had ever led.[7]

Although Nisei soldiers had been in the Pacific Theater from early August, 1942, in Guadalcanal and on through every encounter until the Japanese surrender, there was very little publicity about them. The authorities felt that it was important to keep the Nisei participation secret to have it effective. Even before the attack on Pearl Harbor, the United States Army had realized that in a war with Japan it would be imperative to have men who knew the Japanese language well enough to converse, and to read and translate orders, documents, maps, radio broadcasts, and other military intelligence materials. On November 1, 1941, a month before Pearl Harbor, the first class of the Fourth Army Intelligence School opened in an empty hangar in the Presidio in San Francisco. Five Nisei were recruited as instructors, of the sixty students enlisted, fifty-eight were Nisei and two were Caucasians. While the two Caucasians were sent immediately into the Alaskan campaign, the field commanders were hesitant about using the Nisei. The two Caucasions demonstrated the value of their skills and argued for their Nisei fellow students. After the first few weeks of being given the opportunity to serve, the Nisei interpreters were so effective that more and more requests for them came from the military outposts.

In May, 1942, the War Department Intelligence Service took over the vital work of language training and moved the school to Camp Savage, Minnesota. By this time all Japanese, aliens and citizens alike, were being evacuated from their Pacific Coast homes to the interior. When the classes grew too large, the school was moved to Camp Snelling, also in Minnesota. After concentrated language study and boot training, the Nisei were sent to the combat zone in the Pacific and Asia as interpreters, translators, and intelligence personnel.

Nisei Interpreter In Burma

I was with the 442nd at Camp Shelby when they checked my personnel records and found out that I had had twelve years of Japanese language schooling. So, with 80 to 100 others, I was transferred to Camp Savage for six months of intense military intelligence training. My parents spoke English so I wasn't that proficient in Japanese. The training was very rigorous for me. We had classes in the morning, afternoon, and even in the evenings sometimes - plus we had homework. Some of the eager guys studied after lights out by the light of the coal burning stove or in the latrine where the bulb was on all the time.

After graduation, we were assigned to different units. I was sent to radio intelligence training in Florida. Then we received final field training in California and our unit was the first group to re-enter California after all of the Japanese had been evacuated from the west coast. From California we were put on a boat that took 49 days to get to Bombay traveling south of Australia. Next we rode an ancient, creeky train across India to Asam near the Burmese border.

From left to right: Ed "Bull" Sumida, Kenneth Moriji, Shoji Fujisawa, and I are pictured standing on the signpost on the Burma Road. We were attached to the 10th Air Force for the Burma campaign where we specialized in intercepting air to ground radio messages from Japanese airfields. We were the "ears." We gathered the data. The enemy fighter pilots each had a code name such as "Red Eagle," and the tower would ask, "Kan dōka, me dōka?" or "How's the strength and clarity of the signal?" I still remember the time when an excited voice from the tower yelled: "Aka! Aka! Aka!" or "Red! Red! Red!" alerting the pilots that they were under attack. When the war ended, we were flown out on C47 cargo planes. Some other fellows were in OSS (Office of Strategic Services), the predecessor to the CIA, and their activities were super secret until recently and more exciting.

Ted Tsukiyama
Interviewed on November 17, 1984
Tsukiyama Collection

The Nisei who served in the Intelligence Service translated intercepted messages from the Japanese commanders in the Battle of Midway. Not only did they know the language and the psychology of the Japanese soldiers, but because of their physical features, they were better able to go behind the enemy lines to obtain strategic information. They were so valuable that almost every unit of battalion size soon had one or more of them working in the front lines. To avoid the danger of being mistaken as the enemy, the Nisei soon learned to wear something, usually a sweat shirt, over their uniforms. After some initial suspicion, they earned the trust of the regular soldiers and were treasured and guarded by them.

The Nisei translators contributed toward the victory in the Battle of the Philippines in the San Bernardino Straits. When Admiral Koga, commander of the combined Japanese fleets, was forced to land in guerilla and American-held territory in the Philippines, he was captured with the entire plan for the approaching naval battle. Through tedious work, the Nisei translated the plans and sent them on to Admiral Halsey, Admiral Nimitz, and General MacArthur. With this information the American fleet inflicted one of the worst defeats in naval history on the Imperial Japanese Navy. According to General Charles Willoughby, Chief-of-Staff of Intelligence, the participation of these Nisei "shortened the war in

Technical Sergeant Edwin Kawamoto of Honolulu acted as interpreter and guide to Japanese officers at a conference for the surrender of Chichi Jima to the United States Fleet.

the Pacific by two years." He further commented that: "In spite of the 2,000 to 3,000 Nisei used, 40 percent of whom were Hawaii-born, there has not been a single case of disloyalty or ill feeling. They did their job quietly and with great efficiency."[8]

The work of the Nisei in military intelligence did not end with the war. After V-J Day (Victory over Japan Day), they convinced Japanese officers and soldiers who, believing that surrender would mean torture or death, hid in caves and forest hide-aways to come out and surrender. Additional forays were thus averted. The Nisei were also present when the surrender documents were translated and signed. After the occupation of Japan was agreed upon, they were with the first American troops to land in Japan and assisted with the administration of the occupation. They helped in the communication between the occupation forces and the Japanese government on the national, provincial, and local levels.

I Was Real Mad

My family was sent to an internment camp in Arkansas in 1942, but I remained behind because, with my boss's support, I had been classified "an essential worker." Before the war my father happened to be a truck driver who hauled fish from Kewalo Basin to Hawaii Suisan Company at 'A'ala Market. He was also listed as the secretary of the company. The military was particularly suspicious of fishermen since they go out to sea, and my father was unfortunate in being an officer of the company.

I accompanied my father to the immigration station when he was called in and the interrogator asked: "A truck driver! What's he doing here?"

So I said, "In that case, get him out!"

But the interrogator replied, "No, because once you're processed, I can't do anything about it." So my parents, three brothers, and two sisters were all shipped to Arkansas.

Well, when the call for 442nd volunteers came through, I volunteered; but they had enough men so they said they didn't need me. About three months later in June, 1943, they issued a call for interpreters and translators. I had always liked Japanese school. I was interviewed and tested at the Nu'uanu YMCA and was selected in the first group of over 300 volunteer interpreters. The military was pretty smart in their classification system. There were about twenty sections and the top section stayed back as instructors for later classes.

After training, they put us into teams which included someone strong in Japanese like a Kibei and others who were not as good in Japanese but were good in English. That way, each team had a balance and there were people on the team with different talents. My team was one of two that were sent to a little known MP (Military Police) unit. The army had this grand idea of forming a company trained to process POWs because they were expecting the Japanese to surrender wholesale at the end of the war. We were supposed to interrogate the prisoners, and I was in charge of the interpreters. The other sections were fingerprinting, photography, and records.

After that special MP training, we were sent to New Guinea in 1944. Unfortunately, there were no prisoners! The Japanese either hid themselves or killed themselves instead of surrendering. So, our unit was dissolved; and I was assigned to the Allied Translators Interpreter Service and attached to the Australian Army. There, on a small Pacific island, I did participate in a surrender ceremony. That was interesting.

Before the ceremony, I talked to the interpreter from the Japan side and said: "Let's reverse roles. I can understand what your officer is saying and I can say it in better English than you can. And, you can explain what the Australian officer said in better Japanese than I can. We can also correct each other." But, the interpreter from the Japan side refused. So I struggled, and he struggled. He translated in terrible English.

In the actual ceremony, they followed protocol. First, about four Japanese officers gave up their swords one at a time to an officer of comparable rank on the Australian side. Finally, the highest ranking officers from each side sat down in a tent to talk over the surrender procedure. Although I was only a sergeant, I was treated like an officer by the Australians and received all the privileges accorded the officers.

Well, as the war was ending, I received a letter from my sister saying that they were being released but that my father could not go back to Hawai'i because no alien was allowed to pass through the west coast. My mother was disappointed that my father couldn't return home, and I was real mad! My Commanding Officer said that if I wrote a letter, he would get it to General MacArthur's Headquarters for approval. I wrote the letter (shown below), and my father was allowed to travel across California and back to Hawai'i.

Kiyoshi Yoshimura
Interviewed on November 17, 1984

XY Section, APO 923,
c/o PM, San Francisco, Calif.
2 March 1945

Commanding General,
Western Defense Command,
Presidio of San Francisco,
San Francisco, California.
(Through Channels)

      In recent letters from my family, I have learned that my father, Kuniichi Yoshimura, presently residing at 33-4-A, Rohwer Relocation Center, McGehee, Arkansas, has been forbidden from entering into the West Coast area. This means he cannot return to Hawaii, his home for over 30 years. This is a bitter pill for him to swallow, as it not only shattered his dream foremost in his mind, but also meant his loyalty was still doubted.

      My father came to Hawaii with the sole purpose of making it his new and permanent home. He began work as a plantation laborer and for the last 25 years or more has held the same job, that being a truck driver for a fishing company. He wants to return to Hawaii because he feels at home there among his friends and because we still have property there. I do not know what the authorities have against him, but as far as I know, he has been loyal to the United States.

At present, living together with him, are my mother, Nao (U.S. citizen) and my two youngest brothers, Frederick T. and Albert K. They, I understand, are free to return to Hawaii but they do not want to be separated no matter how strong the yearning for Hawaii may be. There are two sisters and another brother who were also relocated, but one sister got married, while the other sister and brother are at present in Chicago, working and attending school, respectively.

I was also on the original list to be relocated but upon request was released, and remained in Hawaii when the family left for the mainland. In March 1943, the Army lifted the ban on taking in Nisei and offered an opportunity to us. Along with 9,000 others I volunteered, having in mind the combat team which is at the moment distinguishing itself in Europe, but just missed being included in the quota. However, in a subsequent call for interpreters and translators to fight in the Pacific theater, I made it, and after several months training in the States, ended up here in the Southwest Pacific Area.

My career in the Army may not have anything to do with my father's loyalty, but he's proud of me and I don't think he would hurt one by being disloyal to the United States.

The young women of Hawai'i were unhappy when they were discriminated against in their efforts to join the services. Finally, months after the AJA men had been accepted into the Army, they were allowed to join the Women's Auxiliary Corps of the Army. During the recruitment period, fifty-nine women volunteers of all races were finally cleared and inducted. Of this group, twenty-six or almost half were of Japanese ancestry. They performed the same services as WACs elsewhere doing administrative, secretarial, and motor transport work. A few later became interpreters and were sent to Japan for the Army of Occupation.

For those living in Hawai'i, the days following the December 7 attack were filled with uncertainties, fears, and anxieties, for citizens expected additional bombings and a land invasion. Japanese submarines briefly shelled Kahului, Maui, at 5:45 p.m. on December 15. They also fired upon Hilo, Hawai'i, and Nawiliwili, Kaua'i, during the night and early morning hours of December 30-31. Three medium sized bombs fell on the lower slopes of Tantalus in Honolulu at 2:15 a.m. on March 4, 1942. Because of unidentified elements, five daylight air raid alarms were sounded on O'ahu from December 21, 1941, through March 15, 1942. Invariably the unidentified elements later proved to be friendly.

During May, 1942, the public, noting certain activities, became aware that something might happen soon. There was an increase in military preparations and movement, the sudden release of a large number of patients from a hospital in Schofield, O'ahu, the call to duty of the Defense Volunteers to supplement the armed forces, and an urging by the military governor for women and children living near Honolulu Harbor to evacuate the interior.

170

Graduation Day for Hawaiian WACs

I was a secretary at McKinley High School when Miles Cary was principal. He was a wonderful boss. When the war began, they ran short of teachers; and since I was qualified, I was promoted to registrar. My girlfriend called and said we could get silk stockings if we joined the WACs so the very next morning, we registered. I informed the family only after I passed the physical because I was afraid my brothers would be against it. My brothers were older, married, and had children. We had no men to send into the service so I wanted to represent the Fujii family. As it turned out, my family was proud of me.

The photo was taken at our graduation in 1945 when we completed our basic training. I would surmise that, of the 59 graduates, 21 were Nisei. I wanted to work in a motor pool or be a nurse, but the army put me right behind the typewriter again! I served in General Douglas MacArthur's office in the Philippines and General George C. Marshall's staff in Nanking when he was a military advisor.

Ruth Fujii
Interviewed on November 30, 1984
Fujii Collection

Then on June 4, 1942, came the Navy announcement that a Japanese aircraft had attacked Midway Island, 1,300 miles northwest of Honolulu in the Pacific Ocean. Word of United States victory at Midway reached Honolulu two days later on June 6. United States land and carrier based planes had sunk four enemy aircraft carriers and one heavy cruiser. This ended further Japanese threats to Hawai'i. The tables had turned. Japan was now on the defensive. Hawai'i was no longer a defense outpost, but a staging area for offense.

Initial anxieties lessened, and even when the war became a part of the lives of the people, the Hawaiian population continued to support the war efforts. Rules and regulations were eased, and civilian rule was restored on October 24, 1944.

The Nazi collapse on May 8, 1945, ended the European phase of World War II. A ceremony in Berlin on May 9 ratified the surrender terms. This enabled the Allied Forces, specifically the United States Forces, to concentrate on the war in the Pacific. After a series of island-hopping victories from Guadalcanal in August, 1942, through Tarawa, Kwajalein, Saipan, Guam, Philippines, Iwo Jima, and the Okinawan Islands from 1943 through April, 1945, the Allies cut all sea communications leading to Japan. Then on August 6, 1945, an atom bomb was dropped on Hiroshima, Japan, followed on August 9 by another on Nagasaki. The two attacks devastated both cities and killed more than 70,000 persons and injured about 110,000. The Japanese were crushed.

On August 14, 1945, Japan surrendered and the war in the Pacific was over! There was a surge of emotion in the Islands and in the rest of the world. Honolulu spontaneously celebrated V-J (Victory over Japan) Day with the wailing of air raid sirens, impromptu parades, and much dancing. There were tears of joy and gratitude for the end of the war, tears of relief for the many personal anxieties suffered, and tears of sadness for those sons, brothers, and husbands who were never to return home.

In the midst of these celebrations, however, there existed in Hawai'i a group composed primarily of elderly Japanese and Kibei who believed that Japan had indeed won the war. These members of the Hisshō Kai (Absolute Victory Club), who were also known as "Katta Gumi," believed that the victorious Japanese Navy would momentarily sail into Pearl Harbor. To view this triumphant entry, they went to 'Aiea Heights, a hill overlooking Pearl Harbor, to keep their vigil. Needless to say, their trips were in vain. In the face of mounting evidence to the contrary, the group held on to its belief.

172

Trying to emulate their hero brothers and friends of the 442nd Regimental Combat Team, this group of barefooted "soldiers" from 'Ewa drilled daily.

War Records Depository
University of Hawaii

Arguments arose and relationships within their families and with their friends became strained as each side tried to convince the other of the reality of their views.

The war was officially over with the unconditional surrender of the Japanese aboard the *Battleship Missouri* in Tokyo Bay on September 1, 1945. It was now time for the Nisei GIs to leave the battlefields and hospitals and to return home to Hawai'i, which was not only sunshine and surf, but family and friends. During the war, several thousand Japanese American servicemen in their late teens and early twenties had traveled for the first time to the mainland United States, Europe, and the Pacific areas. They had had the opportunity to see and to meet different peoples. In Hawai'i, as children of immigrants, they had looked up to the Caucasians because they held status positions as managers on the plantations or as educated people in the professions. However, in their travels they, for the first time, saw thousands of poor whites barely eking out a living. They also met and fought alongside "Kotonks" who spoke and acted differently from Hawai'i's Japanese. They had had the opportunity to reflect upon their lives, their families, and their communities, and to compare them with those of others.

173

This poignant photo shows a mother receiving her son's silver star which was awarded posthumously.

U.S. Army Signal Corps photo
Rademaker, These Are Americans

We've Done Our Share . . .

My older brother was drafted into the army on November 10, 1941. A month later when the war began, he was transferred into the 100th Infantry Battalion. My younger brother and I joined the 442nd Regimental Combat Team, so my mother and father had three sons in World War II to worry about.

Two months after being sent overseas to Europe, my older brother was killed. He was the oldest son and my father's favorite. I remember his being allowed to drive the family truck for my father at age 12, and my father was so proud of him. When he was killed in action, my father was so devastated that he became ill. That was the one time I sent a letter in Japanese because I wanted my parents to know how I felt. I had written letters home in English before because I had sisters and a brother at home in Hilo. This one time, I had a *Kibei* (American-born but educated in Japan) friend translate it into Japanese for me so that my parents could read what I wanted to say to them.

Much later, during the Korean War, my youngest brother served in the army too. My family has done our share for our country.

Dr. Teruo Ihara, 442nd Veteran
Interviewed in October, 1984

Emotions welled as this father embraced his returning soldier son.

Hawaii State Archives.

Satisfied that they had proven their loyalty and driven by the insights they had gained, the Nisei veterans were convinced that they deserved to be treated as first-class citizens. They had left as young men who more or less accepted their limiting position in the white-controlled society. However, they returned as mature and confident men, determined to make changes in the unfair practices socially, politically, and economically for themselves and their families.

While the war years were difficult times for the Japanese living in Hawai'i, the experiences were not nearly as harsh or as bitter as those of the Japanese on the mainland United States. Whether they were aliens or American citizens, Japanese living in California, Oregon, and Washington were sent away to relocation camps inland. They had been suddenly and inhumanely uprooted from their homes and divested of most of their possessions.

However, because there were objective and humane military and civilian leaders who had spoken up to support the Japanese in Hawai'i, and because the Japanese in Hawai'i were a large and needed group, they were spared the total disruption faced by some 120,000 Japanese on the Mainland. All of these factors made a difference in the experiences and attitudes of the Japanese in Hawai'i as contrasted to those of the Japanese on the Mainland during and after World War II.

August 1946 ushered in a new facet of life for Sgt. S. Fukuda from Kāne'ohe. He is shown taking a look at his discharge papers with his girl, Miss E. Oda, after a parade.

War Records Depository
University of Hawaii

Chapter VIII
THE NEW HAWAI'I

The war had changed the Hawaiian community. The seeds of change in social relationships, politics, labor relations and economics, that had been planted and germinating in Hawai'i even before and during the war, blossomed in the postwar era. These major strands of change occurred simultaneously and can best be explained separately, yet each aspect had an impact on changes in the other areas.

The population of the Islands had ballooned with the influx of defense workers and members of the military. Hawai'i's 1940 resident population had been estimated at 427,884, of which 30,041 was military. By 1945, it had jumped to 814,601, which included 354,734 military personnel. For the first time in its history, Hawai'i's people saw many Caucasians of the working classes - servicemen as well as skilled and unskilled workers - as contrasted with those only of the managerial and professional classes.

The rapid population growth and wartime conditions affected everybody. They continued into the early postwar years. Work was plentiful. The hours were long, staggered, and irregular. But the pay was good. Heretofore dependent family members became independent as more women and young people joined the work force. Family, social, and economic patterns needed adjustments.

In many homes, including those of the Japanese, family solidarity weakened. They no longer had their meals together, let alone saw each other, as their work schedules differed. Although Japanese women had worked on the plantations and in small family businesses in the past, they had usually been able to care for their own youngsters. They took them to the fields or looked after them in between their business chores. In their new jobs, this was not possible and young children had to be cared for by non-family members. Older children came home to empty houses. Without parental supervision, language schools, and Buddhist Sunday schools, the role of traditional Japanese values lessened and peer values became more important. With more unsupervised time and

When family circumstances allowed it, girls went on to business school after graduating from high school to train as secretaries and bookkeepers. Working in an office was much better than working in the fields or in the mill. With the war and the movement of male employees into the military and defense positions, increasing numbers of jobs opened up for women.

Yamaguchi Collection

independence, there was a marked increase in juvenile delinquency in the 40s, most of which was in gambling, vagrancy, and traffic violations.

Frightened and confused alien parents abruptly relinquished their decision making responsibility to their children. Parent-child roles were reversed. In many instances, family assets were transferred to the citizen-children. Parents had to ask their children for help in learning the English language and American customs. Some Nisei, blaming the Issei for the rebuff by other members of the community, were very impatient with their parents. Errors in judgment were made by the youth, who, in their desire to be American, discredited anything Japanese. Any values and customs connected with Japan were considered old-fashioned and, therefore, undesirable. Many of the young people especially disliked Japanese authoritarianism. Established Japanese concepts such as filial piety and obligation were ignored more often.

Confrontations between parents and children, something very uncommon in Japanese households earlier, increased. Arguments erupted over the length of dresses, make-up, style of haircuts, choice of friends, and dating.

No longer did most young people allow their parents to choose their mates. The girls were attracted to the suave, young defense workers and servicemen who were lonesome and who were eager to meet young ladies. They were so much more attentive and romantic than the Nisei boys, many of whom were away at war. Statistics show that the Japanese female outmarriage of 6.3 percent from 1930-1940 increased to 16.9 percent the following decade.[1] Dating and marrying outside the ethnic group were especially frowned upon by the Japanese community. This caused divisiveness and pain within families and ill feelings against the newcomers. Girls who dated the haole workers and servicemen were called names such as "haole meat," "kami-kuzu" (rubbish), and "aburamushi" (cockroach). Parents often disowned their children who dared to marry outside of the group.

On the other hand, there were just as many Japanese families that strengthened their bonds as together they met the problems and did their best through frightening and changing times. They recognized the dilemma they were in and gave up visible Japanese customs. However, they kept those values that they considered to be important to the success of any human being. These included those related to filial piety and other personal and community obligations. The family members supported each other emotionally and worked towards solving the problems faced by any family with growing children. Although parent-child roles needed to be reversed at times, there was still respect for parents.

The parents tried to understand the changes that were being forced upon their children by the changing society, whose efforts to Americanize the Japanese had been intensified. The Nisei were greatly influenced by their peers and teachers at school and by the movies, radio, and books to become like white Americans. The boys flexed their biceps in front of mirrors and worked hard to develop muscles like their hero, Charles Atlas. The young girls collected autographed photographs of their favorite movie stars. They wished they could be fair and have curly hair, large double-lidded eyes, and prominent breasts. Sisters and friends gave each other home permanents. They experimented with curling their lashes and oiling to make them appear longer. They selected styles from Sears Roebuck catalogs and sewed their own dresses. How

Christmastime, 1961. These cousins were at a family Christmas party which, by this time, had become traditional along with Christmas trees and an exchange of gifts. Artificial Christmas trees, table top models tipped with red berries, had appeared in some Japanese homes in the late 1930s.

they longed to live romantic lives in some small mid-western town lined with elm trees! Neither the boys nor the girls realized that within their lifetime, four million people each year would travel from the East and West just to visit beautiful Hawai'i, a home which they were yet to appreciate to the fullest.

Even the fathers, who were probably the most reluctant to change, found the need to assume new roles. The change was especially difficult for the Issei father who had always lived a life in which women were in subservient roles. He had been catered to and had not been asked to do any household chores. He had worked in the yard and the garden, but had not helped in the kitchen. A Japanese male who marketed or cooked was an

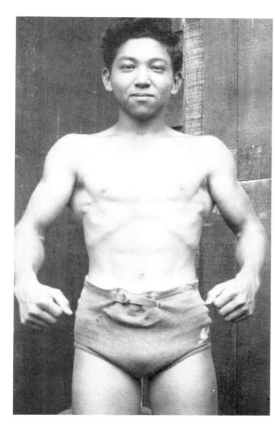

Emulating Charles Atlas.
ca. 1945.

Ochiai Collection

uncommon sight. Because mother had taken an outside job and had less time at home, he now had to help her, including in the kitchen. The sharing of household responsibilities, however, was still not a 50-50 proposition as the woman's job was considered secondary to her husband's and to her home chores. While the men helped within the privacy of the family, they still expected to be catered to in the presence of friends or other family members who did not live with them.

The non-plantation and non-family-business jobs gave the Japanese women greater opportunities to mingle with non-Japanese people. They became more aware of American fashions and served more non-Japanese meals. They gradually depended on and became a part of non-Japanese institutions such as the PTA, Christian churches, and the YWCA.

Along with other families who had sent their men off to war, the Japanese families had followed the progress of the war. They had

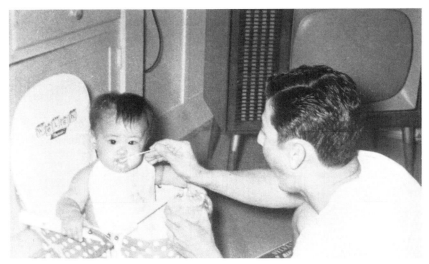

Open your mouth – 1958.
The Issei father left the day-to-day care of his children to his busy wife. Nisei fathers very slowly and gradually began to assume some of the responsibilities of child rearing. This Nisei father, probably one of the few to do so, had attended baby care classes with his wife in anticipation of the blessed event and had learned how to feed, change, and bathe his daughter.

Hazama Collection

shared anxieties as well as pride in the military accomplishments of their men. In some instances, they had become familiar with others through correspondence with families on the Mainland who had befriended their soldier sons and husbands. More and more young people went to mainland schools in the postwar years and mingled with mainland students and their families. Locally, the Japanese families reciprocated the kindness shown members of their families. These opportunities for association gave both the Japanese and the non-Japanese a greater understanding of each other.

The Japanese had been excluded from some of the classified jobs related to secret military matters which paid top wages and salaries. However, their income levels improved during the war and immediate postwar eras. Many went into positions in the Territorial and County governments which had become available when others went into the lucrative defense jobs.

In her dissertation, "Some Aspects of the War Situation Upon the Alien Japanese in Hawaii," Yukiko Kimura of the International Institute of the Honolulu YWCA concluded, that in 1943, that:

. . . physical security does not necessarily give these people a feeling of security. A real feeling of security comes when they feel that they are trusted and allowed to take part in the common cause of the larger community, even at the risks of their lives. Language usage and other old world habits of the alien Japanese may lag behind their spirit and desire. But their having been permitted to participate thus freely and intimately in the war effort of the larger American community has substituted for their earlier feeling of fear, a strong confidence in the leadership and administration of the United States government. In this sense, the experiences they have had since December 7 have helped solve a great part of the so-called Japanese problem in Hawaii, a problem which the last three quarters or half century had not solved.[2]

There was a gradual change, too, in the attitude of Japanese parents toward higher education for their daughters. In the past, great sacrifices had been made by everyone in the family to educate the sons. The girls were expected to contribute their earnings to help their brothers to become doctors, dentists, and lawyers - professions with the higher status. But, as family incomes increased, parents began to have aspirations for their daughters to become teachers or nurses, professions that would readily complement their being wives and mothers.

As the housing shortage eased and incomes were sufficient, married sons and daughters moved out of their parents' homes and set up their own households. This was in keeping with the American concepts of independence and individual rights. In two family households, conflicts often arose because of differences in custom. The Issei mother-in-law expected to set the pattern and have her daughter-in-law adjust to it. The daughter-in-law, in many families, had to cater not only to her husband and her parents-in-law, but to her siblings-in-law. She was the lowest person in the family hierarchy. The Nisei daughter-in-law, however, often perceived her role very differently and rebelled.

With the increase in interracial marriages and the arrival of war brides, Yukiko Kimura studied the in-law relationship in Japanese marriages. On the surface it appeared that there were greater difficulties in interracial marriages as they were a fairly new experience and not yet fully accepted. However, the study showed that there was less conflict in marriages where wives were non-Japanese. The in-laws expected these brides to be different and overlooked their "shortcomings." Greatest conflict and competition occurred when the daughter-in-law came from Japan. The

An education, a mother's legacy to her daughters, 1954.
Like most dutiful daughters of her era, Shigeyo Ochiai worked to help educate her brother to become a school teacher although she also longed for a teaching career. So, she encouraged all of her children to pursue their interests. She and her daughters are departing on their first mainland trip, she - to visit her son and her daughters - to attend graduate schools on the east coast.

Ochiai Collection

184

brides, most of whom had come from urban Japan, felt superior to their in-laws who still followed the customs of pre-war rural Japan and openly criticized them. They got together with their friends from Japan and nostalgically reminisced about their lives in Japan instead of doing housework or going out to work. This caused disharmony as the in-laws were operating under the rural work ethic.[3]

Unlike the Issei, but like their contemporaries of other backgrounds, the Nisei followed the trend of having fewer children. This practice in itself brought on some tensions between the Issei and the Nisei. There were also conflicts arising between the Issei grandparents and the Nisei parents about child rearing. There were questions about how and when to feed babies, when to pick up crying infants, the methods of disciplining youngsters, the use of pidgin English, and the assigning of household tasks.

Beginning in the mid-50s, the care of elderly parents became a growing concern for an increasing number of Nisei families. Traditionally, it was the custom for the *chōnan* (eldest son) to inherit whatever assets his parents had and to care for them. Because they had been taught this value from the time they were young, the older Nisei *chōnans* and their wives accepted this responsibility. If they had been living together, they just continued to do so. However, if they had maintained separate households, the elderly parents usually came to stay with the *chōnan's* family as they became older. It was not as easy for the younger Nisei who had been exposed to more middle class American values. They questioned the custom because they felt that all of the siblings were children of their parents and therefore equally responsible for them. Family meetings were held and alternate decisions were made. In some instances, other siblings, frequently daughters, cared for the parents. In others, parents lived with each child for an equal number of months per year. Still other parents who were ill or immobile were placed in nursing or care homes.

The cost of caring for the parents often added to the problem. Although the Issei had worked diligently since arriving in Hawai'i, most had very limited assets. Their meager earnings had been spent on their daily expenses and on their children's education. In their retirement years, most did have some monthly income. The plantation workers received small pensions, medical coverage, and social security payments. Those who had worked in other small businesses had only social security payments plus medicare benefits since 1965. These limited resources were barely adequate

185

when they were well. However, as they became less able, they needed help. Sometimes the children shared in the expenses. At other times the elderly received aid from governmental agencies. The latter alternative and the sending of parents to nursing homes were unheard of solutions in the Japanese community until the postwar years. Families sometimes endured the hardship of caring for the elderly to save face and to avoid being talked about.

Thus, although the Nisei grew up in mostly hard-working, stable families within a generally homogeneous Japanese community, values and aspirations were changing all the while, gradually at first and more rapidly with the war. The Japanese moved out of the areas of their ethnic concentration and increasingly entered the mainstream of the Hawaiian community physically, culturally, socially, and economically.

In the years following the war, the Nisei's most dramatic impact was felt in the political arena. Their experiences in the battlefields and in their travels had added to their understanding of the words equality, liberty, justice, and democracy. As they returned home, they talked about their pre and postwar experiences and of their future. They believed it was time for Hawai'i to be released from the domination of the haole oligarchy, the paternalistic plantation system, and the Republican Party. The Nisei veterans wanted equality as U.S. citizens and greater economic and social mobility. They wanted what they were entitled to as citizens and not what the oligarchy wanted them to have. They wanted to be in control of their lives.

The Nisei veterans pondered and discussed these concerns as they took advantage of the Servicemen's Readjustment Act of 1944, commonly known as the G.I. Bill of Rights. The G.I. Bill paid the tuition, books, and $75.00 monthly living expenses. It afforded a tremendous opportunity for the Nisei who had been taught to value education, but who could not heretofore afford higher education. The Nisei veterans enrolled in large numbers at the University of Hawaii as well as at mainland colleges. After completing their baccalaureate degrees, many continued and entered graduate programs and professional schools. They re-turned as doctors, dentists, and lawyers.

While the doctors and dentists achieved status as professional people in the community, some Nisei veterans felt that the best and fastest means of facilitating the major changes they desired was through involvement in politics and government.

Historically, the Republican Party had dominated the Hawaiian

On August 15, 1946, these Hawaiian WACs including S/Sgt. Ruth Fujii rode on a float urging veterans to prepare for the future by enrolling in school. The float depicted a classroom scene.

War Records Depository,
University of Hawaii

political scene since soon after Hawai'i's annexation to the United States in 1898. This domination was still evident throughout World War II and for eight years following it. The postwar Democratic Party in Hawai'i continued to be troubled by poor leadership and factionalism. Democratic Governor Ingram Stainback and his administration were friendly with the established *kama'āina* families and were more Republican in their thinking and actions than Democratic. A second group led by the ILWU's (International Longshoremen's and Warehousemen's Union) Jack Hall and other labor leaders focused on changes in legislation favorable to the laboring class. There were also other minor groups led by non-*kama'āina* haole independents such as John A. Burns, O. Vincent Esposito, and Honolulu Mayor Johnny Wilson.

John A. Burns, a haole who had lived most of his life in Hawai'i, was not a member of the ruling white elite. Neither was he, like them, a Republican. As the liaison officer between the Honolulu Police Department and the F.B.I. during the war and as captain of the vice squad, he had witnessed and worked with the problems of the Japanese and the downtrodden. More than anything else, he wanted to break the total control that the oligarchy had over every facet of Hawaiian living. He wanted to give the non-haole citizens a voice in their own government and in their own destinies. He theorized that a strong party composed of these people could wrest control of the Islands from the oligarchy.

Middle-aged and financially limited, John A. Burns was one of several factional leaders who set out to rebuild the Democratic Party in the years following World War II. Beginning in 1946, he met regularly over coffee on Saturday nights with a group that included Chuck Mau, Jack Kawano, Mitsuyuki Kido, and Dr. Ernest Murai. He wanted the support of all the non-haole groups, but he especially sought that of the Japanese and the Hawaiians

---

Breaking the Wall of Prejudice

Dan Aoki joined the Democratic party in 1948 and was one of its leaders during the Burns' years. Although he did not run for public office, he was influential in helping to shape policies. In looking back over the years he said:

> Since becoming the majority party in the State Legislature and capturing the governorship, the Democrats with Jack Burns as their leader have focused all of their efforts on breaking down the so-called wall of prejudice against the non-whites. As far as the Japanese were concerned, it was very seldom that even when they were trained and educated that they came out on top. They were number two at best or number three. We always wanted to make them number one. A good example was the cabinet of the Territorial government. There was never a Japanese cabinet member until Mich Watanabe and Sakae Takahashi in 1950 or 1951. We wanted to get Nisei in positions to prove that they can do the job if given the opportunity. They're qualified to do it. All they needed was a chance to do it. That's what we tried to do all the time.
>
> . . . The election of George Ariyoshi was the climax of it all. He happened to be at the right place at the right time. It's not that we wanted to elect a Japanese governor. No, it's not that idea. We just wanted a non-white person to prove to the people that one doesn't have to be a white person to be a leader.

Interviewed on June 10, 1984

188

because of their large numbers. He was determined to be success-ful in his efforts.

Although Burns realized that his chances at winning the election were slim, he decided to run against the popular incumbent Joseph Rider Farrington for the position of Delegate to Congress in 1948. He believed that in order for the Democratic Party to be a serious challenger to the Republican Party, it needed to field a full slate of candidates. Therefore Burns became a contender.

Burns welcomed the support when a disabled 442nd veteran and University of Hawaii student, Daniel K. Inouye, phoned to offer his help. Along with the then 442nd President Dan Aoki, Burns and Inouye worked hard to persuade the Club members that they individually, and the 442nd as an organization, should become politically active. This was no easy task since the 442nd had been mostly a social club and there was resistance to changing that image. The trio argued convincingly that the men of the 442nd had helped to win the war and it was now time to help build the kind of Hawai'i they had fought for. They needed to build a stronger second party to stand up against the Republicans who had monopolized the scene too long. John Burns, who had earlier been made the first honorary member of the 442nd in recognition of his staunch support of the Japanese during the war, was their man for he held the same dreams that they had – equality, justice, and opportunities for all regardless of race. After many hours of discussion, the veterans were won over; and they helped in the 1948 campaign distributing brochures and making house calls.

Although Farrington was reelected as Delegate by a three to one plurality, Burns had won the active support of a large number of non-haole citizens. He continued to rebuild the Democratic Party, using his Saturday night coffee gang and the newly involved Japanese as his core group. Among the members were veterans Dan Inouye, Dan Aoki, Matsuo Takabuki, Mike Tokunaga, and part-Hawaiian William Richardson. Burns, a widely read man and a devout Catholic, assumed the role of an educator and shared his insights on philosophy, history, economics, and politics. They also discussed details such as effective Democratic Party organization, recruiting of Party members, and the securing and training of candidates. The number of prospective Japanese supporters increased when the alien population was granted the right to naturalization and citizenship with the passage of the Walter-McCarran Immigration and Nationality Act by Congress in 1952.

On February 24, 1955, U.S. citizenship became a reality for these pictured Issei, some of whom had lived in Hawai'i for fifty years. They had prepared for this auspicious day by studying the American Constitution and history at citizenship classes.

Hawaii Times Photo
Yamaguchi Collection

In the 1952 Territorial election, the Democratic Party won half the seats in the House of Representatives. In 1954, however, the Democrats won twenty-two out of thirty House seats and ten of fifteen Senate seats. The Democrats had overcome the fifty years of Republican domination! They were clearly in control of the Territorial Legislature. In this political revolution which heralded a new era for Hawai'i, nearly half of the victorious legislators were AJAs. Among them were Nelson Doi, Stanley Hara, Daniel K. Inouye, Spark M. Matsunaga, and Sakae Takahashi, each of whom was to play a major role in Hawai'i's efforts towards equality and opportunity for all. The one disappointment for the Democrats was the defeat of Burns to Farrington's widow, Elizabeth, by less than 1,000 of the nearly 140,000 votes that had been cast.

The 1955 Legislature was optimistic and idealistic, but inexperienced. They, more than anything else, wanted to break down the existing wall of prejudice and to give all persons equal opportunities. The lawmakers attempted to implement the Democratic Party platform which called for tax law revisions to relieve the low income people, to aid small businesses and labor, and to make educational and land reforms.[4] Numerous bills were introduced; however, few became law.

"I Gave This Arm to Fight Fascists"

In the fall of 1954, six Democratic candidates William Crozier, Masato Doi, Daniel Inouye, Anna Kahanamoku, Russell Kono, and Spark Matsunaga campaigned as a team in the strong Republican Fourth District. Their challenge to the Republicans for a candidate to candidate debate was not answered until a meeting one night at Aina Haina. As one of the Democratic candidates was speaking, a Republican from the audience grabbed the microphone and charged that the Democratic Party had been captured by the ILWU whose leaders were Communists.

Although he wasn't scheduled to be the next speaker, Dan, angered by the charge, sprang to his feet, put his notes into his clenched teeth, and tore them with his only hand and said,

. . . I cannot help wondering, whether the people of Hawaii will not think it strange that the only weapon in the Republican arsenal is to label as communists men so recently returned from defending liberty on the firing lines in Italy and France. Let me speak for those of us who didn't come back– I know I speak for my colleagues on this platform, . . . we bitterly resent having our loyalty and patriotism questioned by cynical political hacks who lack the courage to debate the real issues in this campaign.

I had never before called attention to my disability for the simple reason that I didn't consider it a qualification for public office. But at that moment, blinded with fury, coldly aware that I was engaging in a bit of demagoguery, I held up my empty right sleeve and shook it: "I gave this arm to fight fascists. If my country wants the other one to fight communists, it can have it!"

Inouye, Daniel K.
Journey to Washington, p. 248-249.

The Democrats and the Nisei once again scored victories in the 1956 election. This time John Burns won handily over Delegate Elizabeth Farrington and went to Washington, D.C. to continue Hawai'i's fight for statehood. Dan Aoki, the former 442nd President, went along as administrative aide to Burns. A concern that repeatedly appeared in the statehood issue was the large number of Asians in the Islands, particularly those of Japanese descent. This question and others, like that of the Communist influence in Hawai'i, were repeatedly examined by members of Congressional Committees.

In the spring of 1947, then Governor Ingram Stainback was informed about the presence of Communists in Hawai'i by the Chief of Army Intelligence. Among those named were Jack Hall, Regional Director of ILWU, and waterfront organizers, Ichiro Izuka and Jack Kawano. Also named were educators Dr. John Reinecke and his Nisei wife. More information became available later in 1947 when Ichiro Izuka broke away from the ILWU and the

---

They Are As Good Americans

Dan Aoki served as administrative assistant to John A. Burns when the latter was Delegate to Congress and also when he served as Governor of Hawai'i. The two became acquainted when Burns was made the first honorary member of the 442nd in recognition for the help he had given the Japanese in Hawai'i during the war. Aoki recalled:

Along the way you're going to have to choose whom you're going to go with. The kinds of things a person says and does make you stay with him. When the Hawai'i Statehood Bill was before the Rules Committee, Judge Smith asked Delegate John A. Burns, "How can you ask us for statehood for Hawai'i when only one-third of the people of Hawai'i are Caucasians?"

I happened to be in the room and I heard Mr. Burns come right out and say, "Mr. Chairman, I've studied the Constitution of the United States and nowhere does it say that the United States is for Caucasians. I'm not here asking for statehood because of the one-third of the people of Hawai'i who are Caucasians, but I'm here asking for statehood because of the two-thirds of the people of Hawai'i who are non-Caucasians. My constituents may not look like yours, but let me assure you that they are as good Americans, if not better Americans than your constituents."

You can't help but follow a man who can stand up like that and talk to the leaders in Congress.

Dan Aoki
Interviewed on June 10, 1984

An abandoned ice house served as the background for campaign posters in Waipahu. Although most Japanese Americans were Democrats, Peanuts Kunihisa was a Republican. He was elected to the State Senate in 1959 but was defeated in 1962 and 1966.

Waipahu Cultural Garden Park

There was an increase in Mainland and foreign investments. Personal incomes rose and unemployment was down to 2.7 percent in the 60s. The economic picture, however, changed beginning in the 70s as Hawai'i, like the rest of the nation, suffered a recession and rising inflation. Unemployment and cost of living figures rose while tax revenues fell.

Against this background, the multi-ethnic Democratic legislature under the leadership of progressive and innovative men like Nadao Yoshinaga and Sakae Takahashi worked towards realizing a "New Hawai'i." Revisions were made to the existing tax structure. A graduated income tax based on the ability to pay was enacted to supplant the flat 2 percent tax in 1957. Under the new law, lower incomes were taxed at lower rates and higher incomes at higher rates. Excise or gross income tax rates on production, manufacturing, and wholesaling were lowered and those on retailing were raised.

In order to make home ownership a reality for increasing numbers of people, the Democratic legislature, inspired by Governor Burns, made changes in the land tax laws. The new taxes, computed from revised assessments of property value, were based

197

Sakae Takahashi, who served as Senate minority leader in the 1962 session, is pictured during the opening day ceremonies.

Takahashi Collection

on market value and highest and best use. Faced with higher taxes, the large landowners were thus forced to put vacant lands on the market, much of it as long term lease lands. The Maryland Land Law, which was passed in 1976, gave the Hawaii Housing Authority the right of eminent domain to condemn private property for later resale to lessees. The law was challenged by the large estates, but the U.S. Supreme Court in 1984 declared it to be constitutional as long as there is just compensation. The State also made low interest loans available to qualified first time home purchasers.

Educational concerns at all levels were given top priority. In the public schools, increased appropriations made possible the elimination of book rental and other special fees, lowered the pupil teacher ratio, and installed new programs. Teachers' salaries were raised according to newly established pay scales based on longevity and training. Quality and expansion were also sought in higher

Senator Brian Taniguchi (since 1994); former Representative (1980-1994).

"I was always interested in government service. I was actively involved in student government during my intermediate, high school, and college years. Serving on the Neighborhood Board and working actively in the disadvantaged areas were extensions of that interest. I now represent the people of the Mānoa area where I grew up. I was elected to the Legislature for the first time in 1980 and have been re-elected two times since. I really enjoy doing something for the community where I grew up and serving the people I know."

Interviewed on December 3, 1984

Photo by Russel Yamashita

education. A university system was established to include a network of community colleges, West Oahu College, and the Hilo and Manoa campuses. New departments, such as American Studies and computer science and two new professional schools, the Medical and Law Schools, were added. The legislature also embarked on a program to upgrade the physical facilities at all levels of education.

Workers benefited from planned and repeated raises of the minimum wage, increased coverage by the unemployment compensation fund, and various training programs. Agricultural and seasonal workers came to be covered under workers compensation while government workers were given the right of collective bargaining.

Consideration was given to preserving agriculture and conservation lands through the greenbelt law. The Economic Planning and Development Department was established and charged with the responsibility of addressing concerns about planned and controlled growth. New industries in diversified agriculture and aquaculture were studied and encouraged. Issues related to the planned use of resources, particularly of water, and the protection of the environment from pollution, were faced.

Prominent researcher, Takuji Fujimura, pioneered the development of mass hatching techniques for fresh water prawns while serving as a biologist for the State of Hawaii. The industry that he helped to launch has grown to twenty-two farms with an annual production of 268,000 pounds and an approximate value of $1.3 million in 1983. Fujimura currently serves as a consultant to prawn projects throughout the world.

Photo by C. Richard Fassler
Aquaculture Development Program
Dept. of Land and Natural Resources
State of Hawai'i

Reapportionment was affected with the Supreme Court ruling of one man, one vote. The membership of the State Senate was increased to twenty-five and that of the House to fifty-one. An ethics commission and campaign spending limits were established and the sunshine law was enacted in a move towards a more open government.

Japanese Americans also provided leadership in the various County governments. Shunichi Kimura was first elected as Chairman and Executive Officer for the County of Hawaii in 1965. He continued to serve as Mayor until the election of Herbert Matayoshi, another Nisei, who worked with Japanese American Prosecutor Jon Ono and Council members William Kawahara, Muneo Sameshima, and Stephen Yamashiro over the years. In 1974, Shunichi Kimura was appointed as a judge in the Third Circuit Court, Family Court. On the island of Kaua'i, Democrat Tony Kunimura, who had earlier served as one of the leaders in the State House of Representatives, became its first Nisei County Mayor in 1982. Masato Doi, later Judge Doi, and Patsy Takemoto Mink have served as chairpersons of the Honolulu City Council.

Judge Shunichi Kimura of the Third Circuit in Hilo. Shunichi Kimura was already a leader during his college years. He served as president of the ASUH, the Associated Students of the University of Hawaii, in the early fifties.

Kimura Collection

Among the Japanese American members of the Honolulu City Council have been Ben F. Kaito, George Koga, Toraki Matsumoto, Yoshiro Nakamura, and Matsuo Takabuki. The latter was appointed a trustee of the Bishop Estate, the largest landowner in Hawai'i, on June 18, 1971, by Chief Justice William Richardson of the Hawaii Supreme Court. The Estate had been created for the benefit of Hawaiian children by the will of Princess Bernice Pauahi Bishop, descendant of the Kamehameha lineage. The income derived from the vast land holdings has gone solely to the support of the Kamehameha Schools, which maintains a campus encompassing grades kindergarten through high school, an Extension Division, and an Educational Research Institute. Although there were no questions about Takabuki's ability, there were concerns about his business relationships and his ethnic background. As the attorney for Capital Investment Company, Takabuki was already involved in land dealings in the State. Would there be conflicts? His Japanese ethnicity per se was not challenged. It was the fact that he was not Hawaiian that became an issue for there were those who felt that a Hawaiian would be in a better position to understand the needs of the Hawaiian people. There was much discussion in the community about ethnic pride and the aloha spirit which encouraged cultural sharing and mixing. The initial furor subsided and Takabuki has continued to serve as trustee.

Beginning with the appointment of Masaji Marumoto as Associate Justice of the Territorial Supreme Court in 1956, increasing numbers of Japanese Americans have served in the judiciary. In 1959, Wifred C. Tsukiyama became Chief Justice. In 1984, three of the five members of the Supreme Court were Japanese Americans.

Others such as Masato Doi, Yasutaka Fukushima, and James Wakatsuki have served in the Circuit Courts. Yoshimi Hayashi served as U.S. Attorney in 1968.

Yet another factor that simultaneously contributed to major changes for Hawai'i during this period was the rapid growth of unionism, especially that of the ILWU. It was the first union to organize workers industry-wide, regardless of race or skills. Unions along racial lines had existed on the plantations since the early 1900s. Although each strike had brought on some improvements, the unions were generally not very effective as the employers pitted one ethnic group against the other. In organizing, the ILWU needed to address and to allay suspicions and resentments that one group harbored against the other. In addi-

Trustee for The Kamehameha Schools

I returned to Hawai'i in 1949 after completing my studies at the University of Chicago Law School. Since I was the President of the 442nd Veterans Club, I was chosen as the standard bearer for the Nisei on the Connally Caravan during Hawai'i's drive for statehood. Soon after 1952, before the "Democratic Revolution" in 1954, I was elected to the City Council at a time when the Council and the Legislature were dominated by the Republicans.

I did not apply for the position of Trustee for the Kamehameha Schools but was voted in by the Chief Justices of our Supreme Court in 1971 because of my background in real estate. Although there were other Asian members on the Board, I was the first Japanese to be so honored. My role as a Trustee is very interesting and I feel that I have now been accepted by the Kamehameha Schools and the wider community.

Matsuo Takabuki
Interviewed on December 10, 1984
Kamehameha Schools Photo

203

Justices of the Hawaii State Supreme Court (1984) Left to Right: Justice Yoshimi Hayashi, Justice Edward H. Nakamura, Chief Justice Herman Lum, Justice Frank Padgett, Justice James Wakatsuki.

Photo by Graphic Pictures Hawaii, Inc.
Hawaii State Supreme Court Collection

tion, it was dangerous for the organizers in the early 30s for they had to be discreet, lest they be discovered, fired, and blacklisted. The prospective members, too, were afraid of the same action should they be found sympathetic to the cause.

The National Labor Relations Act of 1935, which was declared constitutional in 1937, gave industrial workers on the plantations the right to organize and engage in collective bargaining. It was not until the passage of the Hawaii Employment Relations Act of May 21, 1945, commonly known as the Little Wagner Act, however, that agricultural workers won the right to organize.

By mid-1941, with the determined leadership of local and mainland ILWU leaders, the waterfront had been organized. The advent of World War II in December, 1941, brought union activities to a standstill and all efforts were directed toward winning the war. The military government not only froze the plantation workers' wages, but made it difficult for them to leave

"Major" Okada

. . . "Major" Okada – the nickname is from his high school baseball days – earned a place in Hawaiian history. After World War II, when the ILWU was struggling for a foothold on the plantations to organize workers there, Okada's personal popularity and connections in the amateur baseball leagues helped open the way.

In addition to Oahu Sugar Company workers, Okada helped organize the plantations in Ewa, Waianae and Waialua. Union work was far more difficult and dangerous 35 years ago. For his activities, Okada was called before the House Un-American Activities Committee hearings here.

. . . Union organizing led to Democratic Party work and Okada was one of the forces that helped the Democrats oust the entrenched Republican Party with its ties to big business and foment the "social revolution" of the mid-1950s which created new opportunities for so many in Hawaii.

. . . Most remarkable about Okada was the man himself. He was warm-hearted, plain and humble – "an Indian, not a chief," he said. But he was a tireless worker for community causes – people causes, really; there cannot be many organizations beginning with the name Waipahu that he was not part of.

Honolulu Advertiser Editorial,
January 6, 1983.
Waipahu Cultural Garden Park Photo

their jobs. Although their wages were substantially lower than those of many others, the plantation workers had to endure.

With the lifting of martial law and subsequent cessation of hostilities, there were renewed union activities. The workers on the plantations were ready to be organized. The leaders made conscious efforts toward racial harmony and unity. Meetings were conducted in three languages – English, Japanese, and Ilocano (Filipino dialect) – to allow understanding and participation by all persons. Rank and file members with leadership potential from the different ethnic groups were trained as leaders. The union embraced the slogan, "An injury to one is an injury to all." By the late 40s, the ILWU claimed a membership surpassing 30,000.

On September 1, 1946, 21,000 sugar workers staged a successful seventy-nine day strike against thirty-three plantations. Faced with a strong union and near drought conditions, the employers relented. Although the union lost on the issue of a closed shop and compromised on wages, it won the virtual abolition of the paternalistic perquisite system. The plantation worker now had greater control over his life. He could make decisions on where to live and how and where to spend his money.

Sugar plantation laborers' rally.
Hawaiian Agriculture Co., Pahala, Hawai'i ca 1947-49.

Hawaii State Archives

Meeting in Secret

Dan Aoki grew up in Puʻunēnē, Maui. Because his father was a Christian minister, Dan lived in a big house with indoor plumbing. He had a good life. But he saw how the plantation people, people that he played with, lived. They traded at the plantation store where they were able to charge. Then on pay day, their charges were deducted first, often leaving the workers with zero cash. Not having any money, they had to charge again. They were caught in the system and couldn't move. They needed to join forces to better their lives.

In recalling the difficult time that the workers had in their attempts at organizing, Aoki recalled:

> In the late 20s and 30s when the workers wanted to organize, they had to meet secretly. It went something like this . . . they'd decide on where they were going to meet. The host prepared something to eat and got some beer ready. He'd pull all his shades down and lock up. A person going to the meeting needed to be careful, too. He needed to have someone he could trust to drive him. When they approached the house where the meeting was going to be held, the driver slowed down, as slow as he could. And then the person opened the door and sort of rolled into the hedges when he found the coast to be clear, especially of the camp police. He'd crawl up to the house and knock in a special way. The host would turn off the lights, let the person in, and close the door. About five or six leaders would meet. . . . Then by word of mouth they'd get the message to the others. Everything had to be by word of mouth. They had to be sure whom they talked to. . . .

Interviewed on June 10, 1984

The ILWU staged an even more devastating strike on the waterfront in 1949. Pointing to a thirty-two cents per hour differential between the West Coast and Hawaiʻi, two thousand longshoremen walked off their jobs and completely disrupted all Hawaiian shipping. Before long, every individual living in Hawaiʻi was affected, as Hawaiʻi was very dependent on shipping. Food and other shortages occurred, businesses failed, and unemployment rose. The public was the victim and there developed strong anti-union sentiments. The fact that Jack Hall and other union leaders had been named as possible Communists in 1947 added to

After over three months of negotiations in 1956, the ILWU and Hawai'i's sugar industry signed an agreement for a new contract. Union negotiators shown signing the agreement were, seated from left, Yasuki Arakaki, Kameo Ichimura, Seiko Shiroma and standing, Jack Hall and Louis Goldblatt.

Waipahu Cultural Garden Park

the public's negative reactions. The leaders had made an unsuccessful attempt in the mid and late 40s to control the Democratic Party and had failed. They were accused of being more interested in the political implications of Communism rather than in the betterment of the working class. The strike was settled 178 days later when the workers won a fourteen cents per hour increase.

Through the long strike, its attendant losses and miseries including the accusations lodged against the union leaders, the rank and file remained loyal to Jack Hall and the ILWU. Threats to their leaders were nothing new to the workers who had earlier weathered the accusations of a Japanese conspiracy and whose supporters had been in prison. It was important to them that Jack Hall and the union were willing to fight for them and that they continued to bring improvements to their lives. Through his tough and determined negotiation stances, the Hawaiian agricultural workers came to be among the highest paid in the world. In January of 1955, Jack Hall was instrumental in bringing the sugar, pineapple, longshore, and other smaller unions into one large strong unit, Local 142.

Unions continued to exert a great deal of influence in the Hawaiian economy and society during the 60s and the 70s as the ILWU and other unions strengthened their positions or entered the Hawaiian scene. The American Federation of Labor (AFL) continued to organize the construction workers along trade lines. Electricians belonged to the International Brotherhood of Electrical Workers, carpenters to the Carpenters Union Local 745, and the plumbers in Plumbers-Fitters Local 675. Bus drivers and truckers were recruited by Art Rutledge and the Teamsters Union while hotel workers were wooed by both the ILWU and Local 5 of the Hotel, Restaurant Employees and Bartenders Union. When the State Legislature granted the right of collective bargaining to government employees, blue collared workers joined the United Public Workers (UPW), clerical and other office workers, including educational officers, the Hawaii Government Employees' Association (HGEA), other educators the Hawaii State Teachers Association (HSTA), Hawaii Federation of Teachers (HFT), and the University of Hawaii Professional Assembly (UHPA). In the spring of 1984 when contract negotiations were not proceeding satisfactorily, UPW, HSTA, the bargaining unit for all public school teachers, HGEA and UHPA formed a coalition and bargained as a unit and won minor medical benefits and pay increases.

Japanese Americans have been prominent in the leadership of the various unions. Among them have been Major Okada, Newton Miyagi, Thomas Yogi, Yasuki Arakaki, and Yoshito Takamine of the ILWU, George Kaisan of the Teamsters, Al Hamai, Barbara Nagaue, and Haroldeen Wakida of HSTA, Russel Okata of HGEA, and Royce Higa, Samson Mamizuka, Thomas Fujikawa, and Akito Fujikawa of the AFL affiliates.[6]

Armed with their college degrees and confident of themselves as Americans, the Japanese Americans have increasingly made themselves available to the mainstream of the Hawaiian business and economic communities. Contrary to widely held beliefs, however, they have not come to dominate the economic scene. As of the 70s and 80s, they have attained, on the most part, supervisory and middle-management positions. Only a few, having demonstrated their capabilities, dedication, and social ease, have risen to the top corporate levels. When Castle and Cooke, one of the Big Five sugar factors, appointed Mitsuyoshi Fukuda as a Vice President of Industrial Relations in 1966, he became the first Asian to attain a Big Five corporate position. By 1984 AMFAC, another Big Five Company, listed Frederick J. Murata, Vice

"Mits" Fukuda

On August 20, 1966, the *Honolulu Star Bulletin* published an article titled: "C & C Names First A.J.A. Vice-President." By being appointed Vice-President of Industrial Relations of Castle and Cooke Inc., Mitsuyoshi Fukuda became the first to be named to the vice-presidency of one of the Big Five companies and the first Asian to be promoted to a high corporate office in the firm's 115 year history.

A graduate of the University of Hawaii and a former teacher, "Mits" Fukuda distinguished himself during World War II. As an ROTC Reserve Officer, he was commissioned a second lieutenant when he joined the 100th Infantry. He was eventually promoted to Army Infantry Major and became the highest ranking Nisei combat officer. When he returned home after the war, he received four job offers. In 1946, he joined Castle and Cooke as an Assistant to the Director of Industrial Relations. According to "Mits": "Some big companies seemed to be willing to do something for the Nisei veterans. Very few AJAs chose to go into big business. Most of the other veterans decided to go back to college or returned to their old jobs. I had no problem fitting in as a new employee, and I was treated very well."

"Mits" credits the war for opening the door to opportunities.

President-Director Corporate Audit, and Charleen K. Ikeda, Vice President-Corporate Secretary in high corporate positions.

Egan Nishimoto left his position as Executive Vice President of Dillingham Land Company to become Executive Director of Development for Hawaiian Operations for CMV, Inc. As such, he is responsible for the over-all management of the Ala Moana Center, the Ala Moana Building, and the Ala Moana Pacific Center. The General Manager of the Ala Moana Shopping Center is Stanley Tabata, another Japanese American.

Still others were appointed as directors of the large companies. Attorney Ralph Yamaguchi was one of the first Asians to be so tapped by AMFAC in 1964. He continued service to AMFAC in the 80s along with Senator Patricia Saiki. Castle & Cooke appointed Betty Y. Hirozawa as an alternate director in 1978 and a director since 1979. She is Vice President-Administration and Secretary-Treasurer of the Hawaii Employers Council. In 1982 Bert T. Kobayashi, Jr., Wallace S. Fujiyama, Glenn A. Kaya, and Richard Mamiya were four of the twenty-eight members of the board at First Hawaiian Bank. An earlier appointee was Governor George Ariyoshi.

Nisei veterans Dan Aoki, Daniel Inouye, Shigeto Kanemoto, and Mike Tokunaga saw the need for a bank to replace the Japanese banks that had existed before the war. Their deliberations led them to Koichi Iida and Tokuyoshi Awamura, Issei leaders in the Japanese Chamber of Commerce. Together they raised the necessary capital in the community and Central Pacific Bank was granted its charter from the State of Hawaii in January, 1954. Iida, who served as the Chairman of the Board until his death, was succeeded by Sakae Takahashi, attorney and legislator. In 1984, Central Pacific Bank (CPB) was the fourth largest bank in the State with sixteen branches. A second Japanese bank, City Bank, was organized in 1959 by Baron Inaba, James Kamo, James Morita, and Mike Tokunaga, among others. With assets of 360 million dollars

Betty Hirozawa.
"I was looking for something new and different in the way of a career. At about that time, there was a lot of labor unrest and the waterfront strikes were going on so I decided to major in labor and industrial relations. I studied at the University of Hawaii for my first two years and then graduated from the Cornell School of Industrial and Labor Relations. For young women interested in this field, I would encourage them not to give up too easily and would advise them to get some experience at the operations level in industry."

Interviewed on December 3, 1984
Hawaii Employers Council Photo

and eleven branch offices on three islands, it ranked fifth among the ten banks in the State of Hawaii in 1984.

Still others participated in the growing Hawaiian economy by joining existing family enterprises or by establishing new businesses. Upon graduation from college, sisters Rose Kamuri Shigemura and Ruth Kamuri Koga joined their father in the operation of the Ritz Department Stores. Nenichi Kaimuri, who had come to

Hawai'i in 1896 at age 15, had worked as a schoolboy in a plantation manager's home. There he had been allowed to study English from a tutor in the company of the manager's children and therefore was proficient in English. He opened a store specializing in women's and children's ready-to-wear clothing on Fort Street in downtown Honolulu in 1938. After a million dollar renovation and expansion in 1960, mens', boys', sub-teens', and home furnishings deprtments were added. A second store in the Ala Moana Shopping Center, a third at Pearlridge Center, a fourth at the Royal Hawaiian Center, and a fifth store, a men's specialty shop at Ala Moana, followed.

Arakawas – "the big store in the little lane" grew to become a large department store "on historic Depot Road, nestled below the O'ahu Sugar Company Mill."[7] Like the old plantation stores, Arakawas stocks everything from jewelry to clothing to appliances to electronics to garden supplies. It was started in 1909 as a

Arakawa Shōten was located on the 'Ewa side of Waipahu Depot Street fom 1912-1947. The upper floor was used as a living quarters for the family and as a hotel. In 1947 the store relocated across the street to an out-of-sight theater building inside a narrow foot-traffic lane. During the war Arakawa Shōten became Arakawas. The store has been in the current building since 1955.

Arakawas Collection

tailor shop by Zempan Arakawa who had come to Hawai'i from Okinawa in 1904 to work in the fields. He started sewing and selling because he was too small to do heavy field work. At his shop he sold *ahina* (denim) pants, *palaka* (checkered) shirts, *kaukau* bags (lunch bags), *tabis* (footwear), *kappa* (raincoats) as well as one-half gallon water cans. Seventy-five years later, Arakawas remains a family business. It is owned by the founder's four sons and one-daughter. Others involved are two brothers-in-law, two sisters-in-law and several nieces and nephews. Goro Arakawa, credit and advertising manager, has been a leader in the study and the preservation of historic Waipahu.

George Fukunaga became the second president of Service Motors in 1960 when he succeeded his father, Peter. By 1969, the business that had started as a repair shop with service as its motto in a two bay garage in 1919 recorded sales of 40 million dollars as automobile, appliance, furniture, and retail divisions were added. Its name was changed to Servco Pacific to reflect its scope of activities. By 1979 it involved 1,100 employees in Hawai'i and 250 on Guam. Its eleven operating divisions are responsible for automotive and marine distributorships, retail dealerships, shopping centers, finance company offices, insurance agencies, electronic and appliance distributorships, department stores, music stores, music schools, and real estate, securities, and advertising agencies. In the 80s, George Fukunaga serves as Chairman of the Board and Chief Executive Officer while his brother, Tom, is the president.[8]

The two sons of Masayuki Tokioka, financier and entrepreneur, have also been active in the field of finance. Lionel Tokioka joined International Savings and Loan Company in 1960 which then had assets of thirteen million dollars. From his initial involvement as a teller and bookkeeper, Tokioka rose to become Chairman of the Board in the late 1970s. In 1984 International Savings and Loan Company, with assets nearing four hundred million dollars, had thirteen branches on the three islands of O'ahu, Hawai'i, and Maui. As Chairman of the Board, Tokioka has been instrumental in guiding the firm in providing additional functions and services. Franklin Tokioka has been with Island Insurance Company, the only locally owned property and casualty company, and National Mortgage and Finance Company.[9]

On Kaua'i, a small grocery and dry goods store started by H.S. Kawakami in 1926 grew to four general merchandise stores by World War II. In the early 1930s, brother Fukutaro also opened his own store in Hanapēpē, Kaua'i. The two brothers merged and formed a parent company in the late 50s that came to include eight Big Save Markets, five Ben Franklin Stores, five snack shops, one restaurant, one cafeteria, one cookie bakery, and sixteen hotel gift shops. Active in the various facets of the corporation are Fukutaro's children, Norito and Tooru Kawakami and their sisters, Yukie Murakami and Mabel Hashisaka, and H.S.'s offsprings, George, Richard, and Charles Kawakami, and their sister Gertude Toma.

Other examples of Nisei who have joined and expanded their family businesses include Tomoo Okuyama of Sure-Save Super Market in Hilo, the Okada and Otani families - wholesalers of fish and other food products, Thomas Kunimune of Kuni Dry Goods, and Sidney Kosasa of Thrifty and ABC Drugs.

Getting in on the fledging garment industry in 1954 with $5,000 and a $30,000 loan was Keiji Kawakami of Iolani Sportswear. He manufactured aloha shirts of colorful Japanese fabrics for local residents and tourists. Over the years the company has expanded its lines to also include mu'umu'us and active sportswear for men and women. By 1984, with son Lloyd as the chief executive officer, Iolani Sportswear and its two sister companies, Young Hawaii and Aloha Tailor, supported over two hundred employees. Although

One of the diversified interests of the enterprising Kawakamis.

Kawakami Collection

215

he had a course in textiles at New York University, Kawakami knew nothing else about the garment industry when he started with four employees. He credits the growth and success of his small beginnings to the collective efforts of persons from many ethnic groups. By the early 80s, he was spending a greater portion of his day in community affairs in appreciation for the opportunities and help he had received over the years.

King's Bakery, which opened its doors in Honolulu in 1963, followed a successful operation that Robert Taira had started in Hilo in 1950 with less than $500. He had gone to baker's school upon his discharge from the U.S. Army after World War II and had created a recipe for Portuguese sweetbread which he featured. The bread was a success with local people, who introduced it to their friends and families around the world. Soon King's Bakery was shipping 30,000 loaves annually to the Mainland. To meet the growing and promising mainland market, Taira opened a California plant in 1977 and a South Carolina plant later. Together the two mainland plants are capable of turning out 3,800 loaves per hour. They supply every major supermarket chain on both the East and West coasts. The operations of King's Bakery have come to involve other family members over the years. Taira's wife and oldest son manage the office and the three coffee shops in Honolulu respectively, his second son the California plant, and his sister and brother-in-law, the South Carolina plant.[10]

According to their in-house publication, *Good Times,* brothers Albert and Wallace Teruya opened the first Times Super Market, a neighborhood store in McCully, on April 29, 1949, with three basic principles – quality merchandise, competitive prices, and excellent service. Over the years they have continued to expand in the size and number of stores. By 1984 there were fifteen stores on O'ahu. Not only has Times been a leader in growth, but it has been at the forefront in bringing marketing innovations to Hawai'i. Its McCully store was the first retail store to have air-conditioning while it was the first major supermarket chain in Hawai'i to use the Universal Price Code (UPC) scanner with electronic cash registers to facilitate accurate check-out. In 1982 Times also introduced an electronic speaker system to orally give the customer the price being entered.

In 1955, a young carpenter opened a real estate firm to sell houses his father's construction company had built. By 1963, the young man was busy handling many other listings as well as acquiring parcels of land for development. The latter acquisitions

Bob Taira and King's Hawaiian Bread

Nisei Robert Taira parlayed a $372 investment into a baking industry with sales expected at over $20 million in 1984. Bob's parents came to Hawai'i early in the century from Okinawa and he grew up on Wailea Plantation on the Big Island. His sister Shizu thinks that he developed his interest in starting a baking business as he traveled as an interpreter in the army. When he returned home, Bob asked his sisters to teach him to bake and he practiced. His mother was a talented cook who always encouraged her large family of nine children to experiment. The sisters enjoyed baking at a time when very few Japanese families owned cookbooks. When Bob showed an interest in baking, a most unusual hobby for a Nisei veteran, his father was understanding and encouraged him.

After his "at home" training, he came to Honolulu to attend a baking school that had just opened. Fortunately, he had an inspirational instructor who left an impression on him. Bob then traveled to Chicago to attend Wilton Cake Decorating School while many other veterans went away to college.

Bob Taira is shown here with loaves of his King's Hawaiian Bread in his Los Angeles plant. The bread is produced in an all automated process which mixes ingredients by computer, weighs, cuts into portions, sets aside for rising, bakes, cools, wraps and packs for distribution. The unassuming local entrepreneur also has other restaurants in Hawai'i and Nagano, Japan, a travel agency, an industrial coating company, and the non-dairy ice cream "Tofutti" franchise in California, Nevada, Arizona, and Hawai'i. Enterprising as ever, he already has other business ideas in mind.

Bob Taira and Sister Shizu
Interviewed in November, 1984
Taira Collection

---

have proven to be a bonanza, for by 1981, Herbert K. Horita Realty, Inc. had built 5,530 single-family homes, 1,427 condominium units, 800 town houses and two hotels with a total of 518 units. By the mid 80s he had added thousands of other units to his firm's credit.

Horita has guided the growth of his firm in all facets of the business – from land acquisition and development to design and sales by researching information and market needs. Studying the mushrooming tourist industry, especially in Waikīkī, he has set about to develop a second major tourist area on O'ahu. The West Beach Development which encompasses 640 acres of land from Kahe to Barber's Point in Leeward O'ahu will have luxury hotels and shopping areas, as well as homes. New beaches will be constructed to attract the tourists. When completed in fifteen to twenty years, the area should provide employment for about seven thousand people.[11]

There are many, many others who have been a part of the struggles of the Japanese for equality in the Hawaiian community. They, along with those mentioned above, and the rest of the community have been instrumental in the development of Hawai'i to become a progressive and outstanding state of the United States.

Chapter IX
THE PEOPLE:
A HUNDRED YEARS LATER

In 1980, one hundred years since the arrival of the Kanyaku Imin (government contract immigrants), the Japanese numbered 240,000. Approximately 13 percent of that number were part-Japanese. They spanned several generations from the small group of elderly Issei, to the Nisei, the Sansei, the Yonsei, and even a few Gosei (the fifth generation). While adjusting to life in a foreign environment and later becoming a part of the multiethnic community, the Japanese have undergone changes in their physical stature, health patterns, life-styles, as well as in the very fabric of their value structure.

The 1980 statistics show the Japanese to be the second largest ethnic group after Caucasians, comprising 24.9 percent of the total population of Hawai'i. Unlike their earlier concentration in the Japanese camps, they have distributed themselves about equally throughout the four counties of the State of Hawai'i.[1]

From June through August is ken *picnic time at Ala Moana Park in Honolulu. Not only Issei, but their children and grandchildren enjoy a day of fellowship and games. Practical items such as toilet paper, canned goods,* shōyu *and pencils are given as prizes.*

Photo by Jerry Fujioka

Table 1

Geographic Distribution of Hawai'i's
Japanese by Counties, 1980

State and County	Population	Percent
State	239,748	24.9
City and County of Honolulu	189,828	24.9
Hawai'i County	24,476	26.6
Kaua'i County	9,775	25.0
Maui County	15,669	22.1

Within the counties, the Japanese choose to live in multiethnic communities; and the majority reside in urban and suburban areas. They are now minorities on the plantations.[2]

In 1980, the Japanese made up the largest civilian work force in Hawai'i with 62,150 male and 56,563 female employees.[3] However, they did not earn the highest incomes. Their median income was the second highest with $23,209 per civilian family as compared to $19,528, the overall family median income. Among male civilian workers, both the Chinese and Caucasians reported higher proportions of professional and managerial workers at 51.6 percent and 44.5 percent respectively. Similarly, the Japanese rank third, after the Caucasians and the Chinese, in the median number of years of schooling with 12.6 years for persons 25 years or older. Only 31.6 percent of the Japanese males and 26.8 percent of the females were employed in high status occupations.[4]

When the *Honolulu Star Bulletin* published a list of "Hawaii's Top Thirty" executives commanding $100,000-$360,000 in annual salaries in 1979, not one Japanese American qualified for this highly selected list.[5] Furthermore, only four out of the eighteen persons earning top salaries of $50,000 or more on "Hawaii's Highest Paid Public Servants" list were Japanese Americans. Thus, for the Japanese in Hawai'i, top executive positions in private industry and in the public sector were still not readily attainable.[6]

Japanese women made up 35 percent of the total female work force in Hawai'i, exceeding their population percentage by 10 percent.[7] This follows the role of women in the Japanese culture and the tradition of work which is an ingrained part of their heritage. In the early years, Issei women joined their husbands in the sugar and pineapple fields and also assumed full responsibility for daily household chores and child-rearing. Nisei and Sansei women today assume their share of the responsibility of earning the family's income.

Work: A Way of Life

We Japanese girls grew up knowing that we would have to work, work, and work. My Nisei mother always worked alongside my Issei father. When he ran a service station, he was the mechanic; and she pumped the gas and kept the books. When we owned a store, he was the butcher, and she did the ordering and managed the rest of the grocery store. All four of us children, two boys and two girls, helped in the store after school and on weekends by stacking cans, sweeping, and doing odd jobs; but we also managed to find time to swim, to climb trees, and to play *mamangoto* (house).

When I was eleven, Pearl Harbor was attacked; and business boomed for our beachside store in Haleʻiwa, Oʻahu. My parents were proud of us because when the truckloads of GIs swarmed in to buy soda, candy, and ice cream, we stationed ourselves throughout the store – each with a box of small change to handle quickly the milling crowd of hot, thirsty soldiers. At these times there was no space in the store for clerk or customer to get to the cash register. We were often given a treat of soda and ice cream after the rush.

Because Okā-san was so busy with the business, she had a young teenager, Kimie-san, staying with us to be in charge of domestic chores. However, Okā-san made it clear that for our own sake, we were to learn to do household chores as well as to cook from Kimie-san. When I got lazy, I was firmly reminded that she was not a maid but a family member and a teacher as far as housework was concerned. And, a super teacher she was! She supervised our chores and our homework. She did not want second best in anything from us, and I owe her a lot.

By age nine or ten, like most girls, I learned to sew kimonos at Japanese school and was sent to a sewing teacher during the summers to learn to draft patterns and to sew my own dresses. This early age for learning to sew was necessary since I was expected to earn money by working in the fields by the time I was twelve years old. I donned thick working clothes and got into open trucks at dawn. I did hoe-hana work in sugar and pineapple fields. By the time I was fourteen or fifteen, I was old enough to pick and lug heavy pineapples in a bag through the rows of sharp, pokey plants for which I was paid 28 cents an hour. My pay seems so meager now, but at the time I was proud to be able to earn some money.

During the war, my classmates and I worked in the potato fields during school days for the war effort. Toward the end of the war, I was lucky enough to be hired first as a salad girl and then as a waitress at the Haleiwa Hotel which had been converted into an Officer's Club. My mother worked as a waitress because my dad's Parkinson's disease prevented him from running a business. I was always under my mother's watchful eyes for she had strict rules about fraternizing with haole officers or GIs who manned the kitchen.

Age sixteen was that magical age when I could finally get out of the hot sun and field work and earn some decent wages at the pineapple cannery. I got up very early to catch the bus to Honolulu. I was fortunate to be employed in the can storage department at Libby McNeill and Libby instead of trimming and packing and worked there every summer throughout my high school days at Mid-Pacific Institute and through my five years of teacher preparation at the University of Hawaii. And, my paychecks were handed over to my parents who used the money for tuition. I even returned during the summers after I became an elementary teacher; for although I was the recipient of a tuition scholarship to New York University, I wanted to earn the rest of my expenses for my master's degree. I appreciated having a job in the cannery through those many years, but those experiences also made me more determined than ever to get an education.

In retrospect, I can see that the tradition of work had become an important value. I not only taught during the school year, but with the exception of a few summers when I had my babies; I've also taught during summer sessions for extra income and gradually developed a specialization in the process. I received a lot of advice and encouragement from my mother and my mother-in-law who said: "You have worked hard for an education so use it. Go to work; we will help you to take care of your children while you teach." I have no regrets – I feel very fortunate to have had a very fulfilling life.

Dorothy Ochiai Hazama

Physically, by 1980, the average height of Japanese men over eighteen years of age was 65.7 inches, which was approximately two inches shorter than the overall average of 67.5 inches for Hawai'i's men in general. They also averaged 146.3 pounds, weighing less than the average 159.5 pounds for the total male population. Japanese women averaged 61.0 inches, or one and one-half inches shorter than the overall female average of 62.6 inches. They, too, weighed less at 116.5 pounds on the average as compared to the average of 127.0 for the total female population.[8]

Data available for 1931-32 provide interesting comparative statistics between the Japanese born in Hawai'i and their predecessors.[9]

Table 2

**Heights and Weights
of Japanese: 1931-32, 1975-80**

	Male		Female	
	Height	Weight	Height	Weight
1931-32				
Born in Japan	61.9 in.*	148.5 lb.	57.9 in.*	113.0 lb.
Born In Hawai'i	63.5 in.*	150.2 lb.	58.6 in.*	103.3 lb.
1975-1980				
All Generations:				
Born in Hawai'i				
and Japan	65.7 in.	146.3 lb.	61.0 in.	116.5 lb.

*converted from metric measures.

The average height for Japanese men and women in 1980, which included all generations, was, indeed, taller than the average for the Issei and Nisei of fifty years ago. However, the weights revealed variations. An interesting finding shows that fifty years

*Nisei parents, Kate and Yutaka
Inokuchi, with their son, Thad.
Kate – 5'3"
Yutaka – 5'6"
Thad – 5'10"
Inokuchi Collection*

223

ago, women born in Hawai'i weighed ten pounds less on the average than their mothers, while they now weigh more than the Issei and Nisei groups' averages of the early thirties. The averages for the males over the study period do not show similar variations.

Cumulatively, the Japanese group's average age of 35.6 years in 1980 makes them the oldest of any of the ethnic groups in Hawai'i. Of the 26,775 people in Hawai'i who are seventy-five years or older, 10,756 were Japanese, making this group the largest group by far in this age category. Furthermore, the statistics show that 17.6 percent or 42,171 of the total number of Japanese were sixty years or older.[10]

One factor contributing to the more mature average age for this group was the fertility rate of the Japanese which, as of 1980, was the lowest among the various ethnic groups. The general fertility rate or the number of live births in a year for every 1,000 females of child bearing age was 50.2. This was far below the rate of 78.8 for all groups combined. Viewed in terms of the Crude Birth Rate, there were only 11.1 births per year per 1,000 Japanese in Hawai'i.[11] This fact, along with the small number of immigrants from Japan in recent years, also accounts for the drop in the percentage for the Japanese in the total population of Hawai'i from year to year.

Life expectancy data reported by the Department of Health showed a total average of 79.66 for the Japanese. The male expectancy average was 77.74 years of age; and the women, as expected, exceeded that with 81.54 years as their average. For decades, the average life expectancy for the Japanese was the longest until the 1980 census. A close scrutiny of the life expectancy figures of the Chinese and Japanese for the decades from 1930-1980, as shown below, depicted a minor change in 1980 from past trends which bears watching.[12]

Table 3

**Life Expectancies
of Chinese and Japanese: 1930-1980**

Date	Chinese	Japanese
1930	60.07	60.07
1940	65.32	66.28
1950	69.74	72.58
1960	74.12	75.68
1970	76.11	77.44
1980	80.24	79.66

224

Waipahu Pension Club ca. 1980.
Membership in Senior Citizens' Clubs and retirement groups are growing in numbers. The multiethnic clubs, to which many Issei and Nisei belong, offer field trips, songfests, and classes in ukulele, crafts, calligraphy, and Japanese and social dancing.

K. Saito Collection

From 1940-1970, the just-born Japanese child in Hawai'i was expected to live, on the average, longer than a child of any other ethnic group. The just-born Chinese child was a very close second. As of 1980, the Chinese child's life-expectancy was longer, albeit only slightly, for the first time in five decades. An examination of data from two major medical projects in Hawai'i may be of interest in understanding some of the causes of mortality among the Japanese.

Major research studies in cancer patterns and coronary disease among the Japanese are worth noting especially since cancer, coronary heart disease, and stroke in that order were the three leading causes of mortality among a large group of Japanese men studied in the Honolulu Heart Program. In contrast, for Hawai'i's population as a whole, cardiovascular disease was the number one killer.

Dr. Laurence N. Kolonel and his associates at the University of Hawaii's Cancer Research Center of Hawai'i have discovered striking variations of incidence rates, cancer sites and types, and health and dietary habits among Caucasians, Japanese, Chinese, Hawaiians, and Filipinos who together comprise 95 percent of the population. In a ten year study from 1967-76, Japanese men and women as well as Chinese and Filipino men were found to have lower incidences of all cancers combined than the Caucasians. The generally slight body build, absence of obesity among Asian groups, and dietary factors seemed to be related to lower risks. Furthermore, according to Dr. Kolonel's report:

> Japanese men and women had more sites of low risk than any other ethnic group. They had significantly lower rates of cancers of the mouth, lung, larynx, bladder, kidney, and brain, as well as lymphocytic leukemia, melanoma, and Hodgkins's disease. In addition to these nine and other cancers for which all ethnic males were at lower risk than whites, Japanese men had significantly less pancreatic and testicular cancers and lymphosarcoma. Besides the above nine cancers which were low for both sexes, Japanese women had significantly less granulocytic leukemia and cancers of colon, breast, cervix (invasive) and ovary.[13]

One type of cancer, with a higher incidence among Japanese and Hawaiian women as compared to Chinese and Filipino women, was in the gallbladder. It was found that Japanese and Hawaiian women consumed more coffee than Chinese and Filipino women. Higher coffee consumption has been associated with increased risk for cancer of the gallbladder.

A study of dietary fat intake among the five ethnic groups indicated that there was a positive correlation between breast cancer and dietary fat intake. Japanese in Hawai'i reported the second lowest dietary fat intake and Japanese women had the second lowest incidence of breast cancer after the Filipino group.

Dr. Kolonel and his associates also compared two groups of Hawai'i's Japanese, Issei, Nisei (which included later generations as well), and Japanese in Japan. The results of these comparisons as reported in a study, "Cancer Patterns Among Migrant and Native-born Japanese in Hawaii in Relation to Smoking, Drinking, and Dietary Habits," revealed that, in general, Hawai'i's Japanese had higher incidences of cancer than those in Japan with the exception of esophageal, stomach, and cervical cancers. Of the Japanese in Hawai'i, Nisei rates were lower than Issei rates for lung, prostate, esophagus, stomach and cervical cancers, but higher than Issei rates for cancer of the uterus and female breast cancer. There were no apparent differences between Japan and Hawai'i Japanese in pancreatic cancer and leukemia.

Of interest, too, were the effects of smoking, drinking, and dietary habits on the Japanese 45 years and older in Hawai'i. Lung cancer incidence correlated positively with rates of cigarette smoking for men and women. Similarly, a relationship was seen between alcohol consumption and esophageal and rectal cancer incidences. Dietary fat intake corresponded with colon cancer rates for men and women, but not with patterns for breast or prostate cancer.[14]

Cancer of the stomach, which is prevalent among the Japanese, was the subject of another study. A comparison was made of gastric cancer among Japanese born in Hawai'i, Japanese in Japan, and Caucasians. The highest rate occurred in the Japan Japanese group followed by the Japanese in Hawai'i. The examination of dietary data indicated a positive association of gastric cancer with consumption of rice, pickled vegetables, and dried/salted fish. The intake of vitamin C in the form of fruits and supplements, on the other hand, tended to be associated with a lower incidence of stomach cancer.[15]

The researchers, in concluding their discussion of cancer patterns, reiterated their "belief that environmental agents cause most cancers" and "dietary factors and nutrition are important elements in the causal web of cancer."[16]

The Honolulu Heart Program has published numerous reports on the prevalence and incidence of coronary heart diseases and the impact of traditional Japanese and westernized life-styles by following a group of 8,000 men living in Hawai'i who were born between 1900-1919. These men have been studied since 1965. The reports on acculturation and coronary heart disease indicate that there was a general pattern of a higher prevalence rate for total heart disease among the more western or acculturated group.[17]

In a ten-year study of the incidence of heart disease among the 8,000 men of Japanese ancestry, it was found that men who developed coronary heart disease had lower average intake of total calories, carbohydrates, starch, and vegetable proteins, and higher mean intake of percentage of calories from protein and fat. Major risk factors were cigarette smoking, blood pressure, serum cholesterol level, and glucose intolerance. It appears that serum cholesterol and blood pressure were especially significant. The mortality rate for men with hypertension was twice that of men with normal blood pressure levels.[18]

Stroke mortality has declined since 1960 for Japanese men in Hawai'i, California, and in Japan. For men of Japanese ancestry in Hawai'i and California, the mortality rate was three times less than that for men in Japan and approximated that of the Caucasians in recent years.[19]   Although many people believe that high shōyu consumption is a key factor, according to these studies, a possible explanation was the greater consumption of animal protein and fat-intake among Japanese Americans. These dietary factors seem to have an inhibiting effect on stroke incidence and mortality.[20]

Therefore, healthwise, as the Japanese in Hawai'i became less traditional and more westernized, the resulting changes brought mixed consequences. As life-styles changed, especially in dietary preferences, the Japanese Americans became more prone to certain types of cancer and to heart disease, which more closely approximated the patterns of the mainland whites, while at the same time, showed a decrease in cancer and stroke which were more prevalent in Japan. Thus, improvement in health appears not to lie in returning to more traditional life-styles or in turning to more western dietary habits and ways but in heeding the outcomes of these valuable studies, which were specific to this ethnic group, and to being informed about the current status overall in health research.

Of the ethnic groups in Hawai'i, the Japanese, especially during the early years, had been the group most opposed to interracial marriages. In the period from 1912-1916, only 0.5 percent of the Japanese grooms and 0.2 percent of the Japanese brides dared to defy the group's customary behavior. For the Japanese, notions of a successful marriage resulting in "purity of lineage" meant an

---

Do We Need A Nakahodo?

It was in the late spring of 1948 when Bum and I decided to be married before the opening of the coming fall semester at the University of Hawaii. He was going to begin his sophomore year and I was going to start my second year as program counselor at the University. We first dated in 1942, kept up a correspondence while he served as an interpreter in the Army, and saw each other regularly after his 1946 discharge. Our families knew each other well for both had operated businesses in the 'A'ala Park area for many years.

Bum had told his parents and my mother about our plans and had gotten ready consent. However, my now parents-in-law felt that we needed to go through *nakahodos* (go-betweens) as was the Japanese custom. *"Nan to itte mo, neko no ko wo morau no dewa naindakara."* (After all we aren't asking for a cat's child, but a precious daughter).

Mr. Sano, a fellow *Yamanashi Ken jin* (person from Yamanashi prefecture) was asked to represent the Komeijis while a neighbor, Mr. Maeda, represented my mother. Because the *Nakahodo* custom being observed for the form only, Mr. Sano did not visit my family officially until the *yuinō* ceremony (engagement gift ceremony).

On the appointed date, Mr. & Mrs. Sano, Mr. & Mrs. Maeda, and my in-laws-to-be came to our house. Neither Bum nor I had been invited. Although I personally thought all of this was old-fashioned and ridiculous, I didn't fuss because I didn't want to antagonize anyone. I only wanted to get married. However, curiosity did get the better of me and I watched the entire formality through a crack in the living room wall. I nearly burst out laughing several times, for it was so funny to see such close friends be so formal with each other. Mr. Sano and Mr. Maeda did most of the talking at the beginning – and both families bowed low and said, *"Yoroshiku onegai itashimasu."* (May I ask for your support and help.) The Komeijis through Mr. Sano presented a tray of gifts which included a bottle of *sake* (rice wine), a large red fish, and an envelope of money. The latter was to be used by the bride for the wedding.

The participants must have felt awkward during the initial formality, for they later relaxed and enjoyed the rest of the evening talking stories and having dinner.

Jane Okamoto Komeiji

Who Needs a Nakahodo?

Bum and I wanted a small wedding, but our parents insisted on a big wedding so we compromised. We planned the small wedding ceremony in a Protestant church, and his parents and my mom planned and paid for a real traditional wedding reception with many of their friends as guests. The reception had the dai ishiki, *or formal portion, which included introductions of the wedding party and the presentation of our backgrounds. This was followed by the* dai nishiki, *or second part, which included professional entertainment with singing and dancing.*

Jane Okamoto Komeiji

arranged marriage with a Japanese mate, preferably one from the same prefecture. Within their own ethnic group, Naichi-Okinawan marriages as well as marriages to one of the *chōrinbo* or *eta* class were forbidden. Needless to say an outmarriage with a *gaijin* (foreigner) was frowned upon.

Marriage in the Japanese family had traditionally been considered as not only a compact between two people, but one that involved the two families. Therefore, the prospective mate's genealogy, including a family health history, was investigated before an agreement was reached. Not marrying according to the prevalent custom, as well as friction and divorce later on, brought *haji,* or shame, to the parties involved.

As shown in the table below, by 1982, 40.5 percent of the Japanese grooms and 47.2 percent of the Japanese brides married mates who were non-Japanese.[21] This change, which accelerated after World War II, was often accompanied by traumatic and tense times within the families.

Table 4

Interracial Marriages among Japanese
Percentage of All Marriages

	1912-1916	1920-1930	1930-1940	1940-1949	1950-1959	1960-1977	1982
Grooms	0.5	2.7	4.3	4.3	8.7	19.6	40.5
Brides	0.2	3.1	6.3	16.9	19.1	28.1	47.2

It is interesting to note that while Japanese women were initially less likely to marry outside their group, they now outnumber the men in doing so. The most frequent choice for outmarriage partners for Japanese brides and grooms was Caucasians followed by part-Hawaiians.

Sociologically and psychologically, "love" was the main reason offered by marriage partners. Some also felt the need to be different and non-traditional while others were attracted by physical attributes, life-styles, and values of other racial groups, especially if they viewed those characteristics as representing a higher status. Realistically, as the percentage of the Japanese population decreased, not only were fewer partners available within the group, but more and more people were in contact with the marriageable partners from other ethnic groups at school and

Hawaiian style wedding. 1982
Sansei John Komeiji and Chinese Hawaiian Kalowena Ching were married with their
parents' blessings. In earlier times, Japanese parents were not as open to mixed marriages.
                                                                    Komeiji Collection

at work. Thus it appears that soon more of the marriages among the Japanese like those of the other ethnic groups in Hawai'i will be mixed marriages.

Because the Japanese over the years valued the sanctity of marriage and the importance of keeping a family intact, divorce was frowned upon by the Issei and the Nisei. As the younger generations began to question the traditional values and accepted the more individualistic American societal values, the divorce rates have risen. In 1982, slightly more Japanese wives (13.4 percent) sought divorces than Japanese husbands (12.2 percent) out of the total number of divorces that year. Since the statistics did not differentiate the ethnicity of the marriage partners, it is not possible to ascertain whether more divorces occurred in in-group or out-group marriages. However, from the divorce percentages from 1982, it can be concluded that the Japanese still had a relatively low divorce rate since they constituted about 25 percent of the population in Hawai'i at that time.

A survey conducted in 1971 involving 477 Japanese in Honolulu from the general population shed some light on how they think and feel by comparing their responses to results from a national character study of Japanese in Japan. In Hawai'i, Issei, Nisei whose

231

ages ranged from forty to sixty, and Sansei twenty years or over were included. Of this group about half or 54 percent had not visited Japan.

The following table from the report on "A Study of Japanese Americans in Honolulu, Hawaii" summarizes personal preferences with a breakdown of items by age.[22]

Table 5

Personal Preference Among Japanese in Honolulu by Age

Items	Japanese	Non Japanese	Preferred Japanese Items by age breakdown				
			20s	30s	40s	50s	60s
Food	38%	32%	35%	46%	32%	38%	48%
Language	12	78	2	6	6	16	48
Movies	24	54	11	16	18	34	56
Radio	18	74	5	6	14	27	52
Spouse	80	6	63	89	81	89	87
Close Friends	60	6	48	59	61	68	69
Music Education*	10	67	13	6	5	8	21

*Japanese music education includes "koto, samisen, and Japanese dancing" and American music education, "piano, ballet, and violin."

The Japanese Americans showed a uniformly strong preference for other Japanese in close interpersonal relationships ("spouses" and "close friends") except for the respondents in their twenties. Language, a major cultural factor, on the other hand, received a very low preference for all groups even among the over sixty age group with a 48 percent rating. English is the everyday spoken language for most with only a limited number, mostly Issei, using Japanese.

In another aspect of the study, about 22 percent of those surveyed reported being fluent in Japanese and about 15 percent stated that they were fluent in both languages. Although not necessarily fluent in Japanese, the majority of the later generations have had some years of exposure and study in the language. More than 80 percent of the Nisei and 29 percent of the Sansei had studied Japanese for more than six years. While there is a continuing study of the Japanese language among the younger generations, there appears to be a marked decrease in the number who are fluent in it.

Therefore, in terms of the use of the media, it is not surprising

In the 1950s, the Japanese in Hawai'i once again resumed their visits to relatives in Japan. This Issei couple is loaded down with candy leis which were welcome gifts in war torn Japan.

Hazama Collection

that most Nisei and Sansei do not read the Japanese language newspapers. Only half of the Japanese American population, mostly Issei and Nisei, listen to the Japanese radio broadcasts. However, the popularity of Japanese television programs does not follow this pattern. Nearly 80 percent, including three fourths of the Sansei, enjoy these programs. Family life dramas and samurai programs seem to appeal to all ages. But, only 13 percent go to see Japanese movies.

It is interesting to note that the Nisei, especially those in their forties, registered a lower preference for Japanese foods and spices than the Sansei in their thirties. One can only conjecture that the wartime "Be American" movement might have influenced these preferences. It is also worth noting the Sansei's interest in Japanese music education.

In other phases of the study, the Japanese in Hawai'i differed somewhat from those in Japan by being less inclined to follow customs and in worrying about money or fame. Weddings and funerals are costly occasions in which the Japanese cultural influences are very evident. When asked about the advisability of having elaborate weddings and funerals, even if costly and complicated, 70 percent in Hawai'i and 37 percent in Japan replied that it "should be according to means." The Japanese Americans seemed to be more practical in their decisions.

Oyakōokō, or obligational respect toward parents, seems to be a value that has persisted over the years in both places. It was considered an important virtue by 53 percent of the respondents

The Vegetable Man

The Vegetable Man *(Yasaiya-san),* a vanishing trade. 1984.
Koichi Watanabe's father-in-law owned a vegetable truck so Koichi bought his own truck and began his business on wheels in 1947. While the Vegetable Man's mobile markets were commonplace in plantation camps and suburbs from the 30s through the 50s, according to Koichi Watanabe, there are only two of them left continuing this work on a full time basis on O'ahu. The vegetable truck actually is a mini-market on wheels offering things a house-wife needs for cooking such as meat, sashimi, bread, fishcake, canned goods, and an array of vegetables. Koichi's truck has two refrigerated sections. He is shown here with his "cash register" around his waist in Mānoa, but he also peddles his wares in 'Ewa on scheduled days.

Photo by D. Hazama

in Hawai'i and 61 percent in Japan. When given a decision making situation of loyalty to parent or benefactor over business obligations, the Japanese Americans exhibited slightly higher concern for filial piety than those in Japan. However, *on-gaeshi*, or repaying obligations to friends and benefactors, received only a 27 percent rating in Hawai'i as an important virtue as compared to 45 percent in Japan.

Although the Nisei and Sansei do not attend church as regularly as the Issei, in general, Hawai'i's Japanese showed a stronger religious inclination with 72 percent indicating a personal faith as compared to only 30 percent in Japan. Of those indicating a personal faith, 50 percent chose Buddhism and 30 percent were of the Christian faith. The Christian influence, especially Protestantism, is much stronger among the Japanese in Hawai'i than in Japan.

Before and since World War II, new varieties of faith, many with healing aspects, have been proliferating in Japan. After World War II, a number of these faiths have found their way to Hawai'i and throughout the world and have attracted a large and growing following for they attempt to help anyone regardless of ethnic or religious backgrounds. Tenrikyō – the oldest of these faiths, Konkokyō, Seichō no Ie, Tenshō Kōtai Jingū Kyō, Church of World Messianity, and one of the most recent arrivals – Mahikari of Hawai'i are some of these faiths. Many of these groups emphasize personal and spiritual purification as a means to attaining mental and physical health.

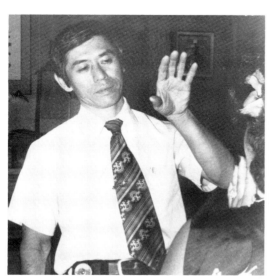

Bobby Toguchi is transmitting Divine Light to purify a fellow member at the Mahikari of Hawaii Center which was established here in 1976. One purpose of Mahikari worldwide is to unify all peoples and religious teachings.

Mahikari of Hawaii

235

The biggest divergence between the Japan and Hawai'i groups occurred in relation to the importance placed on money in child rearing. Only 9 percent of the Japanese in Hawai'i agreed to this statement: "In raising children of elementary age, some people think that one should teach that money is the most important thing." In Japan, 57 percent agreed with that statement. Responses to this item and others, such as on the values of discipline and freedom as well as on traditional attitudes of sustaining a good image of a teacher, revealed the possibilities of distinct differences in attitudes toward education between the two groups.

A very interesting item identified the sex preference of people if they were to be born again. As expected, a very high percentage of men in Hawai'i and in Japan preferred being a man. But, the women showed a greater difference with 73 percent of the American females in Hawai'i wanting to be a woman as compared to 48 percent in Japan. Japanese women in Hawai'i appear to be more content with their role than their counterparts in Japan.

Overall, the Japanese Americans indicated a more positive attitude toward democracy and were more in favor of respecting the rights of individuals, including those of family members. They also expressed a more relaxed life-style and a stronger concern for the protection of their natural environment. Therefore, while Japanese Americans in Hawai'i may still share many attitudes and values with those in Japan, there are now decided differences not only in overt behaviors like language but in the ways in which they think and feel.

By and large, the Sansei and Yonsei have not grown up on the plantations or labored in the sugar and pineapple fields. They have not faced the trauma of being Japanese in wartime Hawai'i. Their loyalty to the United States or their rights as U.S. citizens have never been questioned. Most of them have grown up in comfortable, generally stable two-parent, middle class homes, and attended public or private high schools, often with other Sansei as their closest friends. Their interests were those of typical American teenagers – loud popular music, pets, reading, television, basketball, football, baseball, surfing, and sunbathing.

But the younger generations of Japanese Americans are far more complex and pressured generations than their carefree appearances would indicate. Consciously or unconsciously, especially during adolescence and young adulthood, they experience the need to come to terms with the Japanese values acquired from their closeknit extended families, the American influences from

236

Pitcher Darlene Yoshioka in action. November, 1978.
Darlene's University High School Softball Team won the state championship that year.
Darlene also starred in basketball. She now has a career in communications and is an
accomplished female lead singer for her group.

Yoshioka Collection

their general environment driven home through the schools and the media, and the growing pressures of the local peer culture.

It is important not to stereotype the Sansei and Yonsei for as individuals they vary from being very outspoken and fiercely independent to being passive and dependent, and from being highly Americanized to being more traditionally Japanese. However, some insights into the character of the later generations – their beliefs, values, and behavior – can be understood from research studies conducted mainly among students at the University of Hawai'i.

The Hawaiian Sansei have been characterized as showing a greater need for deference, abasement, nurturance, and affiliation when compared to Caucasians in Hawai'i. They show strong traditional Japanese and peer influences upon their beliefs and values. They expressed a lesser need for dominance, aggression, and autonomy, were seen as more reserved, more humble, more conscientious, more regulated by external realities, and lower in leadership potential than the Caucasian college students. The only

Heading for the surf. 1982.
A surfer is shown with his two prized possessions, his wheels and his surfboard, strapped on the rack. Although surfing was a sport of Hawaiian royalty from ancient times, few could afford surfboards which were heavy and large. With the newer, lighter boards, and a worldwide interest in the sport, there are many avid surfers among the younger Japanese today.

Hazama Collection

dominance expressed by the males was in their attitude toward marriage relationships. The Sansei females were described as being affected by feelings and were more concerned over personal relationships. They were more obedient, suspicious, and apprehensive than Caucasian female students, who were also more self-assured.[23]

Behaviorally, Japanese American students were less responsive in college classes than Caucasian Americans at the University of Hawaii. A high percentage of Japanese Americans, 71 percent, did not participate at all as compared to 9 percent not participating from the Caucasian group. Furthermore, they seemed to accept their passive behavior because they were not dissatisfied with their low verbal performance. However, they were as successful as Caucasian students in terms of acquiring the content covered in the course.[24]

A study of dominance and deference among three groups of college students – Japan Japanese, Japanese Americans in Hawai'i, and Caucasians – revealed that the Japanese American males in

According to the November 5, 1984 edition of Ka leo o Hawaii, *the student newspaper at the University of Hawaii at Manoa, students of Japanese ancestry constituted 35.3 percent of the University's enrollment. While still the largest ethnic group on the Mānoa campus, their percentage declined by 0.1 percent when compared to the figures for the previous year. It has declined by that percentage each year since 1981. Japanese students usually major in business administration, education, math, and engineering and still dominate the undergraduate program; but Caucasian students top the number of students pursuing graduate degrees.*

University of Hawaii

Hawai'i were less dominant in their needs than Japan Japanese males and Caucasian American males. Ironically, the Japan Japanese of today are more like Caucasian Americans. However, the females in Japan and in Hawai'i did not differ significantly. Although the Sansei females were reported to be acculturating more quickly than the males, they were less dominant and more deferent than the males.[25]

A 1981 study of self concepts of student teachers in the College of Education before and after student teaching revealed that Japanese American student teachers' mean scores were generally lower than those of Caucasian student teachers. Although the Japanese group generally increased their scores on a self concept test at the end of a semester of student teaching, the Caucasian group's scores decreased. The Caucasian group's scores still exceeded that of the Japanese student teachers', however, because they initially had higher scores.[26]

239

A look at the close and intense family backgrounds of the Sansei shed some light on the research findings. The Sansei were the first generation of Hawai'i's Japanese to have been in close contact with grandparents, in addition to parents, all of whom placed a high priority on the concept of *Kodomo no tame ni* (for the sake of the children). The Issei and Nisei grandparents and parents have also passed on to them what are essentially the Meiji era values of deference and respect toward parents, elders, and persons in authority, the need to work hard and to be frugal, the desire for education, the importance of family cohesiveness, and a strong sense of obligation. They also imparted a deep sensitivity to social interactions calling for self restraint, self denial *(koraeru)*, and a heightened sense of gratitude and appreciation toward everyone who has helped. It seems that while the young Japan Japanese males have changed in their attitudes toward dominance, many Sansei still reflect the values brought to Hawai'i a century ago.

In one study, the Sansei showed the inculcation of traditional values even more than their parents in their attitude toward the care of the elderly, an important aspect of filial piety. In a study of oyakōkō, or care of parents, Nisei and Sansei over forty years of age were compared with Sansei and Yonsei under thirty years of

In the 1950s and 1960s, photographers found a ready market among young parents, many of whom joined "baby plans" which included annual portraits of the children during their growing years. As cameras became cheaper and better, more and more families began to take their own snapshots.

Hazama Collection

240

My Father

Early on, my father encouraged me to attain a good education. He once told me that one can earn a fortune but that can be lost as well. An education, however, can never be taken away.

When I was an eighth grader, I told my father I wanted to become a lawyer. He was very pleased and told me he would give up everything, even the shirt off his back, in order to make my hopes possible.

That guidance and my parents' generous support have been very much responsible for my educational advancement and whatever measure of success I have been able to attain. Okage sama de.

Gov. George R. Ariyoshi
Ariyoshi Collection

age. Interestingly, the single males below thirty revealed the most favorable attitude concerning the care of the elders in their own homes and in their belief that children should provide financial assistance to parents in their old age. The over-forty age group who had children of their own and had more experiences in the care of parents had changed their attitudes toward oyakōkō because of practical considerations. The responses of the below thirty males, though somewhat idealistic, provided some indication of the continued effect of ingrained values toward filial piety and the deep feelings they have toward parents and grandparents.[27] It is a commentary on the changing times, however, that many elderly may not receive the at-home care from their families that they hoped for in their twilight years.

Since ethnic identity is an important factor in the behavior, attitude, values, and acculturation of Japanese Americans, Dr. Gerald Meredith of the University of Hawaii and Drs. Minoru Masuda and Gary Matsumoto of the University of Washington School of Medicine devised an instrument to study differences among three generations of Japanese Americans. (See Appendix, "The Ethnic Identity Questionnaire," a self administered survey.) They found considerable residual ethnic identification in the Sansei that "reflected a pride in Japanese ancestry, agreement on value of Japanese cultural contributions, desire for the preservation and enjoyment of things Japanese, and a recognition of family kinships."[28]

To explain the Sansei and Yonsei's characteristics only in terms of traditional Japanese values would be too simplistic. They have grown up in a very American system outside and even inside the home. These two cultures share much in common such as the high esteem placed on education, hard work, and frugality. On the whole, the Sansei and Yonsei have maintained the reputation of being "good" students which had been established by their Nisei predecessors.

Another culture, that of their peers, seems to have had a much stronger impact on the Sansei than on the Nisei and has reinforced the importance of being sensitive to interpersonal relationships. It has had a strong effect on their being more passive rather than dominant and verbal.

Many Sansei and Yonsei have managed to survive adolescence and young adulthood without disruptions, and those who established effective study habits and made career goals early in their lives seem to have made the transition into adulthood with greater

242

Sansei Pamela Yamaguchi was the valedictorian of Waipahu High School's 1964 graduating class, just as her mother, Tomoe, was the valedictorian for the eighth grade class of 1935 at Waipahu.

Yamaguchi Collection

ease. For others, the differences in the expectations of the Japanese, American, and peer cultures have created internal conflicts and identity crises.

There are many aspects of the peer culture that run counter to parental values. Play, have fun, "hang loose," "why work so hard," and being one of the crowd are values that have often come into conflict with traditional Japanese and Amercian values. On the one hand, the Sansei and Yonsei, like most young people, want to assert their independence and greatly value freedom of choice. At the same time, they are keenly concerned about "making A" or "making an ass of oneself" before their peers and do not want to "make waves" or disrupt the norm. Some are also critical of the older generation for exploiting the environment for economic development, yet find the ability to earn a good income to be a pressing need. Furthermore, rather than being immediately beneficial, the greater freedom in career choices today, as compared to

Astronaut from Kona

Air Force Lt. Colonel Ellison Shōji Onizuka, the grandson of immigrant sugar workers, was notified on January 16, 1978, that he had been selected as an astronaut. It was the realization of a dream that he dared to dream as a boy growing up in North Kona on the island of Hawai'i, where he helped pick coffee berries on his father's farm. He had, at one time, considered becoming a coffee farmer but was encouraged by his father to get an education so he could make something of himself. He attended the University of Colorado at Boulder and received bachelor and master of science degrees in aerospace engineering. Upon graduation, he entered the Air Force where he was primarily involved in flight testing until his selection as an astronaut.

In a June 7, 1980, address to the graduating class and friends at Kona Waena School, Astronaut Onizuka said:

> I feel awfully lucky to just get this chance. It's only because of [family and friends] that people like me can grow up in the coffee fields of Kona and fly on the Space Shuttle. As Alan

Shepard once said, "It's easy to reach out and touch the moon when you're standing on the shoulders of giants"– and you are all "giants," Thank you for helping me "Be Prepared."

Quotation from Naomi Sodetani in "The Homegrown Astronaut," *Honolulu Star Bulletin*

Onizuka always felt a strong sense of obligation to do well for those who follow. Because he was the first Asian-American astronaut from Hawai'i, he had an additional desire to do his best.

In January, 1985, Lt. Colonel Onizuka experienced a successful flight; but on his next flight on January 28, 1986, he and the entire crew of the Challenger Space Shuttle perished in a tragic explosion. He died a hero while serving his country.

Among the many memorials that continue to honor him are the Astronaut Ellison S. Onizuka Space Center at the Kona Airport, the Challenger Center at Barbers Point, an astronomy base camp on Mauna Kea, and scholarships for science teachers.

---

the more limited opportunities that were available to their parents, often causes confusion and delays in goal attainment.

In the past two decades, there has been a growing desire among the people of all ethnic groups in Hawai'i to be identified as "local." In the Japanese group, this is especially strong among the Sansei and Yonsei. It is believed that the term local was first used during the 1931 Massie trial. Writers who have explored this now commonly used term appear to be in general agreement about this trend and its complex ramifications.

In 1975, Eric Yamamoto, a student at the University of Hawaii, received the E. Hormann Prize Award in Sociology for his paper, "From 'Japanee' to Local." He studied the identity crises among a limited group of Sansei college students who were trying to resolve their cultural and values conflicts and identification uncertainties. Although his sampling was small and there have been changes in the attitudes of students due to shifts in economic conditions, the conclusions still remain viable and sound. He proposed that the solution to the Sansei's identity crises could be found in compromise. The Sansei could accept the ethnic values, goals, and actions of Japanese American parents without becoming like them. This would necessitate an understanding and appreciation of the times and circumstances that brought one's

A popular pasttime. 1982.
These young people are enjoying a relaxing moment of singing and strumming. Hawaiian and American tunes are popular with guitar and ukulele players of this age.

parents' generation to where they are today. A compromise was preferred over the other alternatives which were either to reaffirm traditional Japaneseness and to strongly identify with the established Japanese Americans or to break away from family ties and expectations completely [29]

Glen Grant, in studying race relations among elementary students, provided insights on local ways that apply to youths and older generations as well. After observing children interrelating with one another, he concluded that the local Hawaiian lifestyle did not require the abandonment of cultural ties with one's own ethnic origin as long as the children learned the skills of initiating and maintaining points of commonality with others by friendly interactions.[30]

The establishment of points of commonality can readily be observed among Sansei and Yonsei youths when they first meet someone new to them. This can best be explained through a hypothetical but realistic example of a Yonsei male meeting another college student, a part-Hawaiian in this case, while waiting for their class to begin at the University of Hawaii. They are in adjacent seats. After eye contact is made, the conversation may proceed as follows:

Lincoln School fourth graders, Kristy Nishida (on the left) and Sabrina Lowe, are exchanging stickers and fancy pencils. Boys trade baseball and football cards among friends.

Photo by D. Hazama

Yonsei:	"Eh, Howzit! Where you from?"
Hawaiian:	"Mānoa. Where you from?"
Yonsei:	"Moloka'i. You Roosevelt grad?"
Hawaiian:	"Nah! Mid Pac."
Yonsei:	"No kidding! My kid sister went there. Maybe you know her, Lynn Nakamura."
Hawaiian:	"Yeh, brah! She's my classmate. Small world! Eh, I hear Moloka'i got lotta papio."
Yonsei:	"Pretty good. I just caught some last week. You like fishing?"
Hawaiian:	"Oh yeh! But O'ahu all fished out, brah!"

In a few minutes of conversation, several points of commonality have been established, namely language, high school affiliation, locale, and an interest in fishing. When they leave the classroom at the end of the period, the two exchange firm, elbow up, thumb grip style handshakes, a man to man peer ritual, and a "See you, brah!" parting remark. Each departs with a sense of acceptance and even trust from which a sharing, helping relationship, local style, can be developed. Although the language and handshakes may differ, children, females, and older persons also establish points of commonality with similar topics in a culture where social sensitivity has a high priority.

247

Hawai'i's Racial Mixture

Photo by C. Hazama

Nanette Naioma Napoleon, a freelance researcher and writer specializing in historic graveyards, has documented over three hundred cemeteries in the islands and written a book, *Oahu Cemetery
Burial Ground & Historic Site*. The state's leading cemetery expert
gives lectures and walking tours and featured in newspapers and
magazines and on local and national TV programs. In 1885, her
great-grandfather, Jusaburo Kuroda, arrived in Hawai'i at age
twelve aboard the *City of Tokio* with his parents, who were part of
the historic first group of contract laborers. Jusaburo (aka Frank)
went to school on Hawai'i for just three years before he was
accepted to O'ahu's prestigious St. Louis College and, in 1892,
became the first graduate of Japanese ancestry. This led to a vari-
ety of jobs. Nanette is of Japanese, Hawaiian, Tahitian, Chinese,
Corsican, Spanish, and Scottish descent.

Since the population trend is very clear that with each new
generation more and more people will be of mixed blood, the local
Hawaiian culture, rather than creating an identity problem, could
be the means for the racially mixed to be proud of their several
heritages. And, the people of Hawai'i will all benefit from the
richness this will bring to the quality of life.

Conclusion

Through the hardships and adversities as well as the unique opportunities provided by America and Hawaiʻi, the Japanese, most of whom had originally arrived in Hawaiʻi by "mail order" much like other needed plantation supplies, have remained to become a contributing force in the history and life of the people of Hawaiʻi. They were not the only people who came to the Islands and faced new lives. Similarly, there were many other immigrant groups who, like the Japanese, came and met the challenges and opportunities. Historical conditions both in Japan and in Hawaiʻi, their own values and traditions, as well as their personal needs and aspirations influenced the Japanese to respond to the circumstances in the manner in which they did. And in the process, they developed an identity and a character of their own which has given them a place in the Hawaiian sun.

In comparison with some other groups, the Japanese were helped by several factors in their search for security in a strange land. For one, the planters' policy of racial segregation forced them to live and work with fellow Japanese. This gave them the comfort of some familiarity in a new land. Secondly, they had the strength of numbers as they formed the largest group of laborers that the growing sugar industry needed. Another factor, the Japanese government's intervention in response to the complaints of the plantation workers, brought them moral support and some relief. The arrival of many women helped to establish families, perpetuated important customs and values, and provided stability and a sense of community. The presence of a smaller but influential group of educated and trained people such as teachers, priests, and newspapermen contributed moral and ethical leadership and a voice against injustices.

As their *dekasegi* (leaving home temporarily to work in a foreign country) years of three lengthened to five and then to ten and more, the Japanese began to consider Hawaiʻi their home. Those who remained on the plantations gradually rose to skilled and supervisory positions. A large percentage left the plantations to become independent entrepreneurs or workers in the service and business sectors. All the while, whether they were on or off the plantations, they lived lives that valued children, education, and hard work. They stressed loyalty to the family, the community, and the country, which in the case of the children was America. They worked towards acculturation and acceptance while preserving the basics of their own culture.

Therefore, when the shocking reality of World War II was thrust upon them, they were ready to meet the biggest test of their mettle. The Japanese, aliens and citizens alike, helped in the war effort at home. The story of the young Nisei's loyalty to the United States and their military achievements as members of the 100th Battalion, the 442nd Regimental Combat Team, and the interpreters in the Pacific Theater are now legendary. Their continued participation and accomplishment in the peacetime that followed, especially in politics, helped to change the course of history and brought about the development of the New Hawai'i.

The impact of the Japanese, both visible and invisible, on the local culture can be felt and viewed in nearly every aspect of life in Hawai'i today. Japanese foods are readily available and have

Throw net, a little known early contribution of the Japanese to the Hawaiian culture. The ancient Hawaiians knew the skill of net making. When the Japanese introduced the throw net, the Hawaiians quickly assimilated this method of net fishing; and today, many consider the throw net to be a truly Hawaiian method.

Photo on Moloka'i by Bob Abraham, 1980

become a part of the diet of all of the people. Everyone, regardless of ethnicity, uses the ever present zōri and follows the custom of leaving footwear outside the door. The Japanese as well as those of other backgrounds celebrate Boy's Day by flying carps. Symbols such as the *banzai* (cheers!) and the one thousand cranes (symbols for longevity) are used at many weddings. The Japanese custom of giving *osenbetsu* (money for going away) as well as the attendant custom of reciprocating with an *omiyage* (present) may be witnessed at the airports. Money, instead of flowers or food, is sent to the family of the deceased. *Yakudoshi* (unlucky year) parties are held to chase the bad luck away when men reach forty-two. (See Appendix, "Symbolism at Traditional Celebrations.") The martial arts – jūdō, karate, aikidō – classes interest youngsters and adults from all ethnic groups as do Japanese films and television programs. An increasing number of non-Japanese have affiliated with religious groups that have their origin and headquarters in Japan.

In the arts, flower arrangement and *bonsai* (miniature plants) are hobbies that have a large ethnically mixed following. *Shibui* (elegance through simplicity) Japanese influences are seen in home and garden architecture and decor as well as in fabric and fashion.

Aikidō is the least aggressive and most philosophical of the martial arts. The primary focus is on centering at a point in the lower abdomen, the seat of ki, to develop inner calmness, relaxation, a harmonious integration of self, and oneness with the universe. Aikidō is secondarily a method of self-defense that emphasizes neutralization of an opponent's aggression rather than attack.

Mānoa Aikidō Club

Master carpenter George Furukawa painstakingly laid each tile on the roof, gate, and fence of his beautiful Japanese-style home.

Photo by D. Hazama

These examples of the influence of the Japanese upon the local culture are a testimony to the pride that the Japanese have in their culture and their willingness to share it with others. It is also a tribute to the openness of the people of the other ethnic groups to willingly accept another's culture. Needless to say, the same process of sharing and receiving has been reciprocated whereby the Japanese in Hawai'i have now incorporated the practices and customs of the other groups to be a part of their lives today.

The Japanese in Hawai'i in the 1980s still share physical characteristics and some basic values with their relatives in Japan and those who settled on the mainland United States. But, the Japanese in Hawai'i also manifest differences that set them apart as well. The most outstanding of those differences is in their perception of themselves. The Japanese in Hawai'i take pride in and view themselves as being a part of the people of Hawai'i. At home, they consider themselves as "local" or local Japanese. They frequently differentiate, though not necessarily negatively, the Japanese from Japan or from the mainland United States by dress, mannerisms, or speech patterns. Their sense of identification with and love of Hawai'i are definite and intense.

There is, too, an underlying sense of appreciation for being a part of Hawai'i. Having been one of the larger groups in a state of

Two Nisei professors have been honored at the University of Hawaii at Manoa by having buildings named after them. Watanabe Hall built in 1970 at a cost of $3,283,000 was named after Physicist Kenichi Watanabe, the first local boy to have a building dedicated to him. In 1979, History Professor and a Big Island boy, Shunzo Sakamaki, was also honored by having a $4,867,913 building named for him.

University of Hawaii

Fujio Matsuda, son of immigrant parents and a product of the public schools, served as the president of the University of Hawaii for ten years from September 1974 to May 1984. Prior to his presidency, Matsuda, who holds a Ph.D. in engineering, was Director of Transportation for the State of Hawaii.

University of Hawaii

minorities, the Hawai'i Japanese realize that they have escaped some of the more vicious prejudices faced by those on the mainland United States. Sympathetic to the cruel injustices suffered by their mainland brothers and sisters who lost their possessions and who were relocated into detention camps, they are also grateful for having been spared these experiences en masse. They manifest little bitterness, resentfulness, or anger in their experiences so far. Even the Issei with their *"Shi ka ta ga nai"* (It can't be helped; make the best of the situation) attitude tend to speak with fondness, humor, and pride about their early plantation experiences and feelings rather than resentfully. The Nisei and Sansei express quiet pride and satisfaction in speaking of their accomplishments during World War II and subsequently.

And so – this is the story of a people who galvanized their inner strengths and adventured and risked to better their lives. In the process, they helped to build the Hawai'i of the 80s, a vital and vibrant part of the United States of America. They have learned the lessons of liberty, equality, and justice. They have learned to live with and to respect peoples of backgrounds different from theirs. They have had the taste of success as they progressed from being the lowest outsiders in the Hawaiian hierarchy to mainstream members and even to leaders. This story does not end here, but will continue with the passage of time. What crossroads it will meet and what paths it will take will be dependent on the people, the time, and the circumstances.

Epilogue

It has been twenty years since the publication of *Okage sama de: The Japanese in Hawai'i*. When Bess Press approached us with the idea of republication, we realized that this was a rare opportunity and a challenge: We could bring an up-to-date focus on our people as a whole who have increased in population and become more complex and diverse; and we could expand upon our original story with additional accounts of individual Japanese Americans in Hawai'i who through their hard-earned achievements have contributed at local, national, and international levels. Examples are our Olympic champions, other world-class athletes, and those who have achieved global recognition in fine arts, performing arts, and other creative fields. Also included are the experiences of the courageous young men who internalized their democratic upbringing and expressed their dissent against what they considered to be unfair and un-American practices.

The Diverse and Complex *Nikkei*

The all-inclusive term *nikkei* has been used more and more to describe Japanese Americans in the United States. Dean S. Toji gives this definition: "By the end of the 1970s, the word *Nikkei*, meaning people of Japanese descent (usually those outside of Japan), started to be used by some as a broad inclusive term encompassing the growing diversity among Japanese Americans." He also explained that *nikkei* was an increasingly complex ethnic group. Generational categories such as *nisei* or *sansei* are not clear-cut, discreet groups. For example, some *issei* married early *nisei*, making their children half *nisei* and half *sansei*. Also, the growing number of multiethnic Japanese Americans has made it more difficult to record population data.[i]

The *State of Hawai'i Data Book*, based on the 2000 census, reported the population of Hawai'i's Japanese Americans at 201,764 (which represents respondents who chose "race alone") and 296,674 (which represents respondents who chose "race alone and in combination"). Because the 2000 census used different methodology from previous censuses—the new census allows respondents to choose multiple categories to identify their race—it is more difficult to make comparisons between censuses. By percentage, 201,764 (race alone) is 16.7 percent of the total population of the state of Hawai'i, showing a continued and significant decrease from the high of 42.7 percent reported in 1920. On the other hand, 296,674 (race alone and in combination) is 24.5 percent, or about one-fourth, of the total population. In actuality, the total number of Japanese Americans has increased over the years. However, there has also been a huge increase in the overall total population. Only those who identify themselves as white outnumber those who identify themselves as Japanese.[ii]

Toji's population study on the *nikkei* in the entire United States shows that the total Japanese American population, including mixed-race and mixed-ethnicity people, accounts for over 1.1 million people. Over 60 percent live in two states, California (34 percent) and Hawai'i (26 percent). For Hawai'i he chose to use the larger number ("race alone and in combination") from the 2000 census. He attributed this decrease in Japanese American population from the last census to low birthrate, high rate of out-marriage, assimilation, and a low level of immigration. He also reported that 30 percent of the population was of mixed ancestry. Toji lists Honolulu as the "Top" in Japanese American population among five metropolitan areas. He reported that, in Hawai'i, the number of Japanese Americans grew from 217,000 in 1970 to 297,000 in 2002, but this was an overall loss of 11 percent over the thirty-two-year period.[iii]

The fact that Japanese American women were more likely to intermarry and choose white spouses most frequently was discussed previously on p. 230. Toji reported that Japanese Americans in the early postwar years intermarried with white Americans; but that in the 1980s, there was a shift to intermarriage with other Asian Americans. In 1990, 40 percent married non-Japanese and the majority followed the trend in the following decade. Here in the islands, the part-Hawaiian group needs to be included. In Hawai'i, families of mixed ethnicities are easily observable at many family gatherings.[iv]

Sadly, only a handful of the adventurous *issei* laborers and picture brides who gave us a start to the present population remain. These precious pioneers are now over one hundred years old and are most likely living out their lives in care facilities.

Issei laborer Etsuo Hazama (p. 64–66), his picture bride Tatsuyo (p. 63–64), and their medium-size family of descendants at a New Year's gathering. This photo was taken sixty-six years after their arranged marriage. The family now includes part-Hawaiian and Caucasian granddaughters-in-law, a Filipino-Japanese grandson-in-law, and great-grandchildren who are Filipino-Japanese and Hawaiian-Japanese-Chinese.

Hazama Collection

Ichi Moriguchi

Mrs. Ichi Moriguchi, 101 years old, is one of the very few surviving *issei*. She was born on May 27, 1906, and is now being cared for at Hale Pulama Mau at Kuakini Hospital. Although she can no longer walk and is hard of hearing, this fragile lady can see with her glasses and communicate intelligently with the aid of a small device. Her mind is still sharp and she has a keen memory.

She was born in Fukushima *ken* (province) and soon after birth was a *yōjo* (adopted child). Her adoptive parents doted on her, and she said she was very spoiled. In her teens, she went to Tokyo to work at a *kōba* (factory or workplace) because her friends were going.

Her future husband and his father had immigrated to Hawai'i earlier, and his father revisited his native village to seek a bride for his son. He and her parents arranged a marriage, and he returned home, leaving a photograph of his son with her.

257

The family celebrated Ichi Moriguchi's 100th birthday with her. The happy smile on her face reflects how she has changed. Issei eighty years ago invariably put on stoic, unsmiling faces in front of the camera.

She was seventeen years old when she came by boat to Hawai'i and married Teizō Moriguchi at a temple in Honolulu. Her husband was twenty-four years old. With obvious pride, she said that her husband owned a repair shop and was very skilled at repairing bicycles, radios, and just about anything. She worked at Okazaki Tailor where she learned to use the sewing machine and became skilled at sewing men's pants, an intricate task. She worked there for about ten years and then worked for Haseyama Tailor. She continued to sew men's pants and was very proud of her sewing skill. She said the owner was very kind to her and treated her like family. She was employed there until she retired in her eighties. By learning to sew, she was able to avoid having to labor in the fields in the hot sun.

Ichi Moriguchi was naturalized on April 18, 1957. She and her husband traveled together several times to Japan and attended the Olympic Games on one of their trips. They also visited the continental United States, Canada, and Europe.

Her husband passed away about thirteen years ago. She had three children, but her oldest son and her daughter are gone now. She spoke fondly and appreciatively of her family's kindness and visits. They are her pride and joy.

Interviewed on April 10, 2007

Extended-Family Living Arrangements: An Adaptation to Local Reality

The *nisei* and early *sansei* were raised in nuclear households without their grandparents, who still lived in Japan. As families grew with adult children having children of their own, the situation changed. Dr. Glen Grant accurately describes the dilemma of local people and the adaptation that evolved:

> Due to the lack of available land or housing, it has become impossible in modern Hawai'i for Hawaiians or Asians to maintain a large extended-family residence. As the size of families grew, it thus became necessary to adapt to Island realities. Instead of four generations of a family living under the same roof, the more common American pattern of nuclear family structure has become the norm, especially among the middle classes of all ethnic backgrounds. However, within that kinship circle of separate nuclear families is an economic bond that continues to unite several generations of families which no longer share a single roof . . . . If the mainland youth at the age of 18 to 21 is expected to "fly the nest," in Hawai'i it is not uncommon to find single and married children in their 20s and 30s still living with their parents until they can afford their own home.[v]

In some cases, as *nisei* grandparents age and need assistance or have retired and have space in their homes, one of their children with young grandchildren may return to the nest. This is a mutually beneficial arrangement for all generations under one roof. Adult children may leave to attend college, but subsequently return to their nests until they become financially independent or start their own families. With the high cost of real estate, parents often help children with their down payment or to meet their mortgage payments when they purchase their own homes.

Since both parents usually work, grandparents, if available, baby-sit their grandchildren until they attend preschool. They also provide breakfast to school-age youngsters and transport them to and from school. The elders also baby-sit when parents have special engagements. Some grandparents even prepare dinners and dine together with their children and grandchildren before they return to their own homes. Many grandparents regularly invite immediate family (all their adult children and grandchildren) over for dinner once a week. The support is a way to provide continuous bonding within the extended family and among generations. Thus, the Japanese tradition of placing high value on family and *kodomo no tame ni,* "for the sake of our children," continues from generation to generation.

New Year, Thanksgiving, Christmas, and graduations are joyous occasions for the extended family to celebrate together. They began as nuclear family gatherings during the *issei* generation but grew in size as the families expanded. The food preparation and costs are generally shared potluck style. Glen Grant pointed out, "The importance placed upon the sharing of food and drink with family and friends goes beyond the natural love for the ethnic diversity of the 'local' palate—food is the symbolic reaffirmation of social interdependence." [vi]

The menu at these family gatherings is multiethnic, often including dishes such as Hawaiian *poke, kalua* pig, American ham, roast turkey or beef, mashed potatoes, salad, Chinese noodles, Korean-style barbecue beef, and Japanese *sashimi, tako,* and sushi.

The influence of globalization on Hawai'i's Japanese Americans is most evident at these extended family gatherings. Globalization occurs when a culture voluntarily changes its practices after contact with worldwide sources. Family greetings, especially by the younger *nikkei,* are accompanied by Hawaiian-style hugs and kisses on the cheeks and overt displays of affection, a major change over the years. Smiles and "say cheese" to the camera took years of coaching *issei* because they habitually presented stoic, serious expressions for photographs. Colorful *mu'umu'u* and aloha shirts, pants-outfits for women, shorts and jeans, various hairstyles, ear and body piercings, and sitting and standing positions are all signs of globalization.

Retirees

The *nisei* and early *sansei* are now in their retirement years, and, if still mobile, are enjoying their lives after years of working. If both spouses are still reasonably healthy, they count their blessings because so many of their classmates and friends have had to face the challenge of losing lifelong mates. They baby-sit as needed and volunteer their services at various institutions such as schools, museums, churches, and hospitals. They also have time to pursue their own interests in recreation, travel, and activities which they had sacrificed during their working and child-rearing years.

The retirees still enjoy fishing and now have the means and the time to golf with their friends. Others continue their participation in ball games. There are men's *makule* baseball leagues on all islands. Others enjoy growing flowers and a few fruit trees as well as vegetable gardens in the backyard or community gardens provided by the local government. They make an effort to excercise regularly and can be seen walking at sunrise in their neighborhood or in shopping centers. They laughingly call themselves the "dawn patrol." They also participate in excercise programs such as strength building, balancing, low-impact aerobics, *tai chi* or yoga.

Both sexes love spectator sports and are avid fans of the University of Hawai'i's football, volleyball, basketball, and baseball teams. Seniors attend games with season tickets. There are even some devoted fans that travel to the mainland to support their teams at major games.

These retirees love to travel. As youths, they did not leave the islands until perhaps college, and then there were only few who were so fortunate. After retirement, many have traveled extensively. Their destinations include the continental United States, China, Japan, Europe, and, for some, the ancient and once sacred pyramids of Egypt, the Dalai Lama's palace in Tibet, and magnificent Machu Picchu in Peru. Las Vegas, of course, is a favorite vacation spot for seniors, many of whom fly there several times a year to gamble, see the shows, golf, or shop.

In any social gathering, large or small, the seniors' conversations invariably turn to commiserating over health problems. They share information about various supplements, exercises, and doctors, as well as new medical reports they read or heard about.

There are those who look forward to regular weekly breakfasts or lunches with their cronies at their favorite fast-food or local restaurants where they talk story. Others like to try out various restaurants. At lunchtime in any fast-food restaurants, grandparents giving a treat to their grandchildren is a familiar sight. The scene is even more crowded when elementary schools are on half-day or holiday schedules.

The senior's lives are full and fun-filled, and they are greatful to have these rewarding years of retirement, subsidized by social security and pension payments form their years of hard work.

Lifelong Friendships

In Hawai'i, lifelong friendships were cultivated as early as the first grade (kindergartens were established later). Glen Grant commented on this trait: "Local individuals also belong to lifelong friendship networks that contribute to a social climate where peer group influences, interdependency, and a sense of not sticking out in a crowd have become highly valued behaviors. It is not unusual to find local senior citizens of all racial backgrounds who have maintained friendships with elementary-school classmates throughout their entire life." [vii] This practice has been perpetuated by the *sansei, yonsei,* and *gosei.*

High school reunions at choice restaurants are important annual events, especially for neighbor-island and rural graduates. Although many no longer reside in their hometowns, they will travel, often by airplane, to be with their classmates. Las Vegas is a very popular site for many of these class reunions.

The Working Generations

As adults, the third, fourth, and fifth generations lead busy, active lives. Most are employed and have children, although some no longer feel the pressure to marry and have children, once the expectation for all Japanese Americans. A growing number opt for the freedom that being single provides. Or, they may be married but for whatever reason do not have children. As with the general population, the increasing divorce rate is a reality for *nikkei,* too. For those who have children, whether as a couple or as a single parent, juggling the needs and schedules of adults and children creates many pressures. After-school programs offer parents some relief; for a price, students can do their homework and have supervised fun. After work and on weekends, parents take children to sports practice and music or dance lessons. A small percentage attend Japanese language classes that, unfortunately, tend to be more an after-school activity than a language-learning one. Teachers often are challenged to motivate their students. Thus, those who are parents contribute both their hard-earned money and a great deal of their non-working time to their children's activities. Unlike their parents' or grandparents' more traditional cars, they drive around in SUVs and vans.

The more affluent in any generation often opt for status-symbol vehicle brands like Mercedes, Lexus, and BMW.

Their acculturation to the local American-Hawaiian lifestyle is also evident in their hairstyles and attire. With Hawai'i's warm pleasant climate year round, the trend in clothing has been toward more casual and comfortable attire. Gone are the days when mothers sewed the family's outfits. Today, the vast majority of the *Nikkei* families wear store-bought clothes.

The baby boomers are aware of the importance of good health practices. They are physically active, finding time after work, in the evenings, and on weekends to go jogging, walking, and exercising.

The *Nikkei* Youth

The youth intermingle with a far more cosmopolitan, multi-ethnic population of classmates than their parents and grandparents ever did. They enjoy frequent sleep-overs, play in and out of school, and study with friends of mixed ethnicity. Children are not too aware of these differences, and parents are comfortable with the different ethnic backgrounds of their children's friends, including the inevitable dating partners.

When asked in class for an estimate of the population breakdown by ethnicity in Hawai'i, most students guessed a much higher proportion of Japanese Americans than is reflected on the census. This is probably because Japanese Americans, as reported by the Department of Education in 1992, accounted for 52.3 percent of teachers, the authority figures in schools.

KAREN ARAKAWA
WORLD RECORD
BENCH PRESS & DEADLIFT CHAMPIONSHIPS
WABDL - SEPT. 20, 2003 - HAWAII

Nanea Designs

Sansei Karen Iwamoto Arakawa is a graduate of the University Laboratory School and the University of Puget Sound. She has a degree in Urban Planning and is currently Project Manager for the Pacific Housing Assistance Corporation, which develops affordable housing and provides consulting services to other nonprofit and for-profit groups in this field. She took her first weight-training class in 1997 at age thirty-nine, where she met her future husband. Several years later, she started lifting weights in international competitions. With her great sense of humor, she explains her remarkable achievements: "I set the state record for deadlift in the forty- to forty-six–year-olds, ninety-seven–pound group on my first try because there was no record in my group. On my second try, I set the world record of 187 pounds, but then someone beat that

264

later. So, I waited until I could move to the next age group, forty-seven– to fifty-four–year-olds, ninety-seven–pounds, and set a new world record with a lift of 214 pounds, but someone took it away, too. I still have the Hawai'i records. I'm retired from competitions—maybe—but it's still my favorite form of exercise. You can work out and still talk a lot." Karen enjoys her weight-lifting group, called the Pau Hana Pumpers, at CHART. The PHP range from a ninety-year-old woman to the youngest, a forty-year-old man, with most in their fifties and sixties but a few in their seventies and eighties.

Interview May 8, 2007

However, with affirmative action, this percentage has been decreasing slowly. In *The Superintendent's Annual Report 2006*, Japanese Americans made up 31.2 percent of all public school-teachers, less than 50 percent but still the largest group. On the other hand, ethnic Japanese students in public schools constituted only 9.8 percent of the school population, far less than Hawaiian/part Hawaiian (26.9 percent), Filipino (20.4 percent), and Other (15.3 percent). [viii]

Nikkei parents today, like those of previous generations, continue to place great value on doing well in school and work to have their children attend college, including graduate school. To that end, even middle-income families make sacrifices to send their children to private schools. Students' backpacks are weighted down with heavy textbooks for homework, a practice that now begins at an early age.

Children's favorite pastimes are watching TV, listening to music, playing electronic games, getting together at the malls for shopping or just hanging out, and going to the movies. When riding in a car, they listen to their iPods, oblivious to any conversation.

As adults, *sansei, yonsei,* and *gosei* rely on computer skills for work and socialization. They readily look up information on the Internet and frequently chat online or e-mail friends. Their children from a very young age use cell phones, iPods, and computers. Technologically, some seniors have learned to adapt to modern times. Conversely, many others have been slower to adjust, although they may use the computer to a limited extent, they don't want to deal with the intricacies of the Internet or e-mails. Concerned adult children have convinced their parents to own cell phones to use in emergencies. The generation gap is probably widest in this respect as the world of technology develops at a faster pace.

NOTABLE ACHIEVERS

Beginning at a crucial time soon after the conclusion of World War II and continuing through today, a few individuals have achieved success, fame, and prominence in the fields of medicine, education, creative and performing arts, cuisine, and sports. All of these individuals—artists, writers, a star of stage and screen, musicians, a fashion designer, a culinary innovator, and many in the field of sports, including Olympic medalists and world record holders—were selected because of their recognition and prominence at national and international levels, thus truly enhancing the image of Japanese Americans.

MEDICINE

DR. RICHARD TSURUO MAMIYA
"Superman"

Having come from a poor family that lived under crowded conditions in Kalihi and Pālama, Richard Tsuruo Mamiya had no dreams of going to college, let alone of becoming a doctor. He calls it serendipity that opportunities came his way when he needed them. Mamiya, a three-sport athlete, was offered an athletic scholarship to the then-St. Louis College (now St. Louis High School) and, three years later, another to the University of Hawai'i. He was outstanding academically and athletically at both institutions and was admired as a nice, regular guy as well as a leader.

It was during his junior year at UH that his professors noted his adeptness in dissection and suggested he take an aptitude test. It showed him to be a prospect for medicine. Upon graduation from the University he applied to several medical schools, and decided on the first acceptance—St. Louis University Medical School in Missouri.

In 1950, Mamiya left for St. Louis, Missouri, with his bride, Hazel Ikenaga. He had borrowed $4,000 to help defray costs. During the early years of their marriage and until the children came, Hazel worked and helped out financially.

After earning an M.D. degree in 1984, Mamiya served as a surgical intern, a resident, and also as a senior surgical instructor and surgical chief at various hospitals in St. Louis. He returned to Honolulu in 1961 and affiliated with the Central Medical Clinic as a

general surgeon. Always interested in learning and improving his skills, Mamiya participated in the planning for the University of Hawaiʻi Medical School. He wanted very much to help keep local physicians, including himself, at the forefront of medical progress.

The efforts of many, including Mamiya's, led to the opening of a two-year medical school in 1967 and a four-year school five years later. Mamiya served as chair of the surgical department and organized and ran the integrated training program. During this period, he did cardiovascular research and developed a clinical program. He speaks excitedly about this period, when he believes he was creating and developing worthwhile information and techniques. He is known to have cut in half the time to perform vascular blood vessel grafts, a form of open heart surgery, and his patient survival rate has been excellent. He has shared his techniques and procedures with doctors all over the world. He retired in 1995 after more than ten thousand heart surgeries and twenty thousand other types of operations. He continues to remain active in the community as a consultant and as a philanthropist. He has donated generously from a family foundation to St. Louis School; Punahou School, where his eight children matriculated; and Castle Hospital, thereby continuing to live up to his philosophy of leaving the world a better place than he found it.

Recalled by Dr. Michael Okihiro
January 2007

VISUAL ARTS

ISAMI DOI
Inspiration to Budding Artists

Even into the 1950s, the Japanese, who were busy trying to survive, did not think of art as a sustainable profession. Isami Doi was an anomaly. He started his college career at the University of Hawai'i, majoring in pre-medicine. Unfulfilled, he transferred to Columbia University in New York, first majoring in pre-legal and then in education, but he remained unsatisfied. The chance to go into a field he really liked came when he was befriended by a well-known New York artist who recognized his artistic talents and encouraged him to pursue a career in art. It was a difficult decision, but he realized that art, indeed, was the career he wanted. He made the switch.

By 1927, Doi had shown his work at many New York galleries and was even invited to a one-man show in Paris, an unheard-of opportunity for a budding Japanese-American artist from the Territory of Hawai'i. He felt fulfilled and happy with his decision.

He wanted to help other artists from Hawai'i find success and fulfillment in art as well, and encouraged them to go to New York, the art capital of America, for further training and exposure. A group of young artists, including Japanese Americans, took his advice and ventured to New York, where they studied with leading artists.

Among the "New York group" were Satoru Abe, Jerry Okimoto, Tadashi Sato, and Harry Tsuchidana. Over the years, these New York artists have shown not only in New York, but throughout the country, including in Hawai'i. They have each been recognized with many grants and awards and are included on lists of outstanding artists.

SATORU ABE
Sculptor and Painter

Satoru Abe, one of Hawai'i's living treasures, is a painter and sculptor who has exhibited throughout Japan and the United States. Nature, especially trees, continues to inspire him in both painting and in sculpture. He is greatly influenced by his Buddhist faith. Abe has been in a continuous quest for an understanding of who he is.

"After graduating from McKinley High School in 1945, I worked at various service-level jobs but kept asking myself whether this was all there is to life. Concluding that there must be more, I decided to

Eighty-one-year-old master sculptor Satoru Abe still puts in long hours in his studio and at Satoru's Art Gallery.

go to New York City to study art. This decision was boosted when my *issei* father gave me ready approval. These were the days when the community did not regard art as a worthy and sustainable profession."

"I first went to California during the summer of 1948 and picked strawberries to earn enough to go to New York. Once in New York, I randomly chose to enroll at the Art Students League. Little did I know then that it was the leading art school in the city, if not in America. I painted, but knew that I had much more to learn about technique and color."

"Fortunately for me, upon my return to Hawai'i I met an outstanding painter, Isami Doi, and later saw him often when I returned to New York in 1955. Isami inspired, taught, and encouraged me and several other Hawai'i artists. He has served and continues to serve as a mentor for me. I still talk with him although he's been gone for over forty years."

Abe's quest for spiritual and cultural identity took him to Japan for two years, during which he had two solo exhibits. After the return trip to New York, he enhanced his sculpturing skills at the Sculpture Center. He was awarded a Guggenheim Grant during this period.

Another grant, from the National Endowment for the Arts, brought him back to Hawai'i, where he worked with students from the depressed Nānākuli area on a sculpture, Tree of Knowledge, which continues to inspire students.

"In the early years, my work was motivated by a need for self-fulfillment, but with maturity, took on a more universal perspective. Painting and sculpturing are very different venues. In painting I can set my ideas and work quickly, while metal allows me to create and to extend as I add a piece here and a piece there until I'm satisfied."

Satoru Abe's creations are in both institutional and personal collections around the world. A very soft-spoken, humble, and caring man, he lives a simple life in Honolulu creating art and taking care of himself and his plants while mentoring young artists.

Interviewed on February 10, 2007

Toshiko Takaezu sees, hears, feels, reads—whatever presents itself to her and internalizes and integrates these experiences within her own being. Ultimately, these experiences emerge through her deft hands as new shapes, designs, and color in her creation pieces.

Courtesy International Art Society of Hawai'i

TOSHIKO TAKAEZU
Ceramist

Her ceramic pieces are powerful and calming, like her gracious carriage and speech, but in her pieces, as in herself, there is strength and an understated elegance. To be in her presence and to view her creations is a Zen experience. Internationally known and revered, Hawai'i-born ceramist Toshiko Takaezu receives her inspirations through the environment and the cultures of her Hawaiian and Japanese backgrounds.

Takaezu finds working in clay an exciting and satisfying experience. For her, clay breathes with life; it responds to her just as she responds to it. She is influenced by the process. Although she has an idea of what she wants to create, she also responds to the emerging possibilities she encounters in the process. She builds her pieces with measured technical skill, but her glazes are random and spontaneous. She often walks around her large pieces applying the glaze by pouring or painting.

Toshiko Takaezu began her training at the Honolulu Academy of Arts and the University of Hawai'i and continued her studies at the Cranbrook Academy of Arts in Michigan. She has taught and inspired generations of ceramists at the Honolulu Academy of Arts, the Cleveland Institute of Art, and Princeton University, where she taught for twenty-five years. She retired in 1992 and currently devotes all her time to being a studio artist. Although retired from classroom teaching, she continues to teach and inspire through her creations, which are in more than thirty-five public institutions. She has had many exhibits, including more than forty solo exhibits in Japan and the United States. In 1987, she was declared a Living Treasure of Hawai'i by the Honpa Hongwanji Mission of Hawaii.

As told by Stanley Yamamoto,
Retired DOE Educational Specialist

PERFORMING ARTS AND LITERATURE

<u>Stage and Screen</u>

JAMES SHIGETA
Groundbreaking Actor

During an era in film when mixed-ethnic romances were rare or even taboo, James Shigeta was a groundbreaking pioneer, recognized as the only Asian American actor chosen to star opposite a Caucasian leading lady. The following description of the local *sansei* actor is excerpted from interviews by Henry Ong[ix] and Greg Yano of the *Nichi Bei Times*.[x]

A graduate of Roosevelt High School, James Shigeta aspired during his college years at the University of Hawai'i and later at New York University, to become a teacher and a writer. Tall, exceptionally handsome, and with great audience appeal, he was further gifted with a talent for singing, which he developed through

James Shigeta starred with Carroll Baker in A Bridge to the Sun, a romantic true story. This film was probably his favorite among his many films.

voice training, including opera. He received national attention when he won the Ted Mack Amateur Hour's annual scholarship prize on national television in New York City.

He had found success in Las Vegas as a headliner in "Holiday in Japan" when Paramount Studios picked him to appear in the movie *Walk Like a Dragon*. His first mixed-ethnic romantic lead was in *Crimson Kimono* in 1959. He was awarded the prestigious Golden Globe Award for New Star of the Year. When he first began to receive film roles, he prepared for them by taking acting lessons. He also took full advantage of coaching lessons provided by the old studio system. In 1961, he starred in *A Bridge to the Sun,* considered by many to be his finest performance. The movie version of *The Flower Drum Song* brought him instant international stardom. He has continued to be active in films and on the stage and has toured in *The Flower Drum Song, The King and I,* and *The Fantasticks.* In July 2006, he performed with Nancy Kwan in *Love Letters* on stage in San Francisco.

James Shigeta describes himself as "shy," and "a country boy." He refers to himself as an "actor," never a "star," a term he considers vastly overused. However, nationally and internationally, he has attained stardom.

Correspondence with James Shigeta, February 2007

Literature

LOIS ANN YAMANAKA
Poet, Novelist and Teacher

A locally and nationally acclaimed poet and novelist, Lois Ann Yamanaka roots her stories in her observation of locals, especially

Japanese Americans, as they deal with conflicts within themselves, their families, and community. Her writings include universal and sensitive themes such as coming of age, race relations, family matters, and religion, all based in Hawai'i. Yamanaka enhances the local setting with liberal use of pidgin. Her inclusion of locally used profanity in pidgin further lends credibility to the reality and urgency of the plot.

Keith Kashiwada, Professor of English at Kapi'olani Community College who has adapted Yamanaka's stories for the stage, recalls that "initially her writing was not welcomed by many because they were perceived as crass and demeaning. Using pidgin and profanity orally was bad enough but using them in writing was a no-no. After the initial shock and with the increasing use of pidgin by other local writers, Yamanaka's writings are now sought and praised."

Adding to her legitimacy have been the grants she has received from foundations such as the National Endowment for the Humanities, the National Endowment for the Arts, and the Carnegie Foundation. She has also been recognized with many awards and with invitations to speak about writing. Two of her stories, "Wild Meat and the Bully Burgers" and "Heads by Harry," have been staged.

A *sansei* daughter of educators, Yamanaka first trained as a teacher and taught in Hawai'i schools. In addition to her career in writing, Yamanaka also teaches creative writing primarily to young people at her school, Na'au, in Honolulu.

Information provided by Keith Kashiwada, Professor of English, Kapi'olani Community College

LISA MATSUMOTO
Award-winning Playwright, Actress, and Author

Creative, talented, award-winning playwright, actress, and author of children's books, Lisa Matsumoto was born on August 26, 1964; and her death on December 14, 2007 left the community with a deep sense of loss. However, in an all too brief lifetime, gifted, energetic, multi-talented Lisa left a legacy of creative works that will enrich and inspire others for a long time to come. Lisa received her education at Koko Head Elementary, Niu Valley Intermediate, Kaiser High, and graduated from Mid-Pacific Institute. She received her degrees from the University of Hawai'i

"Share sunshine and laughter wherever you go!"
Lisa Matsumoto

at Mānoa, B.A. in Drama and Theatre and a Master of Fine Arts in Youth Theatre. Her use of pidgin in her playwriting and the Hawaiian environmental settings clearly reflect her feelings toward her local origin.

She is the creator and playwright of the award-winning *Once Upon One Time* trilogy, *Once Upon One Time, Once Upon One Noddah Time*, and *Happily Eva Afta,* for which she won a Poʻokela award for original script. She also received Poʻokela awards for *Das How Come* and *The Princess and the Iso Peanut.* Furthermore, she exhibited another aspect of her gifted personality and received a Poʻokela award for the Leading Actress in her memorable role as Da Wicked Queen in *Once Upon One Time.* Lisa received a special adjudicator's award "for her outstanding contribution to Oʻahu's theatres" and the Elliot Cades Award for Literature 2000 which is awarded to "a proven writer who has published a significant body of work of exceptional quality." She also wrote and co-directed *The Wizard of Oz: Local Style*, a concert adaptation of the popular classic for the Honolulu Symphony.

She is equally famous as an author of children's books which she published in partnership with her cousin Michael Furuya who created the appealing paintings to illustrate their books: *How the B-52 Cockroach Learned to Fly*, winner of the 1996 Ka Pala Pala Poʻokela award for Excellence in Childrens' Books and *Wailana the Waterbug*, the winner in 2000. Other bestsellers are *Beyond*

'Ohi'a Valley: Adventures in a Hawaiian Rainforest, and *The Adventures of Gary and Harry: A Tale of Two Turtles.* Youngsters learned about their fragile environment and the perils of endangered species. *Wailana the Waterbug* inspired by the life of little Alana Dung offered a portrayal of death as a beginning rather than an end. It was adapted for their first large scale musical, *On Dragonfly Wings.*

Matsumoto and Furuya also founded 'Ohi'a Productions, a non-profit organization to provide creative, educational and inspiring theatrical experiences to Hawai'i's children and families. Their entertaining and informative *Educational Road Shows* with an environmental theme proved to be such a powerful vehicle that the Department of Land and Natural Resources began to sponsor video productions of the shows which were donated to every elementary school and library in the State of Hawai'i. *Imagination Soars,* requiring student participation, uses creative drama to promote literacy and personal growth. The *'Ohana Program* stages Broadway style musical productions to create enjoyable entertainment for family togetherness. The immensely popular musical production of her book, *Christmas Gift of Aloha,* at the Ala Moana Center reached many who had not seen her other creations.

In a speech celebrating Lisa's life, her mentor, UHM Professor and Director of Theatre Tammy Montgomery concluded:

In the end, Lisa will outlive all of us. Today, we still produce plays that are hundreds, if not thousands of years old. Long after we are gone, Lisa's books and plays will bring laughter to your children, your grandchildren, their children, their grandchildren and to the mamy audiences of the future.

Outstanding Musical Virtuosos

KENNY ENDO
Classical and Modern *Taiko* Master

Kenny Endo is an internationally known performer and composer, and a leading spirit in the perpetuation and popularization of traditional and contemporary *taiko.* He was born in Los Angeles to an *issei* father and a *nisei* mother from British Columbia, Canada. He had an interest in drumming and started training in western drumming in elementary school when he was about nine years old. "When I heard *taiko* while in college, the sound resonated deep within me; I knew it would become my life's work. But, at that time, I didn't think *taiko* would be accessible to me."

Watching a live performance of Kenny Endo is a thrilling and mesmerizing experience as he pours his heart and soul into the drums through the rhythmic beating of his drumsticks.

Photo by Shuzo Uemoto

He spent six months working on a Native American Reservation where the WWII Japanese-American internment camp, Poston, was located. This experience led Endo to explore his roots further. In 1975, Endo began his studies of the *taiko* with *Kinnara Taiko* of Los Angeles and the San Francisco *Taiko Dōjō*. In 1980, he embarked on a rigorous, ten-year odyssey studying with *taiko* masters in Japan. He is the first non-Japanese national to be honored with a *natori* (stage name equivalent to a master's degree) in *hōgaku hayashi* (Japanese classical drumming). In 1990, with a grant for graduate work from the East-West Center, he moved to Hawai'i, where he earned an M.A. in Ethnomusicology from the University of Hawai'i.

Endo established the Taiko Center of the Pacific, a school of traditional drumming, and serves as its Artistic Director. The Center offers classes to the public through the Kapi'olani Community College's non-credit program. Endo has performed as a soloist with the Honolulu Symphony and the Hong Kong Philharmonic as well as in countries such as the former USSR, France, and Egypt. His ensemble has performed throughout the United States, Japan, Germany, Belgium, England, the Czech Republic, and Canada, in such venues as the Kennedy Center for the Performing Arts and the Smithsonian Institute in Washington, D.C. As a composer, Endo has released three CDs.

Information provided by Kenny Endo and from an interview on April 24, 2007 (see www.kennyendo.com)

Herbert Ohta faced failure squarely and took a risk to pursue a career in 'ukulele. He is a pioneer in the field who has mentored and inspired many, including Roy Sakuma, who himself has taught thousands to play and enjoy the 'ukulele.

Ohta Collection

OHTA SAN
'Ukulele Virtuoso and Solo Artist

Herbert Ichiro Ohta, known professionally as Ohta San, is a renowned and respected musician who has shared his 'ukulele artistry with audiences throughout the world. He is credited with having expanded the 'ukulele's capabilities as a solo instrument. His deft fingers can play a range of moods, from slow and romantic to fast and dynamic, as he interprets Hawaiian, American, Latin, and classical music as well as jazz, rock, and pop.

Soft-spoken and humble, Ohta San credits his *nisei* mother for introducing the 'ukulele to him at age seven; Eddie Kamae, an 'ukulele virtuoso, for teaching him special techniques and for encouraging and inspiring him; and Barbara Smith, an ethnomusicologist at the University of Hawai'i, for teaching him music theory and introducing him to classical music.

When asked about his choice of profession, Ohta San replied,

"I thought about it after my years in the Marines and after I had failed to get a job at Pan American Airways in Hawai'i as a greeter. No matter how hard I tried, I couldn't pass the hearing test on high tones. It was then that I turned to thinking of becoming a professional 'ukulele musician. I love the 'ukulele and I had met some success during my eleven years in the Marines. I had toured with the All Navy Show and had even won a spot on the nationally televised *Ed Sullivan Show*. However, my patient mother reminded me that it was hard to earn a respectable living as a musician—let alone as an 'ukulele player.

"But I decided to give it a try. There were lean times, but I hung on. Soon I learned that playing alone was not the way to go. The way to sell a show was for the soloist to be backed by a small band, including vocalists. As soon as I changed to the new format, we began playing to full houses six nights a week at the 'Ilikai. Fortunately my agent had contracted payment to be the larger of two choices—a flat $2,000 per week or all of the cover charge, which turned out to be as high as $5,000 during some weeks.

"I don't play the Club Circuit any more. I only do concerts. I have met considerable success in Japan and go there at least once a year to enthusiastic audiences. Over the years, I have found that humor must be included at Japanese performances. Fortunately I can patter in Japanese and the audience loves it. Some even jokingly tell me they come to hear me talk and not to listen to my music!"

To reach larger numbers of enthusiasts, Ohta San has written and published *'Ukukele O Hawai'i*, a forty-four-page instruction book, as well as recorded over sixty albums in Hawai'i, the United States, Japan, and France. Ohta San, along with Eddie Kamae, continues to seek ways to expand the audience for 'ukulele and Hawaiian music.

Imbued with the spirit of *gambari* (perseverance), Ohta San has practiced diligently, taken new and uncertain paths, and endured hardships. He has met with much success and, like his mentor Eddie Kamae, is now regarded as an international 'ukulele virtuoso.

Interviewed on April 25, 2007
and *September Morn*[xi]

When he was just four years old, Jake's mother gave him his first 'ukulele lesson. "When I played my first chord I was hooked," says Jake. "I fell in love with the instrument." That love grew into a deep passion to create and innovate.

Photo by Jayson Tanega

JAKE SHIMABUKURO
Passionate 'Ukulele Virtuoso

Known for lightning-fast fingers and revolutionary playing techniques, Jake Shimabukuro is a master of the 'ukulele. The thirty-year-old, fifth-generation, local-born virtuoso shatters musical boundaries, playing jazz, blues, funk, classical, bluegrass, folk, flamenco, and rock. While Jake has great respect and love for traditional Hawaiian 'ukulele music, his mission is to show everyone that his instrument is capable of so much more. Jake views it as an "untapped source of music with unlimited potential."

From a modest beginning performing at a local Honolulu café to his debut on national television in 2005 and live performances in front of crowds of over forty thousand, Jake has had opportunities to demonstrate his incredible virtuosity and amazing stage presence, including appearing with over two dozen nationally recognized musicians.

Jake's musical accomplishments are especially well known in Japan, where his outgoing personality and warm heart have made his name a household word. In 2002, he became the first ʻukulele player from Hawaiʻi to sign with Epic Records International/Sony Music International. Then, in 2005, Jake obtained a U.S. distribution deal for his Hitchhike Records label. In 2006, after a video clip of one of his performances started circulating on the Internet, Jake received emails of support and accolades from places as distant from Hawaiʻi as France, England, Germany, Sweden, Australia, and Korea, where he recently signed distribution deals.

Following the fatal collision between a U.S. submarine and a Japanese fishing vessel in Hawaiian waters in 2001, Jake composed "Ehime Maru" to honor the nine young victims. Proceeds were donated to a fund benefiting the victims' families. Although he did not intend to gain recognition for this private work, "Ehime Maru" did receive worldwide recognition and acclaim.

In 2004, Jake was named the State of Hawaiʻi's goodwill ambassador to Japan and was given "The Japanese Foreign Minister's Commendation" for being an active voice in U.S.-Japan relations. In a ceremony held on September 4, 2006, Jake Shimabukuro was appointed the 160th Okinawa-Uchina Ambassador at the Okinawan State House.

Jake Shimabukuro expresses his passion this way: "I love what I do. I'm forever thankful for music." He further demonstrates this by visiting schools to talk with and play for the children of Hawaiʻi, thus inspiring thousands to learn about and play music.

Excerpts and quotes from Hitchhike Records

Anne Namba at work in her Vintage Kimono Room.

Photo by Leonard Cadiente

<u>Fashion Design</u>

ANNE NAMBA
Internationally Acclaimed Designer

For Anne Yuri Namba, being the second-born daughter motivated her to future success as a fashion designer. She said, "I got tired of hand-me-downs and realized that the only way to avoid

281

them was to sew my own clothes. Fortunately I was always art oriented anyway. Soon I was making clothes for my friends, too." Her interest in fashion led her to New York, where she graduated cum laude from the prestigious Fashion Institute of Technology. For the next six years, Anne worked in New York's garment industry, honing her design and technical skills. During her last year in New York, she worked for the costume design department at the landmark Radio City Music Hall.

In 1985, Anne returned to Hawai'i and worked out of her parents' home designing her own line of one-of-a-kind originals made from vintage Japanese kimono and *obi*. In 1989, she opened her Honolulu boutique in Mānoa Valley, and Anne Namba Designs was born.

In the years since, Anne has taken her "Kimono Couture" to new heights with her stunning designs, which solicit a strong universal appeal. She has greatly influenced other local designers, craftspeople, and home seamstresses to appreciate and utilize Japanese fabrics. Her designs have appeared in Neiman Marcus, the Saks Fifth Avenue Folio Catalog, and Bergdorf Goodman in New York. She has produced fashion shows in Hong Kong, Tokyo, Singapore, Beijing, Shanghai, and many U.S. cities.

Anne's clientele is an extensive list of famous women, including former First Lady Senator Hillary Clinton, Mrs. Sadaharu Oh, wife of Japan's famous baseball star, Ann Getty, Olympic gold medalist Kristi Yamaguchi, Elizabeth Taylor, and Aretha Franklin. Former Hawai'i First Lady Lynne Waihee wore an Anne Namba design while hosting a dinner for the Emperor and Empress of Japan. In addition, Anne was featured on Lifetime Television and in *A. Magazine, Inside Asian America* in a pictorial entitled "Ten Women to Watch."

Anne Namba has successfully combined her artistic ability, her passion for fashion, her ethnic origin, and her western professional training to make a very positive impact on the world of local and international fashion design.

Interview on March 20, 2007 and
http://www.annenamba.com/

Chef Roy Yamaguchi creates his Hawaiian Fusion Cuisine.
Photo: www.royyamaguchi.com

ROY YAMAGUCHI
Master Chef

Tokyo-born and trained in the United States, Roy Yamaguchi has become famous for his creative talents in the culinary arts. He is acclaimed for his inspired Hawaiian Fusion Cuisine, in which he combines exotic flavors and spices with local Hawai'i ingredients, a masterful blending of East, West, and Hawaiian influences.

After graduating at the age of nineteen from the Culinary Institute of America in New York, and after several years of intensive training, Yamaguchi attained the coveted title of Master Chef. His first experience as executive chef was at Le Serene in Los Angeles in 1979. He has also worked at the posh Michael's in Santa Monica and at California Cuisine.

In 1984, he opened his own restaurant in Los Angeles, 385 North. Yamaguchi then moved to Hawai'i in 1988 and opened his first namesake restaurant. There are now thirty-four Roy's: twenty-five in the continental United States, six in the Hawaiian Islands, two in Japan, and one in Guam. Among Yamaguchi's other notable achievements: hosting six seasons of the PBS-TV show *Hawai'i Cooks with Roy Yamaguchi*—seen on more than three hundred stations in fifty states, as well as in sixty countries—and publishing three cookbooks, *Roy's Fish and Seafood, Roy's Feasts from Hawai'i*, and *Hawai'i Cooks: Flavors from Roy's Pacific Rim Kitchen.*

Food and Wine Magazine dubbed Roy's the "crown jewel of Honolulu's East-West eateries," and it was selected one of *Conde Nast Traveler's* "Top 50" restaurants. The *New York Times* described him as "the Wolfgang Puck of the Pacific," and *Gourmet* acknowledged Yamaguchi as "the father of modern East-West cooking." In 1988, he was honored with the prestigious James Beard "Best Pacific Northwest Chef" award, the first chef in Hawai'i to receive this distinction.

His passion for Hawaiian Fusion Cuisine and his business acumen have made a unique impact on the international scene for Japanese Americans and the State of Hawai'i.

Source: http://www.royyamaguchi.com/

SPORTS

Unless credited otherwise, information and photos in this section are through courtesy of Hawai'i Sports Hall of Fame and Cybermuseum [xii]

COACH SOICHI SAKAMOTO
Mentor to Olympic Champions

Soichi Sakamoto (1906–1977) was a science teacher in Pu'unēnē, Maui, when he observed his students frolicking in a plantation sugar-cane irrigation ditch near their school. That was forbidden. Although he knew nothing about competitive swimming, he volunteered to supervise the students and devised his own techniques to teach them how to swim at a time when there were few swimming pools or organized swim programs. He eventually became a swimming instructor at the University of Hawai'i and a legendary coach who attained international fame and recognition for his protégés and himself.

Sakamoto coached a number of Olympic medalists including Thelma Kalama, Bill Smith, William Woolsey, and Evelyn Kawamoto. A strict, dedicated coach, his motto was: "Olympics first, Olympics always!" He was assistant coach for the U.S. Olympic Swim Team from 1952–1956. He is a member of the International Swimming Hall of Fame and the Hawai'i Sports Hall of Fame and Cybermuseum. The swimming facility at the War Memorial Complex in Wailuku, Maui, is named in his honor. His success in developing so many internationally outstanding swimmers has not been equaled in Hawai'i's history.

Coach Sakamoto took his outstanding swimmers to mainland and international swimming meets where they earned medals and recognition.

Komeiji Collection

REFLECTIONS ON COACH SAKAMOTO
by Evelyn Kawamoto-Konno

Coach Sakamoto was a very unique person with many gifts. Besides being a dedicated, technically brilliant swimming coach, he was also a musician, teacher, outstanding leader, and really smart, no doubt about it. He used psychology way back then when we weren't talking about it. He would inject ideas into our heads and continue to talk—encouraging, stimulating, and challenging each of us. Every Sunday, we had a team meeting at the pool. There might have been fifty of us. He talked about winning and focusing, and always inspired us in a strong way. He used psychology, both positive and negative, and it worked. He used different techniques to reach different kids, including bawling us out if he thought that was what we needed.

He accomplished more than just being a master of swimming techniques. To improve himself and enhance his swimmers, he always analyzed and evaluated and actually invented equipment to help build arms and legs. When college swimming coaches from major mainland universities came to participate in swimming meets, they were eager to learn about his teaching techniques and were amazed at how he did things.

There's also the caring side to Coach. We would arrive at the pool at about 4:30 p.m. after school and practice under his watchful eyes until about 10:30 p.m. Then, we would catch a ride home with him. He drove the younger kids to their homes before he went to his house, which was pretty late at night by then. I was truly blessed to be under his care and guidance for six years.

There are coaches, great coaches, and then there's Coach Soichi Sakamoto!

Interviewed on February 15, 2007

OLYMPIC MEDALISTS

Swimming

FORD KONNO

2 Golds (one a world record), 1952
Silver, 1952
Silver, 1956
International Swimming Hall of Fame

YOSHINOBU OYAKAWA

Gold, 1952
International Swimming Hall of Fame

EVELYN KAWAMOTO-KONNO

2 Bronzes, 1952

EVELYN KAWAMOTO-KONNO
Only Female Japanese American Olympic Medalist

I was born and raised in Waikīkī until six years of age, so I learned to swim on my own and developed a love of swimming.

When I was about five, my father became very ill and was hospitalized. As a result, his tailor shop on Beretania Street had to be sold, and we moved to the McCully area. Fortunately, the schools were close to the Department of Public Parks and Recreation, which offered after-school programs. Mrs. Lillian Chan, playground director, encouraged me to participate in all activities, including the 50-yard swimming events at the Waikīkī Natatorium. The official in charge, Thelma Wicke, took me under her wing and truly taught me what aloha means. I *loved* this lady.

In July 1941, my father passed away. My mother now had to raise six children, of which I was the youngest. I can still picture her spending long hours doing laundry to support us.

When I was twelve and visiting my uncle, he said, "You wanna meet Coach Sakamoto? He lives nearby. He's a maker of champions! Do you wanna be a champion?"

He introduced me to Coach Sakamoto, who watched me swim some laps. He said, "OK. She can come to practice." That's how I met the coach who changed my life. A group of us walked to daily practice at the university pool. Gradually, the other girls' interests changed, but I continued because I loved swimming.

I was only fourteen in 1948—an Olympic Year. Coach took me to the U.S. National Olympic trials in Detroit, just for the experience. I qualified in eighth place for the finals but was not good enough to go to the Olympics.

It was a long, long haul of daily hard work, but I qualified for the 1952 Olympics in Helsinki, Finland. I won two bronze medals, one for the 400-meter freestyle and the other for the 4x100-meter relay. I attended only one other event there, because my mindset was to make the team and win a medal.

I attended UH as a freshman for a semester only, and then went to a mainland college on a swimming scholarship. What was most memorable was a number of very caring and kind people who reached out to me with love and hospitality. I'm also truly grateful to all the local people, including sportswriters, radio announcers, friends, relatives, and neighbors, who helped and supported me. Many people helped raise funds to enable me to travel to all the different swimming competitions. Mr. Kramer, for example, gave me a job at his clothing store so that I could earn enough to cover my numerous travel expenses. I'll never forget the kindness of all these people.

Interviewed on February 15, 2007

KEO NAKAMA

World record, mile swim
International Swimming Hall of Fame, 1975
First Moloka'i-O'ahu Channel swim, 1961

TOMMY KONO

Only Olympic Medalist in three Weight Divisions:
Gold, 1952 and 1956; Silver, 1960
Olympic Hall of Fame
One Hundred Golden Olympians, 1996
Seven Olympic and 26 World Records
World Champion, 1953, 1954, 1955, 1957, 1958, 1959
International Weightlifting Hall of Fame
Mr. World, 1954
Mr. Universe, 1955, 1957, and 1961

TOMMY TAMIO KONO
Olympic Champion and Mr. Universe

I was born in Sacramento in 1930 as the fourth and youngest son in the family. My father was a robust man, but I was a very sickly child with eczema as a baby; by two years of age I had asthma. I missed one-third of my grammar school days due to my asthmatic condition. I couldn't participate in physical-education class because physical exertion might bring on an asthmatic attack. Instead, I was required to report to a special darkened room to lie down on a cot for the duration of that period.

When World War II began, our family was sent to the relocation camp at Tule Lake in northern California. This move turned out to be good for my health. Living on a dried-up lake helped my asthma.

Ben Hara, our next-door neighbor at the camp, was into weight training, and I wanted to learn because I thought it would improve my health and build up muscles on my skinny physique. But my dad was opposed to the idea; he told me, How can you work with weights? You're so sickly." He told Ben not to encourage me; so my neighbor said to me, "It's up to you!" I had to sneak out to exercise with weights. I was lucky because I found I liked working with weights. I learned the basics of weight training at camp.

After three and a half years in the relocation camp, our family returned to Sacramento. Nobody I knew there had weights. The Buddhist church had a basketball league, so I participated, and that took me to the Sacramento YMCA where I heard the familiar "clang" of barbell plates. I scraped up enough money to join the Y and happily resumed weight training.

When I was a seventeen-year-old senior, I was invited to

1959 World Weightlifting Championship

T. Kono Collection

accompany an older friend to a weightlifting competition. Other lifters encouraged me by saying, "Why don't you enter, too, since you're going anyway?" So, I trained for two weeks, entered as the youngest member of the team, and took second place in my first competition. There was only one other lifter in my bodyweight class. It whetted my appetite and I realized, "I like this! There's no need to find other players, a team, or a court to keep improving myself."

It was amazing. After two years of lifting weights, at the age of twenty, I received world ranking! Then, the Korean War began, and I was classified as 3C physically because I wore glasses. After the army's short version of basic training, I could choose military schooling as a cook, a medic, or a clerk typist. I decided I'd become a cook because I could work one day and have the next day off for weight training.

The North Korean Army realized that cooks were important to the U.S. Army, for American soldiers' morale depended on the condition of their stomachs. So the North Koreans were targeting and shooting the cooks, and the United States needed to replace cooks on the front line. I was assigned to be shipped out and given two weeks off before reporting for overseas duty. When I returned, my friends, they said: "Hey, your name is on the list. You'll be going for the tryouts as a candidate for the Olympic Team." So, while the other guys were drunk the night before being sent overseas, I was asked, "Where would you like to be stationed?" Someone must have put in a good word for me, perhaps Bob Huffman, who was the coach of the U.S. Olympic Weightlifting Team.

I was assigned to Ft. Mason in the San Francisco area and was put in charge of exercising officers; I could also train for the Olympic tryouts. The army covered all my expenses when I was sent to New York for the tryouts. If I didn't make the team, I would be sent back to San Francisco. Fortunately, I made the team and went to Helsinki for the 1952 Olympics. At that time, the military's thinking was that athletes could do more for the country this way than through serving at the front lines. I feel that I did more for the United States by representing our country in the Olympics. It was good public relations for the country at this time for American athletes, especially U.S. Army personnel, to perform well because the Cold War was going strong with the Soviet Union. I felt that I was able to do more for the United States by winning an Olympic medal than by being a cook in North Korea. It proved to be a feather in the cap for the army.

Three days before the Olympics, I got a telegram from Washington D.C. stating that I was to report to Germany to fulfill the overseas assignment. I served there for one year before my army discharge. While stationed in Germany, I gave numerous exhibitions on weekends for the German public as a special guest-lifter at weekly league weightlifting competitions.

I first came to Hawai'i in 1953 for an exhibition and thought, "This is a nice place!" I came back in 1955, and I've lived here ever since, except for seven years when I was a national and Olympic coach in Mexico and West Germany. I had the privilege of visiting twenty-two countries around the world as a weightlifter, thirteen countries as a coach, eleven countries to conduct clinics, and ten countries as an official.

Interviewed March 28, 2007

HAROLD "ODD JOB" SAKATA

Silver, 1948 Olympics
"Odd Job" in James Bond movie *Goldfinger*
World-class professional wrestler "Tosh Togo"

JŪDŌ

KEVIN ASANO

Silver, 1988 Olympics

BASEBALL

STEERE NODA

Founder (at age 13), Asahi
Nisei Baseball Team
Inspiration for young AJA
players
State Representative,
1949–1958
State Senator, 1959–1962

Lillian Yajima Collection

293

HENRY TADASHI BOZO WAKABAYASHI

Three consecutive championships for Hosei
University, Tokyo Big Six Intercollegiate
Base League
First Japanese American in Japan
Professional League, 1936
MVP Japan Professional League, 1944 and
1947
Japan Baseball Hall of Fame, 1964

WALLY YONAMINE

Credit: Michael Okihiro

First post-war Japanese American player,
Japan Professional League
Eight championships in 10 seasons
MVP Japan Professional League, 1957
First foreign born manager, Japan
Professional League, 1972
Japan Baseball Hall of Fame, 1994
Donated $200,000 to Hawai'i High School
Athletic Foundation, 2006
"Living Treasure," Honpa Hongwanji
Mission of Hawai'i, 2007

LENN HARUKI SAKATA

First AJA in U.S. Major League
Shortstop, World Champion Baltimore
Orioles, 1983
Gonzaga Hall of Fame, 1988
Coach, Vancouver 1988–1990
"50 Greatest Sports Figures in Hawai'i,"
CNN Sports Illustrated, 2002

LENN HARUKI SAKATA
First AJA in Major League

While completing his junior year at Gonzaga University in Spokane, Washington, Lenn Sakata was drafted by the Milwaukee Brewers. He spent a few years in the minors, including a couple of years with Spokane as part of the Pacific Coast League, it was then that he had a chance to play before his family and friends in Hawai'i. In 1977 he was called up by the Milwaukee Brewers but only saw limited action. He was traded to the Baltimore Orioles and had a few good seasons with them, including 1983 when the Orioles won the World Series.

Sakata subsequently continued Major League play with Oakland Athletics and the New York Yankees before concluding his playing career of 545 games in 1987. During his eleven-year playing career in the majors, he is credited with 163 runs, 296 hits, 46 doubles, 4 triples, and 25 homeruns.

Sakata has since continued his baseball career as a manager or coach for various professional teams on the West Coast and in Japan. It is widely believed that he is probably only a step away from becoming the first Hawai'i-born Major League coach. Sakata has gained the respect of many for his unflinching love and commitment to baseball and for his patient and skillful teaching of the fundamentals to many prospective major league players.

As related by Dr. Michael Okihiro,
author of *AJA Baseball in Hawaii*

DEREK TATSUNO

First to win twenty games in a season
and 234 strikeouts, national records
Broke NCAA record by striking out
234 batters, 1979
First team All-American, 1978–1979
National College Baseball Hall of
Fame, 2007

TWO OUTSTANDING COACHES

LES MURAKAMI
University of Hawai'i's Famous Baseball Coach

Baseball coach Les Murakami began his career in 1971 as a part-time head coach. He began with minimal support for his team—no scholarships, no baseball field, and no equipment. During the next thirty years, he built an NCAA Division-I power with full scholarships, an on-campus stadium named after him, and an all-collegiate schedule. He became one of the best coaches in college baseball history, posting a total of 1,079 wins.

During his career, Murakami coached over four hundred college players; seventy-six of whom went on to play professional baseball, an enviable record. His induction into the American Baseball Coaches Association Hall of Fame in 2000 stands out among his many awards. Under his leadership, the University of Hawai'i team won the Western Athletic Conference Championship six times and went to the NCAA tournament eleven times. He has had an immeasurable impact on Hawai'i's baseball players and fans alike.

DAVE SHOJI
Renowned Women's Volleyball Coach

Mainland-born Dave Shoji has been the head volleyball coach at the University of Hawai'i since 1975. Since then, his teams have attained national recognition as a perennial ranked NCAA team

Coach with an enthusiastic enrollee in 2006 UH summer clinic

Photo by Neal Hazama

and have won four NCAA championships under his skillful guidance. His teams have won twenty games or more twenty-six times and he has coached thirty-five All-Americans. A few have gone on to play at the international level.

Of all active head volleyball coaches, he has the highest winning percentage in his thirty-year coaching career. Besides numerous Coach of the Year honors, he received the prestigious USA Volleyball All-Time Great Coach Award. His dedication to his players, on and off the court, has been an inspiration to his players and has had a major impact on younger athletes as well. Interest in volleyball in the Hawaiian Islands has soared with the widespread exposure of Coach Shoji and his players due to much-anticipated televised games and tournaments. He and his volleyball players have also nurtured youths through clinics and community outreach.

OTHER WORLD CLASS ATHLETES

Bowling

HIROTO "HIRO" HIRASHIMA

Pioneer in obtaining equal rights for Japanese-American bowlers
and other minorities
American Bowling Congress (ABC) Hall of Fame, 1965
First minority on ABC Board of Directors
Founder, Hawai'i State Bowling Association

KOTARO "TARO" MIYASATO

Seven-time Hawai'i Match Game Champion
Sanctioned 300 game at the All-Star Tournament
in Philadelphia, 1965

<u>Weightlifting</u>

EMERICK K. ISHIKAWA

World record, U.S. National Weightlifting Championships, 1944

<u>Boxing</u>

PAUL FUJII

World Boxing Association Junior Welterweight Champion

<u>Long-distance Running</u>

NORMAN K. TAMANAHA

"Father of Long-Distance Running" in Hawai'i
Fifth Boston Marathon at age forty-five, 1952

Kotaka Collection

<u>Karate</u>

GEORGE KOTAKA

Gold Medal, World Karate Federation Championships, 2002
(Recognized by International Olympic Committee)
Passion for teaching youth at International Karate Foundation
which was established in 1966 by his father, Chuzo, a renowned
sensei and champion.

Golf

DAVID ISHII

University of Houston NCAA championship team, 1977
Hawaiian Open Gold Tournament Champion, 1990
Five Japan Airlines Rainbow Open titles
Twelve Japan PGA titles
Six Hawai'i Pearl Open titles
Two Mid Pacific Open championships

DEAN HIROSHI WILSON

Afuji Cup title, 2000
Japan PGA Championship title, 2001
Japan PGA Match Play Champion, 2001
UBE Kosan Cup title, 2001
Tsuruya Open title, 2002
Gateway to the Open-Mizuno Open title, 2002
Champions' Challenges 2003 and 2004 with Mike Weir
The International champion, 2006
Top 30 on the money list, 2006

Wilson Collection

TADD FUJIKAWA

American Junior Golf's Second Team All-American, 2006
O'ahu's U.S. Open qualifier, beating professionals and amateurs, 2006
Sony Open qualifier, 2007, youngest amateur in fifty years on PGA Tour
Hawai'i Pearl Open title, 2007
50th Annual Mid-Pacific Open winner and youngest champion, 2008

TADD FUJIKAWA
Up and Coming Golf Star

In January 2007, Tadd Fujikawa, a sixteen-year-old Moanalua High School sophomore, gave everyone something to cheer about when he not only made the cut at the Sony Open but also did so as the youngest amateur in fifty years on the PGA tour. After being as high as fourth place and playing in front of a large gallery of fans, he then went on to tie for twentieth place against some of the best professional golfers. The following month, he showed that his talent was for real by stunning everyone with a victory at the 29th annual Pearl Open, considered by many to be the toughest local tournament.

Three generations celebrate yonsei Tadd Fujikawa's win.

Fujikawa Collection

In a *Honolulu Advertiser* article, Garret Hayashi, Tadd's Mid Pacific Country Club golf coach and caddie during the Sony and Pearl Opens, is quoted as saying, "The best part of his game is his mental approach. He is really mentally tough. To him, anything is possible. It's fearless golf. Him being sixteen, I think, has a little to do with it, but a lot of it is just Tadd."

In addition to his exceptional gift for golf, his engaging smile and personality also endear him to his fans and fellow golfers. He is described as exuberant, unfailingly courteous, and respectful to fellow golfers, fans, and golf course staff. He is always humble and appreciates learning from professionals. Tadd signed autographs hours after the Sony Open and wrote a thank-you letter to "Officers, Directors, Members, Staff, Sony Open Volunteers, Fellow Golfers and Caddie." He is genuine in his appreciation of others and so are his parents, Lori and Derrick Fujikawa, who raised their only child to be what he is today. Lori was quoted as saying, "We will never forget all that the people of Hawai'i have done for us."

According to his mom, Lori, five-foot one-inch Tadd Fujikawa was premature, a 26-week baby at birth. He was given only a 50-50 chance to survive. There was the added fear that he might never be normal. At age three, he started jūdō lessons and became a four-time national champion. At one point, he even aspired to go to the Olympics in jūdō. His parents, who golfed for fun, started him on golf lessons at age eight to strengthen his forearms for jūdō. Tadd took to golf and by age eleven, he had to choose between it and jūdō. He felt he had accomplished what he wanted to do in jūdō, so he turned his sights to golf. It was his decision to make, and his parents accepted it.

Tadd practices golf every day. His mom said, "For golf, he has sacrificed being with friends, like going to the movies with them." In 2006, he was an American Junior Golf's Second Team All American and was Hawai'i's U.S. Open qualifier, the youngest ever to play in the U.S. Open. In 2005, he decided to make a sacrifice and chose to move up to the next age division. When the American Junior Golf Tournament was cancelled due to Hurricane Katrina, the decision seemed like a mistake; but it was eventually rescheduled, and he came in third. He then placed second in a tournament in Georgia, firmly establishing himself at the national level. So, his decision paid off after all; and from the end of 2005 to 2007, his game has improved.

He continues to practice and work very hard. His mom recalled, "In December 2006, when Tadd qualified for Sony Open's one exemption spot for an amateur; he worked even harder and sacrificed his Christmas day and evening and the same for New Year's in order to practice."

Tadd has been featured in *Sports Illustrated* and appeared on the cover of *Golfweek* and *Golf World* magazines. He has been on the national golf channel on television and has had international coverage in Japan, Korea, and China. With his family's support, Tadd took the bold step of turning pro on July 12, 2007 at age 16. he became the youngest player to record a hole-in-hole in the 18 year history of the Nationwide Tour on September 21, 2007. On April 21, 2008, at age 17, he won his first tournament as a pro in the 50th annual Mid-Pacific Open and became its youngest champion in four years. Golf fans locally, nationally, and internationally are eagerly waiting to see more of Hawai'i's young golf phenomenon who has created so much interest and excitement in his sport.

Sources: Interview on April 13, 2007
Additional material from *The Honolulu Advertiser* [xiv]

MILITARY

GENERAL ERIC K. SHINSEKI
First Asian American Chief of Staff

General Eric K. Shinseki

Hawai'i Herald

"My name is Shinseki—and I am a soldier." This is how the army's thirty-fourth chief of staff, General Eric Shinseki, introduces himself to his audience. He is the first American of Asian ancestry to attain the rank of full general and the first to be appointed to the army's top job, chief of staff.

As army chief of staff, General Shinseki sought to transform the army to be better able to respond swiftly to catastrophes world-wide. World conditions changed drastically since the end of World War II, and conventional tactics and equipment of that era were no longer effective. He advocated a more mobile army, using Stryker Brigade Combat Teams equipped with upgraded procedures, equipment, and ammunition. His effective appeal to Congress resulted in billions of dollars toward the transformation. Throughout his four years (1999–2003) as chief of staff, General Shinseki did not waiver from his commitment to transformation even while he fielded objections from the highest levels of government.

A West Point graduate, he is a thrice-wounded veteran of the Vietnam War. During his army career, General Shinseki served in various command and staff posts in the United States and Europe, with both U.S. and NATO forces. He was also assigned to various posts in the Pentagon.

Eric Ken Shinseki was born in Līhuʻe, Kauaʻi, in November 1942 and was educated in Hawaiʻi's public schools. Upon graduation from high school he was appointed to the Military Academy at West Point and graduated in 1965 with a Bachelor of Science Degree. He earned a Master's Degree in English Literature from Duke University and later taught at West Point. In his rise to the top position in the army, he has also matriculated at the Armor Officer Advanced Course, the U.S. Army Command and General Staff College, and the National War College.

General Shinseki credits and expresses gratitude to the members of Tom Brokaw's "greatest generation", particularly:

> the members of the 442nd ,100th Battalion, Military Intelligence Service, and the 1399th Engineers for having bought for me and my generation our birthrights as American citizens. Because of what they and others of their generation did on those distant battlefields so many years ago, I have lived my life without suspicion, without limitation, with the full rights and privileges of citizenship, and with the opportunity to compete.

To honor this great and humble soldier and strategist, the Hawaii Army Museum Society, in conjunction with the U.S. Army Museum, has established the Shinseki Gallery in Battery Randolph at Ft. De Russey in Waikīkī and has commissioned military correspondent Richard Halloran to write a biography of him. An Endowment Fund in the name of General Shinseki has also been established in the Public Schools of Hawaiʻi Foundation.

"Is Eric K. Shinseki the Next Great AA Leader?," April 21, 2003 http://www.goldsea.com/Air/Issues/Shinseki/Shinseki.html

---

CAPTAIN BRUCE I. YAMASHITA

Bruce I. Yamashita's academic credentials include a B.A. from the University of Hawaiʻi, a year at the International Christian University (ICU) in Japan, and a degree in law and international relations from Georgetown University. In 1989, the thirty-two-year-old *sansei* from Hawaiʻi reported to the Marine Corps Officer Candidate School (OCS) in Quantico, Virginia, to achieve his goal of serving his country as an officer in the U.S. Marine Corps. Aware of the rigorous physical program at OCS, Yamashita had trained

Captain Bruce I. Yamashita, USMC challenged the establishment to fight for justice.

Hawai'i Herald

vigorously prior to enrollment. He was also aware of the deliberate harassment to build character that was part of the training program. From the first day he found himself to be the butt of ethnic jokes and derogatory and demeaning taunts by the trainer sergeants, including the following:

"You speak English?"
"We don't want your kind around here. Go back to your country."
"During World War II, we whipped your Japanese ass."
"Yamashita, quit bowing. This is America, man."[xv]

One sergeant even spoke to him in Japanese throughout the nine-week training period and insisted that the reply be made in Japanese. A fellow trainee who had witnessed the daily harassment remarked, "Why didn't you just join the Japanese Army?" At first he thought the harassment was part of the training, but soon realized that he was being singled out, and that the remarks were racial.

Yamashita endured the unfair and demeaning treatment and kept his focus on becoming an officer in the Marine Corps. He was certain that he was passing all academic and physical tests and would soon receive his commission. However, two days before graduation, he was notified that he had been disenrolled and would not be graduating because of unsatisfactory leadership. The assessment had been made by his fellow trainees, who had been influenced by the demeaning and derogatory treatment toward him.

Shocked, dejected, and confused, Yamashita returned to Hawai'i where he passed the bar exam. His thoughts, however, were on his experiences at OCS. At first he found it difficult to share his deepest thoughts, but the situation changed when he learned that racial discrimination and harassment were forbidden at the army's OCS.

Yamashita embarked on a campaign in June 1990 to bring the unfair treatment that he had endured to the attention of the Marine Corps, not only because he believed he deserved the commission, but also because he did not want anyone else to receive the kind of treatment he had received. He wrote letters, made telephone calls, and talked face to face with many whom he thought could help with righting the wrong. He was reassured many times that the Marine Corps policies were based on fair treatment and that race and gender discrimination had no place there. His complaints were downplayed and there was no action. During one encounter, it was even suggested that he was trying to fault others for his failure.

Believing that the racial harassment was unjust, the Hawai'i Legislature in 1991 asked Congress to commission Yamashita and to punish the Marine officers who had inflicted the unfair treatment. Through Sen. Dan Inouye's efforts, Congress passed legislation requiring Defense Department schools to certify that "appropriate measures have been taken to publish and enforce" regulations prohibiting racial discrimination. The Japanese American Citizen's League (JACL) also became a major part of the protest and used all of its resources to bring about justice.

A ten-month investigation by the Navy Inspector General verified that "some rather crude remarks based on his ethnicity" were made that "were uncalled for," and a formal apology was issued. On March 18, 1994, after a four-year effort, Bruce Yamashita was finally commissioned as a captain in the Marine Corps.

Yamashita followed his belief that "patriotism is not just going off to war. Sometimes we have to fight the cause in many different ways." He is indeed an American, one who is aware not only of his rights, but also of his responsibilities.

Source: *Honolulu Star-Bulletin* [xvi]
and *San Francisco Examiner* [xvii]

Lt. Ehren Watada risked his career to follow his convictions.

LT. EHREN WATADA

After working hard to achieve his rank in the military and after careful and painful deliberations, twenty-eight-year-old Hawai'i resident and 1996 Kalani High School graduate Lt. Ehren Watada made a life-changing decision, fully realizing that the consequences could lead him to a court-martial, a possible prison term, and a dishonorable discharge. In June 2006, Watada's courageous actions and pronouncements became national news and attracted international attention on the already controversial war in Iraq. He became the first officer to publicly refuse deployment to Iraq. He was charged with that and four charges of conduct unbecoming an officer for his statements against the war.

During pretrial court hearings in the case, Watada's attorney, Eric Seitz, sought an opportunity to argue the legality of the war, saying it violated army regulations that specify wars are to be waged in accordance with the United Nations charter. However, in January 2007, Military Judge Lt. Colonel John Head ruled against this; Lt. Watada and his lawyer were denied the opportunity to debate the legality of the war in Iraq. The judge also barred several experts in international and constitutional law from testifying about the legality of the war. Seitz stated that the proceedings were "almost comical" and "an atrocity." He concluded: "There's really nothing for us to say in this courtroom." Seitz and Watada rejected a plea deal that would have resulted in the equivalency of a dishonorable discharge and an eighteen-month prison term.

The anxiously awaited trial for Watada's court martial began on February 5, 2007. On the third day, when Watada was scheduled to

307

take the stand in his own defense, Judge Lt. Colonel Head unexpectedly announced a mistrial despite the fact that both sides were in agreement that the case could move forward. Seitz responded that he would seek dismissal of the charges on double jeopardy grounds and was prepared to appeal the case all the way to the U.S. Supreme Court if necessary.

In response to the Army refiling all charges, the defense sought dismissal on double jeopardy grounds, which was denied. After unsuccessful appeal through the military court, a civilian federal district court issued a preliminary injunction on November 8, 2007 to halt Watada's retrial. A final decision is still pending.

Watada's case caused a heated polarization of opinions worldwide. Antiwar groups across the United States applauded his actions and supported him while some members of the military and their families as well as some veterans felt he had no right to decide the legality of the war. Locally, a representative of CodePINK, which had maintained a vigil for Watada outside Honolulu's Federal Building during the trial, said the mistrial was "an incredible turn of events."

The newspaper *Military Families Voice of Victory,* a critic of Watada, quoted a few *nisei* veterans' reactions recorded in California that called Watada's refusal to deploy "a shameful act," "a disgrace," and "bringing shame upon Japanese Americans."

At a panel discussion at the JCCH, "1st Lt. Ehren Watada: Dissenter or Deserter?" Dr. Jonathan Okamura of the Ethnic Studies Department of the University of Hawai'i at Mānoa provided a historical overview of prior acts of dissent against participation in the U.S. military by Japanese Americans. He cited draft resistance in internment camps during World War II and the "burn the draft cards" campaign during the Vietnam War in which several *sansei* participated.

1st Lt. Watada eloquently presented this challenge to all Americans:

> Apathy and detachment from this war by the majority of the American people has been the basis for this tragedy from the start. Whether you agree with me or not, I only ask that [you]...find out everything there is to know about this war, take a position one way or another, and if you believe that this war is illegal and immoral—ask yourself what you are willing to do to stop it. The American citizen owes that to the soldiers who are fighting and dying in Iraq every day.[xviii]

Sources: Karen Kakasone, JACL Honolulu Chapter, *The Honolulu Advertiser* [xix]

PRESERVING OUR HERITAGE

*Dr. Dennis Ogawa
Collection*

*Dr. Dennis Ogawa has successfully
excelled in two separate worlds—
academia and business—with a common goal of building pride in self
and the diverse local community.*

DR. DENNIS M. OGAWA
Academic and Entrepreneur

Soon after he arrived at the University of Hawai'i as an instructor in speech communication, Dr. Dennis Ogawa was involved in advocating the establishment of an Ethnic Studies Department. He served as its first chairman for two years (1970–1972) before transferring to the American Studies department. In the classroom as well as at lectures and workshops in the community, he talked about pride in one's identity and diversity as an integral part of Americanism. His classes in Japanese Americans in Hawai'i taught students, particularly the large numbers of *sansei* Japanese Americans, that they were not any less American when they believed and practiced their parents' values and customs. He introduced the terms multiethnic and multicultural as well as such values as *okage sama de* (I am what I am because of you) and *kodomo no tame ni* (for the sake of the children). His classes at the University helped legitimize diversity and its relevance to the spirit of aloha.

In 1982, Dr. Ogawa chanced upon a collection of 28,000 photos from the *Nippu Jiji,* known later as *The Hawai'i Times,* a leading

Japanese-language newspaper. He rescued them from going to the rubbish heap and established the Hawai'i Times Photo Archives Foundation to preserve and make the photos accessible to the public.

Dr. Ogawa's publications include: *From Jap to Japanese: The Evolution of Japanese American Stereotypes* (1971); *Jan Ken Po: The World of Hawai'i's Japanese Americans* (1973); *Kodomo no tame ni: For the Sake of the Children* (1978); *Ellison Onizuka: A Remembrance* (1986); *Hawai'i's YAKUDOSHI Guide Book* (1990); *An Unlikely Revolutionary: Matsuo Takabuki and the Making of Modern Hawai'i* (1996); and *First Among the Nisei—Masaji Marumoto* (2007).

Even while teaching large classes, Dr. Ogawa participated in the wider Hawai'i community. Forever the educator, he started a paid prime-time Japanese cable channel to enhance cultural ties with Japan, thereby strengthening cultural diversity in Hawai'i. Programming for the new Hawai'i channel, Nippon Golden Network (NGN), includes highly rated newscasts and films. The number of subscribers grew from five thousand in 1982 to well over eighteen thousand by 1996. One of NGN's most widely viewed programs shows the same-day quarterly sumō tournaments, which are popular with persons of varied ethnicities. According to Dr. Ogawa, "The switchboard at NGN lights up like a Christmas tree whenever there are interruptions in the showing of the sumō programs."

When queried about his reasons for coming to Hawai'i from California, Dr. Ogawa replied,

> I had wanted to teach at the University of Hawai'i ever since an earlier trip here when I met some local residents. They were so welcoming—so open, caring, and giving. They literally took me in with open arms. I knew then that I wanted to be a part of this very special place that I could call home. It was *the* place for me and my family. It's been about forty years, but I still feel the same about this place. I am glad that I came.

Over the years, Dr. Ogawa has provided leadership in promoting diversity in Hawai'i, resulting in Hawai'i's reputation as the showcase of multiethnicity and multiculturalism. He came as a *kotonk* (mainland *nikkei*) but has transformed into a son of Hawai'i and a *kama'aina* in spirit.

Interviewed April 25, 2007

The 1985 celebration of the arrival of the *Kanyaku Imin* (Government Contract Workers) finally enabled the reluctant *issei* and *nisei* to see that they had played important roles in the development of Hawai'i. They gradually regained their pride in their ancestors as well as in their achievements. They began to share their stories but also realized the urgency to gather more stories as well as rapidly disappearing artifacts to preserve for both future generations of Japanese Americans and the wider multiethnic community.

Thus, they established the following organizations to carry out their mission of preservation and dissemination of the history and culture of the Japanese in Hawai'i.

JAPANESE CULTURAL CENTER OF HAWAI'I (JCCH)

The Honolulu-based Japanese Cultural Center of Hawai'i, established in 1986, strives to "be a vibrant resource, strengthening our diverse community by educating present and future generations in the evolving Japanese-American experience in Hawai'i." JCCH has been realizing its mission objectives through diverse means, which are open to all interested persons.

The permanent exhibit Okage Sama De showcases the over one hundred year Japanese experience in Hawai'i in the historical gallery. The adjacent community gallery features short-term exhibits detailing specifics of the Japanese experience. Ancillary offerings such as lectures and panel discussions augment the exhibits. This arrival scene shows an immigrant family with its baggage as well as their important passports and contracts.

JCCH

311

The Collections Committee receives, catalogues, documents, and stores historically and culturally significant artifacts donated by the public. Collections are used for exhibits as well as for the popular outreach programs of discovery boxes for the schools and rediscovery boxes for the elderly. Depicted here is a student trying on a kimono, probably a first-time experience.

JCCH

The Resource Center is the primary repository for materials that document the evolving Japanese American experience: books in English and Japanese; photos; archival collections of manuscripts, periodicals, pamphlets, and AV materials; videotaped interviews, diaries, and journals; and oral history transcripts.

The volunteer staff fields questions and serves as a source of information for the community. They also conduct some research. The traveling exhibit "Dark Clouds over Paradise" was researched and organized by JCCH volunteers. In their effort to preserve former World War II internment sites, the Resource Center's Hawai'i Confinement Sites Committee is currently involved in fieldwork to identify internment camps in Hawai'i. In this photo, they are trying to locate evidence of the exact location of the internment camp at Hono'uli'uli on O'ahu.

JCCH

312

Local Japanese festivals are celebrated throughout the year with multiethnic partici-
pants and have become fun ways for people to learn about the Japanese culture in
Hawai'i. The New Year's Festival located at JCCH and at neighboring Mō'ili'ili
Field draws more than ten thousand participants annually. In the Japanese tradition,
mochi is a must for New Year, as it symbolizes strength and cohesiveness for the
family. Other demonstrations, hands-on activities, sales, and performances also share
aspects of the Japanese culture as practiced in Hawai'i.

JCCH

Since its inception in 1989, JCCH in partnership with the Hawai'i Hiroshima
Heritage Study Group (H3SG) has conducted twenty-five workshops for over two
thousand participants statewide. Dr. Bernice Hirai shares a koseki tōhon, a family reg-
ister, with workshop participants in Hilo. Through the workshops, hundreds of fami-
lies have been able to compile their genealogies.

JCCH

HAWAI'I UNITED OKINAWA ASSOCIATION (HUOA)

The Hawai'i United Okinawa Association is the umbrella organization for fifty locality and interest clubs statewide. It counts on the involvement of the members of its member clubs in all of its activities. HUOA's facilities are located in the Waipi'o Gentry Business Park in Central O'ahu.

The large Albert T. and Wallace T. Teruya Pavilion hosts many cultural performances, conferences, classes, banquets, and receptions. Its entrance is guarded by shiisaa, a lion, by Okinawan ceramist Isamu Nakamura, of clay mixed with soil from various parts of Hawai'i and Okinawa.

A second building, the Yeiko and Kameko Higa Building, houses the HUOA offices, a display area for historical and cultural artifacts, meeting rooms, and a gift shop.

HUOA

A bevy of colorful banners representative of the fifty Okinawan locality and interest clubs belonging to HUOA adds color to a parade in Waikīkī. Each is held by a representative of the club. The banners are also used at picnics, festivals, and other community events.

HUOA

314

Classical dance performances at the annual Okinawa Festival. Note elaborate costumes and hairdos.

The Issei Garden honors the Okinawan immigrants who were recruited by Kyūzō Toyama, the father of Okinawan immigration. The inscription on the boulder depicts Toyama's vision: "Let us set out and let the five continents be our vision."

The Maui Okinawa Cultural Center, a HUOA member organization, founded in 1992 displays household furnishings, tools, and musical instruments honoring the first-generation immigrants and their descendants.

HAWAI'I JAPANESE CENTER

The Hawai'i Japanese Center in Hilo was organized as a successor to the Hawai'i Shima Japanese Immigrant Museum, which had been established earlier by Mr. Kiyoshi Ōkubo, long-time editor and publisher of the *Hilo Times*. The Center's collection includes his extensive collection of books, newspapers, artifacts, and other memorabilia as well as significant materials donated by others. Currently serving as president is Dr. Masafumi Honda, Associate Professor of Japanese Studies at the University of Hawai'i at Hilo.

The new Hawai'i Japanese Center (HJC) is located near Hilo Airport in a former warehouse. Advisor Gladys Sonomura says, "It's remarkable! The warehouse is being transformed by volunteers into a community center, one in which lectures, exhibits, and meetings will be held." HJC opened in late fall 2007.

HJC

The Hawai'i Japanese Center conducted this annual Kamon Workshop in September 2006. The workshop drew many participants from the community who were eager to find their family crests. It is interesting to note that most of the members of this particular group are students from Waseda University, Tokyo Kasei University, and Tokyo Gakugei University. They were joined by local students from the University of Hawai'i at Hilo.

HJC

316

OTHER MUSEUM SOURCES

Although the previously discussed organizations have the only galleries in Hawai'i focused solely on the Japanese experience, there are some other important museum sources where valuable information about early Japanese immigrants is available.

A glimpse into one of the exhibit rooms shows the scale model of a half-roofed plantation house, which allows the visitor to view the interior. A pair of fighting cocks is visible in the background.

A&B Sugar Museum

Alexander & Baldwin Sugar Museum

The Alexander & Baldwin Sugar Museum in Pu'unēnē, Maui, is well worth visiting. It is dedicated to preserving and presenting the history and heritage of the sugar industry and the multiethnic plantation life that it engendered. It has accomplished these goals in a creative, intriguing, and interesting manner.

The Alexander & Baldwin Sugar Museum encompasses six exhibit rooms in a former plantation house, which adds a unique character and flavor. The Plantation Room includes photos and fascinating exhibits showing the rich, multiethnic nature of plantation communities and plantation life, including such artifacts as religious and household items, and an outstanding scale model of a worker's camp house, a star attraction. A video presentation created by an award-winning filmmaker shows how cane is processed into sugar.

The museum opened its doors to the public in 1987 under the capable directorship of Gaylord Kubota, who continues to serve to this day. It has received local, state, and national recognition for its imaginative exhibits and exceptional contributions. Awards include a Certificate of Commendation from the American Association for State and Local History, a State Preservation Award from the Historic Hawai'i Foundation, two Kāhili Awards from the Hawai'i Visitors' Bureau including the Kāhili Award for Architecture and Interior Design in 1993, and several Preservation Awards from the Maui Historical Society. After a traveling historical photo exhibit was displayed at the Smithsonian's Festival of American Folklife on the National Mall in Washington, D.C., the A&B Sugar Museum received a Certificate of Appreciation.

Reenactment of washing and bleaching rice bags to recycle for other uses.
Hawai'i's Plantation Village

The Hawai'i's Plantation Village

The Hawai'i's Plantation Village in Waipahu, O'ahu, is a unique and interesting museum: it is a walking museum with thirty-two authentic structural replicas and a few original buildings, spread out across fifty acres. It is the only museum on O'ahu dedicated to preserving and showcasing the lifestyles of Hawai'i's multiethnic sugar plantation workers.

A central gallery with displays of fascinating artifacts and relics and information on arrivals is among the attractions to the Village, but the most unique aspect here is the outdoor walking tour, which takes a visitor back in time into fully furnished homes of Hawaiian, Chinese, Portuguese, Puerto Rican, Japanese, Okinawan, Korean, and Filipino immigrants. There are also community buildings, taro patches, and other gardens from the plantation era. *Kama'aina* can come away with a deeper understanding and appreciation of our roots by walking inside the small kitchens, living rooms, and bedrooms furnished with artifacts from the plantation days.

The educational organization was established in 1976 under the visionary leadership of "Major" Okada, in collaboration with community members who had labored on the plantations and with the support of local government officials. The Hawai'i's Plantation Village is a valuable resource for our schools. Since it opened in 1992, 190,000 students have visited the Village.

Neighbor Island Museums

The Lyman House Memorial Museum in Hilo and the Kaua'i Museum have Japanese immigrant artifacts on display among broader coverage of Hawaiian Culture and History. At the Grove Farm Homestead on Kaua'i, a visitor can walk into a furnished Japanese cottage on the grounds; researchers are welcome to use the Grove Farm Plantation Records and Papers left by the Wilcox family. This invaluable repository includes information about Japanese laborers.

OUR ENVIRONMENT

Like other immigrant groups, in a relatively short period of time the *nikkei* have been successful in many endeavors and have contributed much to progress locally, nationally, and globally. We have worked hard, seized opportunities, and utilized our creative minds effectively. As we face the future, we must not only be concerned with our advancement, but also remind ourselves of our responsibilities as stewards of Planet Earth. The planet must sustain not only the present population, but equally, if not more importantly, future generations.

Scientists, environmentalists, and philosophers repeatedly remind us that the damages we have inflicted on the planet have attendant negative consequences. We are currently witnessing global climatic changes that have resulted in increasing numbers of hurricanes, floods, water shortages, parched lands, and poor air quality. Unless something is done now to curb and eliminate these negative conditions, the planet, and especially our islands, will eventually be unable to sustain life.

Most of the world's leading countries have investigated or are investigating the problem individually or with others and have begun to make changes that will lessen the current negative impact. Much more needs to be done, and all efforts must be expended to act faster and to bring more nations and people into the common effort.

One local architectural firm, John Hara Associates, Inc., has been designing structures with sustainable features for almost forty years. The Honolulu Board of Water Supply and Hawaiian Electric Company have been reminding the public to conserve water and electricity. The City and County of Honolulu as well as some businesses have encouraged their workers to take the bus or carpool.

As individuals we, too, must take up the challenge to use less water, electricity, and gas. Turning off the faucet immediately, using energy-efficient appliances wisely, and using compact fluorescent light bulbs are examples of everyday changes that will not only improve our lives, but certainly help toward saving the planet for future generations. We can also recycle paper, aluminum, glass, and plastic so new resources would not have to be tapped. In the meantime, we must be prepared to deal with disasters by having emergency supplies ready and by protecting our homes from structural damages.

Most of us have heard of these measures, but the question that remains is how many of us have acted on these solutions? Now is the time to begin if we have not already done so.

John Hara, SAIA
Award-Winning Architect

Sansei architect John Hara has incorporated innovative designs and sustainable features into his projects for close to forty years. In November 2006, Hara was honored with the State Governor's Award for Distinguished Achievement in Culture and the Arts, its highest individual award and the first given to an architect. His ailing father, himself a multi award-winning architect, was in attendance.

While a student at Punahou School, he developed his interest in music and played the oboe in the Honolulu Symphony as a sophomore. At the University of Pennsylvania, he pursued both architecture and music. He finally decided on architecture and worked and studied in Europe for two years before returning to Hawaiʻi. A walk through the state-of-the-art Case Middle School on the Punahou hillside makes one realize how truly fortunate the people of Hawaiʻi are that he decided to become an architect and to return home.

Hara explained that architects have always been concerned with the environment, but ecology was the term being used earlier. Now people talk about sustainability. The islands are blessed with much sunshine and trade winds, so it is natural to take advantage of these factors in building structures that are open. He added that, in 1980, when designing the Punahou gym, he incorporated natural lighting through the roof, used daylight for heating water, and featured other ecological elements. Recently, the savings from these features were computed to be in the millions of dollars over the years.

He said that a nationwide certification system known as LEED

321

(Leadership in Energy Environmental Design) has been established. His design for the Case Middle School at Punahou became Hawai'i's first—one of only a few nationwide—to achieve LEED's prestigious Gold status for Design. Self-regulating air conditioners and lighting; a unique chiller system which produces ice at night when Hawaiian Electric (HECO) offers discounts and uses it for cooling during the day; innovative water conservation devices such as waterless urinals and low-flow toilets; and components made of recycled rubber and milk cartons are but a few of the sustainable features. Among the awards that the firm received in 2005-2006 are: the AIA Sustainablility, AIA Mayor's Choice, Build Hawai'i Merit, HECO's Project of the Year and Innovation in Design. [i]

John Hara has truly made his mark as the architect for the present and the future with his worldview of architectural design with a strong Asian—especially Japanese—influence and with his practical contributions toward the conservation of energy and natural resources. His greatest "once in a lifetime" challenge is in the immediate future as the designated architect for the 500-acre University of Hawai'i–West O'ahu campus. Hara said, "The campus should replicate the sense of what was there. Because of the history of the area, I feel strongly it is appropriate to have a sense of place. This was a plantation." Thus, when enrolled at the new West O'ahu campus, students of all ages will learn to appreciate the beauty of the architectural design and the importance of sustainability, thanks to the designs of John Hara's "green" buildings.

Interviewed on May 9, 2007

HOPES AND DREAMS
A Letter to Youths of Japanese Descent

You have been and you continue to be a very important part of our lives. Your living enriching, fulfilling, and contributing lives means a great deal to us. We have in our own limited ways tried to contribute to your well being as well as that of our community and nation. But in you, we see our hopes and dreams for an even better Hawai'i and an even better world. Allow us to share with you some of our thoughts as we conclude our story about the struggles and successes of the Japanese in Hawai'i.

Okage same de, we were born into a rich and unique multicultural society and into families that treasure children. As you seek your identity and develop your potential to become responsible, participating citizens, we hope that you will select wisely to retain the best that each of the cultures – your American heritage, your Japanese legacy, and the local culture, a product of the sharing of the different ethnic groups – has to offer.

Okage sama de, we do live in the best country in the world. True, as Japanese in America, we have faced some injustices. But so have the other immigrant groups. The courage and perseverance of our predecessors and peers have brought us to this junction in which you have a greater number of options available to you. We hope that whatever paths you opt for, you will always stand up for freedom, for equality, and for justice for all. We hope that you will retain those values that have proven to be the strengths in the legacy from your grandparents and your parents, some of which are the belief in strong family ties, hard work, and perserverance *(ganbari)*, education, and sensitivity and humility in relating to others.

There have been aspects of our Japaneseness that have tended to inhibit many of us from reaching our fullest potential, especially the over-humbleness and modesty that have eroded our self-confidence and self-image, and the lack of risk-taking and experimentation for fear of failure and attendant *haji* (shame). We hope that you will be flexible and versatile in judging the time and place for humbleness and assertiveness, for leadership and for followership, as well as for certainty and uncertainty. We hope that you will know when to be dependent on your family *(amaeru)* and when to assert your independence.

For many of our generation, the inadequacy of our communication skills prevented us from articulating our thoughts and ideas. Many times this deficiency made others look upon us negatively and suspiciously. You have much to share. You have increasing opportunities to share your insights, concerns, and feelings. Make the most of them by becoming effective communicators. There is a place for standard English, for Japanese, as well as for pidgin. Know each well and use it appropriately.

Okage sama de, our adventuresome forebearers by historical accident came to one of the most beautiful places in the world whose people with their aloha have been extremely accepting of all peoples. There is a great deal we can gain by adopting their concepts of *mana* (spiritual energy bestowed from a supernatural source which can be increased or decreased depending on use), *kōkua* (help), *laulima* (cooperation), *lokomaika'i* (generosity), and *lōkahi* (harmony and balance) among many others. We can also benefit from their respect for their land *('āina)* and its resources.

As we Japanese in Hawai'i achieved some measure of success in schools, in the professions, in politics, and in business, we have also incurred animosity from some members of other ethnic groups. We hope that you will allay this negativism by your caring, your sense of fair play, and your willingness to help them. Unless all peoples have a sense of security and identity, the racial harmony that Hawai'i stands for will elude us forever.

In our youth, our parents thought that we were lacking in appreciation and did not know the meaning of *okage sama de.* It has taken time, many experiences, and maturity for us to realize that we are what we are and where we are because of many people, including our parents.

With time and maturity, we have found that we who are Japanese Americans are fortunate indeed! Our lives are blessed with the bests that many peoples and heritages have to offer. We hope that you, too, will grow to the same appreciation. It is our desire that this book, in some small way, will strengthen your identity as a Japanese in Hawai'i and will extend your appreciation of your legacy and heritage. Then we hope that your identity and appreciation will enable you to give of yourselves to building a better and better Hawai'i and world for all.

Afterword

It is an honor to be asked to write the afterword of this new edition of *Okage Sama De:, The Japanese in Hawai'i.* We are grateful to the authors, Jane Komeiji and Dorothy Hazama, who by sharing and recording their own stories as part of the history of the Japanese coming to Hawai'i, have created an invaluable gift not only for their children but for many generations to come.

At its simplest, *okage sama de* can be translated to mean gratitude and appreciation. But the nuances of this very Japanese phrase mean much more. *Okage sama de* is gratitude coupled with the highest respect and admiration. It is recognition of a generous debt owed that can never be fully repaid. As documented in the book, the *issei* came to Hawai'i dreaming of opportunity and a better life. We—*nisei, sansei, yonsei, gosei*—are what we are because of the hard work, sacrifice, and dedication of the *issei.*

When I was 8 eight years old, my mother left Japan for Hawai'i with my two brothers and me. Our life in Japan had been a struggle. For most of my eight years, Because ofdue to family circumstances, for most of my eight years, I lived with my maternal grandparents and was very close to my grandmother. I remember crying for days after I left her on the dock at Yokohama as we sailed to Hawai'i.

Traveling in steerage on the *SS President Cleveland,* I had my first taste of pink strawberry ice cream and experienced a shower after years of *furo* bathing. They were wondrous distractions that helped to ease my initial sense of strangeness and loneliness. But ice cream and showers were hardly enough to relieve my mother of the fear of leaving what was familiar and the anxiety of the unknown. My mother, on her own with three young children and, fleeing an impossible marriage in Fukushima, Japan, sailed to Hawai'i with the universal hope of a better life.

Currently, I am a U.S. Congresswoman representing the second district of Hawai'i. I feel humbled as I walk to work in the shadow of the U.S. Capitol dome. My admiration for my mother's determination and courage and my gratitude to her for bringing me to a country that provided the opportunity for education are the elements of *okage sama de* to me. Her sacrifices can never be repaid except in the way I live my life.

Today, —almost a quarter of a century after the first edition of this book, immigration continues to be one of the challenges of the 21st century. The hope for the American dream brings hundreds of thousands of people to the United States every year. The history of the Japanese in Hawai'i is one strand of many strands contributing to the richness of Hawai'i's multicultural society. The immigrant heritages of all Americans have enriched who we are and what we have become. The promise of America continues to call upon us to do our part to honor those who came before us. *Okage sama de...*

M

Mazie K. Hirono
Member of Congress

Appendix A
Games and Recreation in the Early 1900s

Although there were no television sets, electronic games, or fancy toys during the early 1900s, the people managed to relax and have fun as a relief from the routine of working from dawn to dusk or from studies in English and in Japanese. Many of the activities are still enjoyed in the 1980s.

Trees, whether in the backyard or neighborhood, were like old friends to the youngsters. Climbing them to play tag with friends, or to just plain daydream, were happy experiences which broke the monotony of mile long walks from school to home.

Swimming and fishing were favorite pastimes for young and old alike. And, if the ocean were not readily accessible, many plantation youngsters swam in irrigation ditches or fished in the reservoirs.

Ulua, the shore casters' prize catch.
Fishing is probably the most popular and enduring sport among the several generations of Japanese in Hawai'i. Having come from an island community and being accustomed to fish as a major food item, the Japanese enjoyed fishing, which provided both food and recreation. It also allowed participation by youngsters and thus each new generation became "hooked" on fishing. While shore casting is still popular, more and more people now own boats and even take fishing expeditions to Christmas Island and Alaska. Enthusiasts regularly watch the locally produced television program, "Let's Go Fishing," and read Hawaii Fishing News.

Hazama Collection

'Ōhi'a-'ai (mountain apple), mango, and guava picking seasons were times to look forward to. Sometimes, the entire family took their poles with small, wire-rimmed cloth bags attached to the ends and hiked into lush valleys and gulches. What fun it was to count the pickings and to share them with neighbors!

Family picnics and outings on rare special holidays were events to remember, especially since mothers and fathers worked long hours on the plantation or in their private businesses. Small family stores and service stations closed only for New Year's. Once a year, on New Year's, country people packed delicious bentō lunches and wore new outfits to picnic at places like the Honolulu Zoo, Kapi'olani Park, or scenic Punchbowl. Riding the streetcar in Waikīkī was another thrilling adventure.

Before theaters were built, Japanese moving pictures were shown in open spaces and playing fields. The movie goers sat on hard benches or on mats in the area which had been marked off by long, white pieces of cloth. The coming attractions were announced throughout the camps via a loud speaker system mounted on a truck or a car.

When theaters were built, youngsters carried their precious pennies and nickels and walked several miles to see the movies. Cowboy, Tarzan, and samurai warrior movies fired the youngsters' imagination. Children spent many hours swinging on banyan rootlets playing Tarzan, sword fighting with sticks, or galloping on broom stick handles.

Girls played "mamangoto" by the hour pretending to be grown-up ladies, especially mothers. They dressed up in their mommy's old high heeled shoes and fancy dresses. Tiny "mothers" washed rice in pots with just the right wrist motion except that the grains were of sand rather than rice. They sliced hibiscus buds and leaves, their meat and vegetables, with the sharp edges of the tops of cans. Rubber dolls that could drink "milk" and wet their diapers were very special Christmas presents and the envy among friends.

Little girls also enjoyed games like jacks, bean bags, string games, hopscotch and games using seeds. Each girl owned a little drawstring cloth bag of jacks and a set of home-made bean bags. The girls exhibited their small muscle dexterity by challenging each other with jacks and elephant ear seeds. They flicked a seed at other seeds with deadly accuracy with their thumbs or caught the tossed seeds on the backs of their hands. Expert jugglers tossed three to six bean bags into the air and around their backs or under a leg without dropping them. A circle of string created designs of one to twenty "eyes" or "brooms" as individuals or partners adroitly twisted their fingers and wrists.

Fūsendama

Fūsendama, fragile balls made from thin paper and imported from Japan, came in bright pink, red, or yellow. They were blown up like balloons and volleyed back and forth by pairs or groups of girls.

Tops and Yo-yos

Yo-yo season started when the stores received their supplies. The most desirable colors sold out quickly to boys and the few tomboys who had been saving their pennies and nickels. Yo-yo was an individual game in which each player worked to perfect fancier and more intricate routines like "Around the World" and "Baby's Cradle." While tops also could be an individual game, boys devised their own "fight-fight" challenges between whirling tops to see whose top could topple the other's.

Stilts and Walking on Cans

Somehow, it was always a challenge to be taller, and boys and girls loved to walk on stilts and cans. It was tricky to see how long one could balance and walk on stilts two and a half feet off the ground. The beginner's stilts started at about a foot off the ground until the skills of mounting and balancing were mastered.

Walking on cans was another home-made game calling for balance and coordination. Strings were attached to a pair of cans and the walker carefully manipulated one foot at a time by pulling on the string with the hands. In some areas, a very sticky substance from beans was used on the empty cans and stuck directly onto the bare feet.

Jan-Ken-Pō or Paper and Stone

Jan-Ken-Pō, in which two opponents used their fingers to shape scissors (two outstretched fingers), stone (fist), or paper (open hand), was the way individuals and teams decided who would go first. Who goes first in marble games or which team would have the privilege of running through the lines first was decided by Jan-Ken-Pō.

Jan-Ken-Pō was also a game in itself requiring only the hands. A player used his right hand to Jan-Ken-Pō and the fingers of the left hand to keep a tally of wins. Two players chanted "Jan-Ken-Pō" and simultaneously swung the fists sideways in rhythm showing their scissors, stone or paper on "Pō." Scissors won over paper because scissors could cut paper; paper won over stone because it could wrap a stone; and stone stopped the scissors and thus was the winner. Children became experts at Jan-Ken-Pō, took a solid standing stance as they faced opponents, and gave a vigorous and rapid "Jan-Ken-Pō!!" as they faced each other in deadly earnest. In a slight variation, Jan-Ken-Pō with only paper and stone signs was the way to choose up sides for a team. All players chanted "Jan-Ken-Pō" until on one "Pō" an even number of papers and stones showed up to decide the team memberships.

Team Games

"Water," "Steal the Flag," and "Bean Bag Tag" were favorite team games while children were waiting for the Japanese school bell to announce class time. In "Water" teams took turns manning the lines to tag the opponents as they tried to dart and dodge their way from one end to the other. All the waiting students needed to start the game was to draw the lines in the sand or the ground and choose up sides.

For "Steal the Flag" a little handkerchief or a piece of cloth was magically transformed into a treasure. Each team tried to steal the other's flag without being tagged in enemy territory. If caught, one landed in "Prison" until rescued by a daring teammate. Speed, boldness, and adroitness were greatly admired in these team games; and these qualities were needed to sneak into the enemy's circle. Anyone daring enough to venture into enemy's territory and stick a foot into the enemy's circle was safe as long as a foot was inside the circle. Then, the final challenge was to steal the "Flag" and to dash back across the line in home territory for a victory.

The "Bean Bag Tag" was a game of deception. The two teams each carried a single bean bag. The game began with a huddle in which the team decided who would actually hold the bean bag. When the members came out of the huddle, everyone had a hand in the shirt or skirt so that there was no way to detect the real holder of the bean bag. Opponents dashed after each other as if to hit to "kill" until the real holders finally showed their weapons and everyone except the holders scattered away in a frenzy. Anyone hit by the bag was "dead," and the game ended when one team knocked out all members of the opposing team.

So, the resourceful boys and girls found ways to have a lot of fun and exercise with some friends, a large playing area, and pieces of cloth or two bean bags.

The Flat Tires of O'ahu Sugar Company
The garage gang's team shows their sense of humor and friendship in the choice of their name.

Waipahu Cultural Garden Park

Boxing was a popular sport encouraged by the plantation management as a recreational outlet. The weight categories allowed for individual differences and being on a team brought together young men of various ethnic groups. Boxing does not seem to appeal to Japanese youths today.

Waipahu Cultural Garden Park

331

Baseball

The boys and men loved to play baseball. Every plantation had a league with several teams. The workers in the mill, the garage, and the field gangs had their own teams; and they competed vigorously with each other for the championship and the right to play against other plantations' championship teams.

Appendix B
Girls' Day Display

by Lianne Takemoto

Emperor   Empress

Three Court Ladies

Five Musicians

Two Ministers with Bows

Three Deputy Chiefs

Household Effects

Household Effects

The most important dolls for the Girls' Day display are the Emperor and the Empress, who together are called the *Dairi-sama*. They are always placed on the top tier, the male on the right and the female to the left of the display. The *Dairi-sama* only would be sufficient in a small display. There is usually an arrangement of peach blossoms with the *Dairi-sama*.

The three court ladies *(sanin kanjo)* with their banquet trays and dishes come on the second tier while the five musicians *(gonin bayashi)* are placed on the third. The ministers with their bows and arrows *(yadaijin)* occupy the fourth tier while the deputy chiefs *(jichō)* are on the fifth level. Household effects and small trays of mochi are placed on the sixth and seventh tiers.

Appendix C
Oshōgatsu - New Year's Day

Many Japanese families in Hawai'i continue to celebrate New Year's Day in a modified traditional manner. A few do so with an understanding of the reasons for the different customs, but most follow the customs because they had observed their parents doing so.

Over the years, some of the practices have changed. Sometimes it was because of the unavailability of the materials. At other times it was a melding of the practices from the different prefectures. The influence of the non-Japanese can be seen especially in the foods. In spite of the changes, recent visitors from Japan have been heard to say that the Japanese in Hawai'i celebrate New Year's more traditionally than do the Japanese in Japan today. The Hawai'i

Japanese continue to follow the customs of the Meiji era that the early immigrants brought with them.

The Japanese see the New Year's as the opportunity to begin the year with a clean state. Debts are paid, quarrels are settled, houses are cleaned, baths are taken, and new clothing is worn for the occasion. They also believe that the New Year brings good luck. In Hawai'i the Japanese have adopted the Chinese custom of burning firecrackers to welcome the luck. They are reluctant to sweep away the residue because it would mean sweeping away the luck.

Beginning with New Year's Eve, many go to the temples and shrines. The Shinto shrines are especially popular at this time of the year. People may be seen standing in long lines awaiting their turn to receive the blessing. The first ritual is for the worshipper to wash his hands and to rinse his mouth at the special basin located just inside the *torii* gate. He then goes up a few steps toward the main shrine where he receives a cleansing from the priest who sprinkles water on him from a leafy branch. The priest also waves a wand of white prayer papers to bless the worshiper. The people sip *sake*, receive amulets, and donate money.

Not only are the houses cleaned, but special decorations symbolizing positive characteristics are set up. A few families use the traditional *kadomatsu* (gate pine) ornament at the doorway. Three stems of bamboo with their ends cut at a slant are arranged with two kinds of pine, a rough bark and a smooth bark, which are tied together. In Hawai'i most families purchase bundles of pine and bamboo branches and use them instead. The bamboo represents great strength coupled with gentleness while the evergreen pine signifies constancy and longevity. It is believed that families displaying the *kadomatsu* will live long and happy lives.

A New Year's offering, *osonae*, of two mochi, a strip of konbu, and a citrus is placed over *saiwai-gami* (happiness paper). The saiwai-gami depict one or all of the seven gods of good luck or symbols representing them. The mochi represent the sun and the moon. The smoothness and the roundness of the mochi signify harmony. The seaweed, konbu, is used because it sounds like a part of the word for happiness, while the citrus is placed because the Japanese word for a kind of citrus is *dai-dai*, which also can mean generation to generation. Sometimes dried persimmons are placed alongside for health and success. Osonae are put in honored places around the house.

Another ornament is the money tree. In old Japan, temple worshippers were given bamboo stems with miniature good luck symbols. Among the symbols are a treasure boat, a sea bream, a gold coin, a money box, a die, a fan, and a target and arrow. Today plastic "branches" may be purchased and displayed.

Mochi (rice cake) is a must at New Year's. Although most families today buy their mochi, there are still some who gather a few days before the first of January to pound their own. A special kind of rice is soaked overnight, then steamed in square wooden trays over an outdoor stove. The rice is then put into a wooden or cement mortar and pounded with long handled wooden mallets. In between the pounding, another person turns the rice over, timing the motion so his hand isn't hit. When the rice becomes smooth and elastic, it is transferred to a table where others break off small clumps and shape them. Sometimes small balls of sweetened beans are put in the centers.

A must at breakfast on New Year's Day is *ozōni*. For this dish toasted mochi is put into a broth along with other ingredients such as vegetables and fish. The kind of broth and the accompanying ingredients except for the mochi vary from prefecture to prefecture. Mochi is eaten for strength and for family cohesiveness. Sometimes youngsters vie with each other to eat mochi equivalent to their ages.

During the day friends, neighbors, and families call on each other. In recent years, the all-day open house has changed to lunch or dinner. Special food known as *osechi ryōri* is served. Musts are *kuromame* (black beans), *kazunoko* (herring eggs), *konbumaki* (seaweed roll), *kinton* (mashed sweet potato and chestnut), and *kamaboko* (fish cakes). There is a reason for each dish. Kuromame is for health, kazunoko for fertility, konbumaki for happiness, kinton for wealth, and kamaboko for happiness and luck. Besides the osechi ryōri, Hawai'i tables are graced with turkey, ham, fried noodles, salad, *sushi* (rice rolled in seaweed), *nishime* (vegetables cooked in stock), sashimi (raw fish), and cooked red fish. The number of dishes as well as the number of items in each dish must be odd numbered, but never nine.

335

Appendix D
Memorial Services

After a Buddhist funeral, other memorial services to express love and respect for the deceased are held at designated times. The first such service, *shonanuka* or *hatsunanuka,* is held on the sixth day after the death. Subsequent services are held every seventh day until the forty-ninth day, *shi jū-kunichi.* In Hawai'i, family members and close friends usually gather either at the temple or at the deceased's home for the shonanuka and the shijū-kunichi services. The other services at seven day intervals are observed by the immediate members of the families only. Another service is held on the 100th day *(hyakka-nichi).*

Families also practice *shōjin,* abstaining from eating foods of animal origin until after the shonanuka service. After the service, the group partakes in a *shōjin-age* (end of shōjin) meal. Some families abstain from eating animal foods until the *shijū kunichi* and have their shōjin-age then.

Anniversary services are held on the 1st, 3rd, 7th, 13th, 17th, 33rd, and 50th years. With the exception of the first year service, the others are held a year earlier because of the Japanese style of counting. Temples in Hawai'i generally notify the families about these special anniversary services.

Appendix E
Symbolism at Traditional Japanese Celebrations

The traditional customs can best be observed at festive occasions such as weddings and specially significant birthdays. While Japanese symbols and even the practice of celebrating special birthdays are still popular and have even been adopted by non Japanese in Hawai'i, the meanings behind the symbols are not always understood. Knowledge about these practices and symbols can add new dimensions to appreciating the Japanese heritage.

To the Japanese, certain birthdays must be observed and are of major importance because they stand for auspicious years or calamitous years in a person's life. In the life of a man, the 42nd year *(yakudoshi)* is considered the most calamitous and for women, the 33rd year. To ward off misfortune, festive celebrations are held on these birthdays. The Japanese system of counting age begins at birth, so that a person by the American style of counting would be 41 and 32 respectively.

The 61st birthday or kanreki marks the beginning of one's second childhood and the auspicious years. Traditionally, a person wears a crimson cap to indicate one's second childhood and red is used in the decor for this occasion. The 70th birthday or *koki*, the rarely reached age, is the second auspicious time. The 77th birthday, *ki no ji*, is a year of gladness marked by the wearing of a red *chanchan ko* or loose coat over the clothes. The final and most honored celebration is held on the 88th birthday *(beiju)* when a person earns the right to wear the crimson cap and the chanchan

Beiju no iwai.
Issei Kame Okamoto was honored by her family on her eighty-eighth birthday with a surprise dinner. She wore a red cap and a red jacket. In the background, 1,000 red cranes are suspended from bamboo branches to wish her continued long life.
Okamoto Collection

ko. Silver and golden wedding anniversaries are also occasions for celebrations.

The Japanese believe in *engi* which, when broadly translated, means lucky or unlucky omens attached to certain objects. Hence, particular symbols such as mochi, cranes, bamboo, turtles, and *tai* (a red fish) are important at weddings and special birthday celebrations. *Mochi*, which also means "to have" conveys wishes for wealth to the person being honored. The two rounded mochi which are stacked symbolize the sun and the moon; the two for increased good fortune and the roundness for harmony. The bamboo *(take)* is considered a lucky plant, one which is constant, devoted, and flexible.

The graceful crane *(tsuru)* and the sturdy turtle *(kame)* also denote long life and happiness.

There is a saying:

Tsuru wa sennen	Cranes live a thousand years
Kame wa mannen	Turtles live 10,000 years

If one crane symbolizes 1,000 years, what better way is there to symbolize long life than with the 1,000 cranes or 1,000 thousand years!! Therefore, the display of 1,000 handmade *origami* cranes is the focus of attention, and in recent years, has been presented in very ingenious and aesthetic ways.

At a wedding dinner, a whole red fish is conspicuously displayed at the head table. The sea bream *(tai)* represents *medetai* or happiness and must be served whole because to cut it would mean cutting away some happiness. And, whenever the occasion demands, a rousing *"Banzai! Banzai! Banzai!"* is in order. This Japanese hurrah stands for *ban*, 10,000, and *zai*, or years. When shouting *"Banzai,"* a person is participating in a tradition which originated in 200 B.C.

Appendix F:
Tracing Your Roots

If you are interested in tracing your roots, you should begin immediately, for with the passing of the older members of the family, much family history is being lost. Fortunately, with the current interest in genealogy, there are "how to" books available at the Mormon Church libraries, the Hawaii State Library, and the bookstores. Go through some of the materials to find out what kinds of information to look for and how to record them. When you decide on or devise a recording system, you are ready to start your research. The following is a minimal listing to get you started.[1]

1. Check your home sources first. Talk with older members of your family including great-grandparents, grandparents, parents, uncles and aunties, and older cousins. Look through family albums, family Bibles, *ihai* (mortuary tablets) which may be found in the Buddhist altar. Check tombstones as they are often inscribed with birth and death dates.

2. Consult community sources.
   a. The Hawaii State Archives has a record of arrival dates of all immigrants who came before 1900 as well as a list of Hawai'i residents who served in World War I.
   b. The Japanese Consulate in Honolulu has the record of arrivals after 1900 in Japanese. Therefore, you need to present your family name in kanji (Chinese characters) for the search.
   c. The U.S. Immigration and Naturalization Service in Honolulu also has records of arrivals after 1900.
   d. The Hawaii Immigration Heritage Center at the Bishop Museum has the passenger lists of arrivals between 1885 and 1900 which often include village and prefecture of origin.
   e. The State of Hawaii Board of Health has the Hawai'i birth, marriage, and death records.
   f. Churches and temples may have membership records.
   g. City directories (1880-date) for all islands and provide addresses and occupations and are available at the Hawai'i State Archives.
   h. Telephone directories, available in microfiche at the Hawaii State Library, give addresses.

3. Write to a relative in Japan and ask for a *koseki tōhon,* a household register, for research purposes. If you know the name and

---

[1]For a more complete listing of local sources, including addresses and phone numbers, consult *Searching for Family Histories through Genealogical Sources and Oral History* which was issued by the Office of Library Services of the State Department of Education in March, 1981. It is available in the Hawaiian Room at the Hawaii State Library.

address of your ancestors' township government, you can write to them directly for your *koseki tōhon*.[2]

4. Write to your ancestors' temple for any information recorded there, especially in their *kakochō* (death register). One may need to send the kaimyō (Buddhist name) of the deceased ancestor. This may be founded on the face of the ihai.

[2]Consult *Family History for Japanese Americans, 1980, by Greg Gubler* as a general guide for research in Japan.

Appendix G:
The Ethnic Identity Questionnaire

Dr. Gerald Meredith, an academic evaluation officer at the University of Hawaii, and Drs. Minoru Masuda (now deceased) and Gary Matsumoto of the Department of Psychiatry at the University of Washington School of Medicine developed this 50 item questionnaire for the purpose of quantifying the extent of ethnic identification among three generations of Japanese Americans. Since its development in the 1960's, it has been used in various studies. The instrument and key are included here with the permission of Dr. Gerald Meredith. The questionnaire can be self administered and self corrected by anyone interested in assessing one's own ethnic identity level or "Japaneseness."

340

Instructions. Listed below are a number of statements about which people often have different opinions. You will discover that you agree with some, that you disagree with others. Please read each statement carefully, then circle the letter that indicates the extent to which you agree or disagree with it. Answer every statement, even if you have to guess at some. There is no right or wrong answer.

Strongly Agree	Agree	Undecided	Disagree	Strongly Disagree		
SA	A	U	D	SD	1.	A good child is an obedient child.
SA	A	U	D	SD	2.	It is all right for personal desires to come before duty to one's family.
SA	A	U	D	SD	3.	Japanese Americans should not disagree among themselves if there are Caucasians around.
SA	A	U	D	SD	4.	I especially like Japanese foods.
SA	A	U	D	SD	5.	A good Japanese background helps prevent youth from getting into all kinds of trouble that other American youth have today.
SA	A	U	D	SD	6.	It's unlucky to be born Japanese.
SA	A	U	D	SD	7.	It would be more comfortable to live in a neighborhood which has at least a few Japanese Americans than in one which has none.
SA	A	U	D	SD	8.	When I feel affectionate, I show it.
SA	A	U	D	SD	9.	It is a duty of the eldest sons to take care of his parents in their old age.
SA	A	U	D	SD	10.	Japanese Americans who enter into new places without any expectation of discrimination from Caucasians are naive.
SA	A	U	D	SD	11.	I think it is all right for Japanese Americans to become Americanized, but they should retain part of their own culture.
SA	A	U	D	SD	12.	A wife's career is just as important as the husband's career.
SA	A	U	D	SD	13.	In regard to opportunities that other Americans enjoy, Japanese Americans are deprived of many of them because of their ancestry.
SA	A	U	D	SD	14.	It is all right for children to question the decisions of their parents once in awhile.
SA	A	U	D	SD	15.	In the Japanese community, human relationships are generally more warm and comfortable than outside in American society.
SA	A	U	D	SD	16.	I would not feel any more tendency to agree with the policies of the Japanese government than any other American would.

Strongly Agree	Agree	Undecided	Disagree	Strongly Disagree	

SA A U D SD 17. The best thing for the Japanese Americans to do is to associate more with Caucasians and identify themselves completely as Americans.

SA A U D SD 18. I am apt to hide my feelings in some things, to the point that people may hurt me without their knowing it.

SA A U D SD 19. It is a shame for a Japanese American not to be able to understand Japanese.

SA A U D SD 20. Japanese people have an unusual refinement and depth of feeling for nature.

SA A U D SD 21. I would be disturbed if Caucasians did not accept me as an equal.

SA A U D SD 22. It is unrealistic for a Japanese American to hope that he can become a leader of an organization composed mainly of Caucasians because they will not let him.

SA A U D SD 23. I don't have a strong feeling of attachment to Japan.

SA A U D SD 24. I am not too spontaneous and casual with people.

SA A U D SD 25. It is not necessary for Japanese American parents to make it a duty to promote the preservation of Japanese cultural heritage in their children.

SA A U D SD 26. An older brother's decision is to be respected more than that of a younger one.

SA A U D SD 27. Socially, I feel less at ease with Caucasians than with Japanese Americans.

SA A U D SD 28. The Japanese are no better or no worse than any other race.

SA A U D SD 29. I always think of myself as an American first and as a Japanese second.

SA A U D SD 30. Although children may not appreciate Japanese schools at the time, they will later when they grow up.

SA A U D SD 31. Life in the United States is quite ideal for Japanese Americans.

SA A U D SD 32. When in need of aid, it is best to rely mainly on relatives.

SA A U D SD 33. It is better that Japanese Americans date only Japanese Americans.

SA A U D SD 34. Parents who are very companionable with their children can still maintain respect and obedience.

SA A U D SD 35. Once a Japanese always a Japanese.

Strongly Agree	Agree	Undecided	Disagree	Strongly Disagree		

SA A U D SD 36. Good relations between Japanese and Caucasians can be maintained without the aid of traditional Japanese organizations.

SA A U D SD 37. It is nice if a Japanese American learns more about Japanese culture, but it is really not necessary.

SA A U D SD 38. It would be better if there were no all-Japanese communities in the United States.

SA A U D SD 39. Japan has a great art heritage and has made contributions important to world civilization.

SA A U D SD 40. Those Japanese Americans who are unfavorable toward Japanese culture have the wrong attitude.

SA A U D SD 41. I believe that, "He who does not repay a debt of gratitude cannot claim to be noble."

SA A U D SD 42. To avoid being embarrassed by discrimination, the best procedure is to avoid places where a person is not totally welcomed.

SA A U D SD 43. I usually participate in mixed group discussions.

SA A U D SD 44. Many of the Japanese customs, traditions, and attitudes are no longer adequate for the problems of the modern world.

SA A U D SD 45. I enjoy Japanese movies.

SA A U D SD 46. It is a natural part of growing up to occasionally "wise-off" at teachers, policemen, and other grownups in authority.

SA A U D SD 47. A person who raises too many questions interferes with the progress of a group.

SA A U D SD 48. I prefer attending an all-Japanese church.

SA A U D SD 49. One can never let himself down without letting the family down at the same time.

SA A U D SD 50. Interracial marriages between Japanese Americans and Caucasians should be discouraged.

Scoring key for the
Ethnic Identity Questionnaire

Each item in the questionnaire has 1 to 5 points, depending on which way the scale goes. If "Strongly Agree" is designated with a value of 5 points, "Agree" would be worth 4 points, "Undecided" would be 3 points, etc. If "Strongly Disagree" is designated with a value of 5 points, "Disagree" would be worth 4 points, and so on.

1. SA	11. SA	21. SA	31. SD	41. SA
2. SD	12. SD	22. SA	32. SA	42. SA
3. SA	13. SA	23. SD	33. SA	43. SD
4. SA	14. SD	24. SA	34. SD	44. SD
5. SA	15. SA	25. SD	35. SA	45. SA
6. SD	16. SD	26. SA	36. SD	46. SD
7. SA	17. SD	27. SA	37. SD	47. SA
8. SD	18. SA	28. SD	38. SD	48. SA
9. SA	19. SA	29. SD	39. SA	49. SA
10. SA	20. SA	30. SA	40. SA	50. SA

The total score of the 50 items can then be compared with the following Mean Total Ethnic Identity Scores provided by the developers of the Ethnic Identity Questionnaire. As noted, the higher the score the stronger the identification with "Japaneseness." There were no significant male-female differences in the scores, therefore, only the combined score is presented here.

Mean Total Ethnic Identity Scores:

Issei	Nisei	Sansei
163	153.46	143.76

Appendix H
Survey On Japanese Superstitions

This survey of traditional Japanese superstitions, attitudes, and beliefs from Dr. Gerald M. Meredith is reprinted here with his permission. Initially, he found a high degree of superstitious belief among Japanese American females as compared with males.

Purpose: The purpose of this survey is to examine the extent to which Japanese Americans in Hawai'i believe in and practice Japanese Superstitions.

Instructions: To each superstition stated below please indicate
                 by circling:
                 1. whether you are familiar with it (YES or NO)
                 2. to what extent you believe in it (which will be
                    abbreviated in the following manner):

                 SB = Strongly Believe
                  B = Believe
                  U = Uncertain
                  D = Disbelieve
                 SD = Strongly Disbelieve

1. The number "4" (shi) is bad luck because it means death.
   a. Are you familiar with this superstition: YES   NO
   b. How much do you believe in it: SB   B   U   D   SD

2. Certain ages such as "42" (shi-ni) are bad luck-thus you need
   to make big parties during these birthdays to prevent anything
   bad from happening.
   a. Are you familiar with this superstition: YES   NO
   b. How much do you believe in it: SB   B   U   D   SD

3. Going to a Japanese Temple to pray on New Years Day will
   give you good luck for the year.
   a. Are you familiar with this superstition: YES   NO
   b. How much do you believe in it: SB   B   U   D   SD

4. If you cut your nails at night, you won't see your parents when
   they die.
   a. Are you familiar with this superstition: YES   NO
   b. How much do you believe in it: SB   B   U   D   SD

5. Carrying an amulet (omamori) with you or putting Japanese
   charms in your house or car prevents bad things from
   happening.
   a. Are you familiar with this superstition: YES   NO
   b. How much do you believe in it: SB   B   U   D   SD

6. The Northern direction is considered bad luck (associated
   with dead people), so you shouldn't sleep or build your house
   facing that direction.
   a. Are you familiar with this superstition: YES   NO
   b. How much do you believe in it: SB   B   U   D   SD

7. Placing Mochi (rice cake) in your house or car for New Years Day will give you good luck for the year.
   a. Are you familiar with this superstition: YES   NO
   b. How much do you believe in it: SB   B   U   D   SD

8. You must mourn for a person for 49 days after he/she dies because his/her spirit is still present.
   a. Are you familiar with this superstition: YES   NO
   b. How much do you believe in it: SB   B   U   D   SD

9. If your second toe is longer than your big toe, it means you will be more successful than your parents.
   a. Are you familiar with this superstition: YES   NO
   b. How much do you believe in it: SB   B   U   D   SD

10. If you do something bad (such as steal, cheat or be disrespectful to parents), you will be punished by God (get "Bachi").
    a. Are you familiar with this superstition: YES   NO
    b. How much do you believe in it: SB   B   U   D   SD

11. You should have ceremonies or church services to mourn for the dead at certain times of the year - (e.g. Obon ceremony or anniversay of death).
    a. Are you familiar with this superstition: YES   NO
    b. How much do you believe in it: SB   B   U   D   SD

12. One thousand cranes (tsuru) represent long life and good luck (thus brings good luck when made and displayed for weddings and birthdays).
    a. Are you familiar with this superstition: YES   NO
    b. How much do you believe in it: SB   B   U   D   SD

13. Misfortunes usually occur in cycles of 3- (e.g. Deaths or accidents in family).
    a. Are you familiar with this superstition: YES   NO
    b. How much do you believe in it: SB   B   U   D   SD

14. When serving tea, you're not supposed to pour backwards (with your hand twisted to sidewards (direction) - it represents pouring water over a dead person.
    a. Are you familiar with this superstition: YES   NO
    b. How much do you believe in it: SB   B   U   D   SD

346

15. Certain parts of the year may be unlucky for you to get married so you plan out your wedding according to a time of the year that is lucky.
    a. Are you familiar with this superstition: YES   NO
    b. How much do you believe in it: SB   B   U   D   SD

Superstitions: Practices in Daily Life
                (please circle appropriate answer)

1. Do you carry an amulet (omamori) or have Japanese charms in your house or car: YES   NO
2. Do you follow any traditional New Year practices such as going to a Japanese temple or putting Mochi in your house:
                                                            YES   NO
3. Do or did you ever cut your nails at night:
                                                            YES   NO
4. Do or did you ever go to a Japanese service or ceremony to mourn for your loved ones: YES   NO
5. If you practice any of these superstitions, is it mainly because:
    1. you believe in it
    2. your parents or relatives make you do it
    3. your family or friends do it (so you just follow their practices)
    4. other (Please state): _____
Are there any other superstitions that you believe in or practice?

Notes

Introduction

1. U.S. Department of Commerce, Bureau of the Census 1982, Part 13-p. 13.
2. Schmitt 1977, p. 25.

Chapter II

1. Lydecker 1910, pp. 10-11.
2. United Japanese Society 1971, p. 48.
3. Takaki 1983, p. 71.
4. United Japanese Society 1971, p. 59.

Chapter III

1. United Japanese Society 1971, pp. 74-81.
2. Ibid., pp. 89-92.
3. Ibid., p. 91.
4. Ibid., p. 112.

Chapter IV

1. Wakukawa 1938, p. 124.
2. United Japanese Society 1971, p. 162.
3. Wakukawa 1938, p. 136.

Chapter V

1. United Japanese Society 1971, p. 172.
2. Wakukawa 1938, pp. 242-244.
3. United Japanese Society 1971, p. 193.

Chapter VI

1. United Japanese Society 1971, pp. 165-166.
2. Wakukawa 1938, pp. 296-297.
3. Compilation Committee for the Publication of Kinzaburo Makino's Biography 1965, p. 66.
4. United Japanese Society 1971, p. 201.
5. Ogawa 1973, pp. 112-149.
   Daws 1968, p. 319
6. U.S. Congress 1937, pp. 247-263.
7. Ibid., pp. 304-305.

Chapter VII

1. Beekman 1982, p. 83.
2. Rademaker 1951, p. 31.
3. Ibid., p. 7.
4. Ibid., p. 46.
5. Tanaka 1982, p. 80.
6. Shirey 1946. p. 101.
7. Lind 1946. pp. 159-160.
8. Rademaker 1951, p. 86.

Chapter VIII

1. Lind 1967, p. 108.
2. Kimura 1943, p. 28.
3. Kimura 1957, pp. 70-76.
4. Democratic Party Platform
5. Rosegg 1979, p. A-4.
6. Hawaii (State), Department of Labor and Industrial Relations 1984.
7. *Honolulu Advertiser,* "Arakawas," 5-1-84.
8. *Honolulu Star Bulletin* 12-1-69, p. D-14; 3-8-79, p. D-1.
9. Interview with Lionel Tokioka 7-84.
10. Taylor 6-29-80.
    Pietschmann 1984, p. 65-66.
11. *Economic Salon* 1970, pp. 14, 16, 34.
    Honolulu Star Bulletin 2-25-79 10-25-79, 2-17-81.
    Honolulu Star Bulletin 2-25-79 10-25-79, 2-17-81.

Chapter IX

1. Hawaii (State), Department of Planning and Economic Development, *Geographic Distribution of Hawaii's Racial Groups, 1970 and 1980* 1982, pp. 11-12.
2. Ibid., p. 3.
3. Hawaii (State) Department of Health, *Population Characteristics, 1980* 1982, p. 11.
4. Ibid., pp. 11-12.
5. Maneki 4-5-79.
6. Whitefield 5-10-79.
7. Hawaii (State) Department of Health, *"Population Characteristics, 1980,* p. 11.
8. Hawaii (State), Department of Planning and Economic Development, *State of Hawaii Data Book 1983.* p. 97.
9. Hawaii (State), Department of Planning and Economic Development, *State of Hawaii Data Book 1982* p. 84.
10. U.S. Department of Commerce, Bureau of the Census 1982, p. 27.
11. Gardner and Nordyke 1985. Table 20.
12. Hawaii (State) Department of Health, Research and Statistical Report #47 1982, pp. 5, 7.
13. Kolonel 1980, p. 1128.
14. Kolonel, Hinds, and Hankin 1980, p. 330.
15. Kolonel and others 1981, p. 2478.

16. Kolonel 1980, p. 1131.
17. Reed and others 1982, p. 894.
18. Yano, McGee, and Reed 1983, p. 569.
19. Takeya and others 1984, p. 270.
20. Kagan and others 1980, p. 17.
21. Hawaii (State), Department of Health Statistical Report 1982, p. 51, Table 61.
   Lind 1967, p. 108.
22. Suzuki and others 1972, p. 13, Table 4.
23. Fenz and Arkoff 1962, pp. 67-89.
   Meredith 1966, pp. 171-180.
   Meredith 1965, pp. 41-49.
24. Hutchinson, Arkoff, and Weaver 1966, pp. 321-325.
25. Arkoff, Meredith, and Iwahara 1962, pp. 61-66.
26. Hazama 1981, pp. 98-100.
27. Takaki and Tanji 1980, pp. 90-95.
28. Masuda, Matsumoto, and Meredith 1970, p. 205.
29. Yamamoto, Eric 1974.
30. Grant, 1978.

Pg. 262

Selected Bibliography

Allen, Gwenfread
    1950   *Hawaii's War Years 1941-1945.* Honolulu: The University of Hawaii Press.

AMFAC
    1964   Annual Report
    1970   Annual Report
    1975   Annual Report

Anthony, J. Garner
    1975   *Hawaii Under Army Rule.* Honolulu: The University Press of Hawaii.

Arkoff, Abe
    1959   "Need patterns in Two Generations of Japanese-Americans in Hawaii." *Journal of Social Psychology* 50:75-79.

_____, *Gerald Meredith, and Shinkuro Iwahara*
    1962   *"Dominance-Deference Patterns in Motherland Japanese, Japanese-American, and Caucasian-American Students." Journal of Social Psychology* October, pp. 61-66.

Beekman, Allan
    1982   *The Niihau Incident.* Honolulu: Heritage Press of Pacific.

Castle and Cooke, Inc.
    1967   Fiscal Year Annual Report
    1971   Fiscal Year Annual Report
    1973   Fiscal Year Annual Report
    1978   Fiscal Year Annual Report

Chinen, Karleen
    1984   "Hole Hole Bushi: Voices From the Canefields, Songs of the Heart." *The Hawaii Herald.* May 4, pp. 6-7.

Coffman, Tom
    1972   *Catch a Wave: A Case Study of Hawaii's New Politics.* Honolulu: University Press of Hawaii.

Compilation Committee for the Publication of Kinzaburo Makino's Biography
    1965   *Life of Kinzaburo Makino.* Honolulu: Hawaii Hochi.

Daws, Gavin
    1968   *Shoal of Time.* Honolulu: The University Press of Hawaii.

Day, A. Grove
    1968   *Hawaii and Its People.* Des Moines: Meredith Press.

DeFrancis, John Francis
    1973   *Things Japanese in Hawaii.* Honolulu: University Press of Hawaii.

Democratic Party
1954   Democratic Party Platform.

Economic Salon
1974   "Horita the Master Planner." October.

Ethnic Studies Oral History Project
1977   *Waialua and Haleiwa: The People Tell Their Story.* 9 vol. Honolulu: Ethnic Studies Oral History Project, University of Hawaii at Manoa.
_____ and United Okinawan Association of Hawaii
1981   *Uchinanchu: A History of Okinawans in Hawaii.* Honolulu: Ethnic Studies Program, University of Hawaii at Manoa.

Feher, Joseph
1969   *Hawaii: A Pictorial History.* B.P. Museum Special Publication 58. Honolulu: Bishop Museum Press.

Fenz, E.D., and Abe Arkoff
1962   "Comparative Need Patterns of Five Ancestry Groups in Hawaii." *Journal of Social Psychology* 58: 67-89.

First Hawaiian, Inc.
1975   Annual Report
1982   Annual Report

Fuchs, Lawrence H.
1961   *Hawaii Pono.* New York: Harcourt, Brace & World, Inc.

Fujiya Hotel, Ltd.
1950   *We Japanese.* Yokohama: Yamagata Press.

Gardner, Robert W., and Eleanor C. Nordyke
1985   *The Demographic Situation in Hawaii, Revised Edition.* Honolulu: East-West Population Institute, East-West Center. Forthcoming publication.

Glick, Clarence E.
1950   "A Haole's Changing Conceptions of Japanese in Hawaii." *Social Process in Hawaii.* 14:1-10.

_____ and others
1958
"Changing Attitude Toward the Care of Aged Japanese Parents in Hawaii." *Social Process in Hawaii.* 22: 9-20.

Grant, Glen
1978   "Race Relations in the Hawaiian School: The Haole Newcomer." *Kodomo no tame ni* (D. Ogawa, ed.). pp. 588-596.

Harada, Margaret N.
1960   *The Sun Shines on the Immigrant.* New York: Vantage Press, Inc.

Harrington, Joseph D.
1979   *Yankee Samurai.* Detroit: Pettigrew Enterprises, Inc.

Hawaii (State), Department of Education, Hawaii Multicultural Awareness Project.
1979   *Shaping of Modern Hawaiian History.* Honolulu.

_____ , Office of Library Services
1981   *Searching for Family Histories through Genealogical Sources and Oral History.* Honolulu.

_____ , Department of Health
1982   Life Tables by Ethnic Groups from Hawaii, 1980. Research and Statistical Report 47 (Robert W. Gardner). Honolulu .

1982   *Population Characteristics 1980, Statistical Report 1982.* Honolulu.

_____ , Department of Labor and Industrial Relations
1984   *Labor Organizations and Affiliates, 1983-1984.* Honolulu.

_____ , Department of Planning and Economic Development
1965   "Demographic Correlates of Interracial Marriages in Hawaii." *Demography.* Vol. 2.
1973   *Community Profiles for Hawaii.* Honolulu.
1982   *The Geographic Distribution of Hawaii's Racial Groups, 1970 and 1980.* Statistical Report 152. Honolulu, January 15.
1982   *State of Hawaii Data Book 1982: A Statistical Abstract.* Honolulu, November.
1983   *State of Hawaii Data Book 1983: A Statistical Abstract.* Honolulu, December.

_____ , Department of Health and Department of Planning and Economic Development
1976   *Ethnic Structures in Hawaii.* Issue #6. (Dr. D. D. Lee) Honolulu.
1981   *Population Report.* Issue #13. (P.T. Kawaguchi, S. Nishi, and R. C. Schmitt) Honolulu.

Hazama, Dorothy
1981   "A Comparison of Student Teachers' Self Concepts and Instructional Style Preferences Before and After Student Teaching." Ed. D. dissertation. Nova University.

Hirayama, Laura
1982   "Day of Remembrance." *Hawaii Herald.* Vol. 3, No. 4. February 19.
1982   "Labor and the AJA Women." *Hawaii Herald.* Vol. 3, No. 6. March 19.

Honolulu Advertiser
1983   "Hideo 'Major' Okada." January 6.
1984   "Arakawas." May 1.

Honolulu Star Bulletin
1969   "History of Servco Pacific, Inc." December 1.
1975   "Childhood of Lumber Toys Led to Success in Housing." Hawaii 200 Progress Edition. February 25.
1979   "Celebrates 60th Anniversary with Free Trade Show Showing Its Goods and Services." March 8.
1979   "West Beach Project, A Developer's Dream." October 25.
1979   "Shivers, Ching, and Eleanor Roosevelt." December 6.
1979   "The Fight to Get Into Battle." December 6.
1981   "Horita Stays Atop Building Trends." February 17.

Hunter, Louise H.
1971 *Buddhism in Hawaii.* Honolulu: University of Hawaii Press.

Hutchinson, Sandra, Abe Arkoff, and Herbert B. Weaver
1966 "Ethnic and Sex Factors in Classroom Responsiveness." *Journal of Social Psychology.* 69:321-325.

Inouye, Daniel
1967 *Journey to Washington.* Englewood Cliffs: Prentice Hall, Inc.

Kagan, Abraham, and others
1980 "Factors Related to Stroke Incidence in Hawaii Japanese Men." *Stroke.* 11(1): 14-21.
1981 "Serum Cholesterol and Mortality in a Japanese-American Population." *American Journal of Epidemiology.* 114(1):11-20.

Kawakami, H.S. (told through Tom Coffman)
1976 *From Japan to Hawaii, My Journey.* Honolulu: Sturgis Printing.

Kimura, Yukiko
1943 "Some Aspects of the War Situation upon the Alien Japanese in Hawaii." *Social Process in Hawaii.* 8: 18-28.
1957 "War Brides in Hawaii and Their In-laws." *The American Journal of Sociology.* 63(1):70-76. July.

Kitano, Harry H. L.
1976 *Japanese Americans, The Evolution of a Subculture.* Second Edition. Englewood Cliffs: Prentice-Hall, Inc.

Kobayashi, Victor, ed.
1983 *Building a Rainbow: A History of the Buildings and Grounds of the University of Hawaii's Manoa Campus.* Honolulu: Hui o Students, University of Hawaii at Manoa.

Kodama-Nishimoto, Michiko, Warren Nishimoto, and Cynthia A. Oshiro
1984 *Hanahana: An Oral History Anthology of Hawaii's Working People.* Honolulu: Ethnic Studies Oral History Project.

Kolonel, Laurence N.
1980 "Cancer Patterns of Four Ethnic Groups in Hawaii." *Journal of National Cancer Institute.* 65 (5). November.

_____, M. Ward Hinds, and Jean H. Hankin
1980 "Cancer Patterns Among Migrant and Native-Born Japanese in Hawaii in Relation to Smoking, Drinking, and Dietary Habits." *Genetic and Environmental Factors in Experimental and Human Cancer.* Edited by Gelboin, H. V., and others. Tokyo: Japan Science Social Press, pp. 327-340.

_____ and others
1981 "Association of Diet and Place of Birth with Stomach Cancer Incidence in Hawaii Japanese and Caucasians." *The American Journal of Clinical Nutrition.* 34:2478-2485. November.

Kotani, Roland
1982 "Hawaii's Gubernatorial Race: The Ethnic Factors." *Hawaii Herald.* 3(20):1,10,11. October 15.

Kuykendall, Ralph S.

1938   *The Hawaiian Kingdom*. Vol. 1, *1778-1854: Foundation and Trans-formation*. Honolulu: The University of Hawaii Press.

1953   *The Hawaiian Kingdom*. Vol. 2, *1854-1874: Twenty Critical Years*. Honolulu: The University of Hawaii Press.

1967   *The Hawaiian Kingdom*. Vol. 3, *1874-1893: The Kalakaua Dynasty*. Honolulu: The University of Hawaii Press.

_____ and A. Grove Day

1961   *Hawaii: A History from Polynesian Kingdom to American State*. Englewood Cliffs, N.J.: Prentice-Hall, Inc.

Lind, Andrew W.

1946   *Hawaii's Japanese: An Experiment in Democracy*. Princeton: Princeton University Press.

1967   *Hawaii's People*. Third Edition. Honolulu: The University Press of Hawaii.

Lydecker, R.C.

1910   *Memorandum on the Introduction of Foreign Laborers into the Hawaiian Islands*. March 8.

Maneki, Ray

1979   "Two Top $300,000 a Year on Executives' Payroll List." *Honolulu Star Bulletin*. April 5.

Markrich, Mike

1984   "Retracing the Evolution of the Hawaiian Throw-Net." *Honolulu Star Bulletin*. May 20.

Masuda, Minoru, Gary H. Matsumoto, and Gerald D. Meredith

1970   "Ethnic Identity in Three Generations of Japanese Americans." *Journal of Social Psychology*. 81:199-207.

McGee, Daniel, and others

1982   "Within-person Variability of Nutrient Intake in a Group of Hawaiian Men of Japanese Ancestry." *The American Journal of Clinical Nutrition*. 36:657-663.

_____ and others

1984   "Ten Year Incidence of Coronary Heart Disease in the Honolulu Heart Program: Relationship to Nutrient Intake." *American Journal of Epidemiology*. 119(5):667-676.

Meredith, Gerald M.

1965   "Observation on the Acculturation of Sansei Japanese Americans in Hawaii." *Psychologia*. 8:41-49.

1966   "Amae and Acculturation Among Japanese-American College Students in Hawaii. *Journal of Social Psychology*. 70:171-180.

Miyamoto, Kazuo

1944   *Hawaii End of a Rainbow*. Rutland, VT: Charles E. Tuttle Co.

Miyasaki, Gail

1973   "Working Women." *Hawaii Herald*. February 16.

Mulholland, John F.
1970 *Hawaii's Religions*. Rutland, VT: Charles E. Tuttle Co.

Murayama, Milton
1959 *All I Asking for is My Body*. San Francisco: Supa Press.

Murphy, Thomas D.
1954 *Ambassadors in Arms: The Story of Hawaii's 100th Battalion*. Honolulu: University of Hawaii Press.

Nordyke, Eleanor C.
1977 *The Peopling of Hawaii*. Honolulu: East-West Center.

_____ and Y. Scott Matsumoto
1977 "The Japanese in Hawaii: A Historical and Demographic Perspective." *Hawaiian Journal of History*. 11:162-174.

Oda, Lorraine
1983 "A Fresh Start." *Hawaii Herald*. January 21.

Ogawa, Dennis M.
1973 *Jan Ken Po*. Japanese American Research Center.

_____
1978 *Kodomo no tame ni: For the Sake of the Children*. Honolulu: The University Press of Hawaii.

Okimoto, Elaine
1982 "Hawaii's Japanese-Americans and Interethnic Marriages." *Hawaii Herald*. Vol. 3, No. 12. June 18.

Pietschmann, Richard J.
1984 "Made in Hawaii." *Western's World*. pp. 65-66. June.

Potter, Norris, and Lawrence Kasdon
1979 *Hawaii Our Island State*. Honolulu: Bess Press Inc.

Pollack, Earl S., and others
1984 "Prospective Study of Alcohol Consumption and Cancer." *The New England Journal of Medicine*. 310:617-621.

Rademaker, John A.
1951 *These are Americans: The Japanese Americans in Hawaii in World War II*. Palo Alto: Pacific Books.

Reed, Dwayne, and others
1982 "Acculturation and Coronary Heart Disease Among Japanese Men in Hawaii." *American Journal of Epidemiology*. 115(6):894-905.

Rogers, Terence
1977 *Adjustment in Intercultural Marriage*. Honolulu: University of Hawaii Press.

Rosegg, Peter
1979 "The Jack Kawano Story." *Honolulu Advertiser*. January 5.

Sato, Hank
1976 "Honouliuli: Oahu's Little Known World War II Internment Camp." *Honolulu Star Bulletin*. March 18.

Schmitt, Robert C.
  1977   *Historical Statistics of Hawaii.* Honolulu: The University Press of Hawaii.

Shirey, Orville C.
  1946   *Americans: The Story of the 442nd Combat Team.* Washington: Infantry Journal Press. December.

Smyser, A.A.
  1979   "He Saved Island AJAs from Mass Internment." *Honolulu Star Bulletin.* December 6.

_____

  1982   "The 100th Infantry Battalion." *Honolulu Star Bulletin,* June 5.
Sodetani, Naomi
  1984   "The Homegrown Astronaut." *Honolulu.* Vol. 19, No. 5. pp. 66-69, 118-123.

Suzuki, Tatsuzo, and others
  1972   "A Study of Japanese-Americans in Honolulu, Hawaii." *Annals of the Institute of Statistical Mathematics.* Supplement 7.

Takaki, Lillian K., and Jan S. Tanji
  1980   "Attitudes Toward Care of the Elderly: A Study of Three Generations of Japanese-Americans in Hawaii." Master's thesis, University of Hawaii School of Social Work. May.

Takaki, Ronald
  1983   *Pau Hana: Plantation Life and Labor in Hawaii 1835-1920.* Honolulu: University Press of Hawaii.

Takeya, Yo, and others
  1984   "Epidemiologic Studies of Coronary Heart Disease and Stroke in Japanese Men Living in Japan, Hawaii, and California: Incidence of Stroke in Japan and Hawaii." *Stroke.* 15(1):15-23.

Tanaka, Chester
  1982   *Go For Broke: A Pictorial History of the Japanese-Americans 100th Infantry Battalion and the 442nd Regimental Combat Team.* Richmond, CA: Go for Broke, Inc.

Taylor, Lois
  1980   "Robert Taira, King of Sweetbread." *Honolulu Star Bulletin.* June 29.

Toyama, Henry, and Kiyoshi Ikeda
  1950   "Okinawan-Naichi Relationship." *Social Process in Hawaii.* 14:51-65.

Tsukiyama, Ted T.
  1978   "Varsity Victory Volunteers." *Honolulu Star Bulletin.* December 7.

  1982   "A Story of Unsung Valor and Devotion." *Honolulu Star Bulletin.* April 9.

United Japanese Society of Hawaii
  1964   *Hawaii Nippon Jin Imin Shi.* Edited by Publication Committee, Dr. James H. Okahata, Chairman. Honolulu: United Japanese Society of Hawaii.

1971 *A History of Japanese in Hawaii.* Edited by Publication Committee, Dr. James H. Okahata, Chairman. Honolulu: United Japanese Society of Hawaii.

United States Congress
1937 *Hearings Before the Joint Committee on Hawaii Statehood.* 75th Congress, 2nd Session (October 6-22).

United States Department of Commerce, Bureau of the Census
1982 *Census of Population: 1980 vol. 1, General Population Characteristics, Part 13, Hawaii.* Washington, D.C.

Uyehara, Yukuo
1980 "The Horehore-Bushi: A Type of Japanese Folksong Developed and Sung Among the Early Immigrants in Hawaii." *Social Process in Hawaii.* 28(1980-1981):110-120.

Vitousek, Betty M.
1979 "The State of Mixed Marriages in Hawaii." *Honolulu Star Bulletin.* February 16.

Wakayama, Mary
1983 "Giving Gifts in Hawaii." *Hawaii Herald.* Vol. 4, No. 12. June 17.

Wakukawa, Ernest K.
1938 *A History of the Japanese People in Hawaii.* Honolulu: The Toyo Shoin.

Warinner, Emily V.
1956 *Voyager to Destiny.* Indianapolis: Bobbs-Merrill.

Whitefield, Debra
1979 "Hawaii's Highest Paid Public Servants." *Honolulu Star Bulletin.* May 10.

Wright, Theon
1966 *Rape in Paradise.* New York: Hawthorne Books, Inc.

Yamamoto, Eric
1974 "From 'Japanee' to Local: Community Change and the Redefinition of Sansei Identity in Hawaii." (Paper, E. Hormann Prize Award in Sociology, 1975.)

Yamamoto, Joe, and Mamoru Iga.
1983 "Emotional Growth of Japanese American Children." Chapter 10 in *Psychosocial Development of Minority Group Children.* New York: Bruner Mazel.

Yamamoto, Loren, Katsuhiko Yano, and George Rhoads
1983 "Characteristics of Joggers Among Japanese Men in Hawaii." *American Journal of Public Health.* 73(2):147-152.

Yano, Katsuhiko, Daniel McGee, and Dwayne M. Reed
1983 "The Impact of Elevated Blood Pressure Upon 10-Year Mortality Among Japanese Men in Hawaii: The Honolulu Heart Program." *Journal of Chronic Diseases.* 36(8):569-577.

Revised Edition: References

Books

Clark, Jean and Diane Dods. *Artists of Hawaii*. Honolulu: University of Hawai'i Press, 1996.

Ethnic Studies Oral History Project and United Okinawan Association of Hawai'i. *Uchinanchu, A History of Okinawans in Hawaii*. Honolulu: Ethic Studies Program, University of Hawai'i, 1981.

Kanahele, George, ed. *Hawaiian Music and Musicians, An Illustrated History*. Honolulu: University of Hawai'i Press, 1979.

Niiya, Brian, ed. *Japanese American History: An A–Z Reference from 1868 to the Present*. Los Angeles: Japanese American National Museum, 1993.

Ogawa, Dennis M. *An Unlikely Revolutionary: Matsuo Takabuki and the Making of Modern Hawaii*. Honolulu: University of Hawai'i Press, 1996.

Okihiro, Michael M. *AJA Baseball in Hawaii: Ethnic Pride and Tradition*. Honolulu: Hawai'i Hochi Ltd., 1999.

Stone, Scott S. S. *Living Treasures of Hawai'i*. Honolulu: Honpa Hongwanji Mission of Hawai'i, 2000.

Toji, Dean S. "The Rise of the *Nikkei* Generation." *The New Face of Asian Pacific America: Numbers, Diversity and Change in the 21st Century*, p. 73–78. Eric Lai and Dennis Arguelles, editors, *AsianWeek* newspaper of San Francisco and UCLA's Asian American Studies Center, 2003.

Yamashita, Bruce I. *Fighting Tradition: A Marine's Journey to Justice*. Honolulu: University of Hawai'i Press, 2003.

Newspapers

Alton, Helen. "Legacy of Retired Queen's Surgeon Lives on in the Hearts of Patients" *Honolulu Star Bulletin*, July 29, 2004.

Chin, Steven A. "A Matter of Honor: The Bruce Yamashita Story." *San Francisco Examiner*, April 4, 1993.

Gonser, James and Treena Shapiro. "Case Middle School state of the art." *Honolulu Advertiser*, March 28, 2005. http://thehonoluluadvertiser.com/article/2005/Mar/28/ln//ln11p.html.

The Honolulu Advertiser, articles on Tadd Fujikawa: February 7, 2007, February 12, 2007, and May 13, 2007.

The Honolulu Advertiser, articles on Lieutenant Ehren Watada: February 4, 2007, February 6, 2007, February 7, 2007, February 8, 2007, February 10, 2007, February 24, 2007, and May 19, 2007.

Interview of Kiyoshi Okubo in July 1991 and quoted by Patsy Y. Nakayama. *The Hawai'i Herald,* October 3, 2003.

"Is Eric K. Shinseki the Next Great AA Leader?," April 21, 2003, http://www.goldsea.com/Air/Issues/Shinseki/Shinseki.html.

Kakesako, Greg K. "Marines face civil rights lawsuit." April 20, 2003 and "Journey to justice," September 21, 2003. *Honolulu Star-Bulletin* from http://starbulletin.com/2003/04/20/news/story5.html and http://starbulletin.com/2003/09/21/news/story6.html.

Nakama, Wes. "Mamiya has the Heart of a Champion." *The Honolulu Advertiser,* June 11, 2006.

Magazines, Booklets, Concert Program

The 54th Cherry Blossom Festival. "7th Annual Hawaii International Taiko Festival." March 19, 2007.

Grant, Glen, "Mixing the Plate: The Multi-culturalization of Hawaii's Japanese Americans." *Japanese American Museum Quarterly,* vol. 12 no.2: pp. 13-19.

International Art Society of Hawai'i, brochure for exhibit. "Kuilima Kākou", Hawai'i-Japan Joint Exhibit, October 17, 2004.

Japanese Cultural Center of Hawai'i, "Historical Campsites Uncovered!" by Shayna Coleon in *JCCH Legacies, March 2006.*

Japanese Cultural Center of Hawai'i. *Grand Opening Souvenir Booklet,* May 21, 1994.

Japanese Cultural Center of Hawai'i. *Zenshin-To the Future.* 2003.

Salkever, Alex. "The Man with the Golden Network" *Hawaii Business.* pp. 44-48. January 1996.

Online sources

A&B Sugar Museum. http://www.sugarmuseum.com/sugar.html.

Anne Namba. www.annenamba.com.

Hawai'i Sports Hall of Fame and Cybermuseum (with exhibits at Bishop Museum and Honolulu Airport) from http://www.hawaiisportshalloffame.com/.

Hawai'i United Okinawa Association. http://www.huoa.org/.

Hawai'i's Plantation Village. http://www.hawaiiplantatonvillage.org.

Jake Shimabukuro. www.jakeshimabukuro.com.

Japanese Cultural Center of Hawai'i. http://www.jcch.com/.

Kenny Endo. www.kennyendo.com.

Watada, Lt. Ehren. in *Pacific Citizen.* Japanese American Citizens' League. http://www.pacificcitizen.org.

Ohta-San Bio compiled by Sharon Ku'uipo Kana'e Paulos from programs for "Ohta San in Concert 2002" and "The Hawai'i Daughters' Guild 30th Annual Holoku Ball," *September Morn*: Monday, 3/30/02 at http://www.geocities.com/sptmbrmrn/033002-4.htm.

Ong, Henry. "Leading Man Emeritus." *GoldSea Asian American Daily* from http:/goldsea.com/Personalities2/Shigetaj/shigetaj.html.

Punahou Case Middle School awards. http://www.ack-inc.com/schools/case.htm.

Yamaguchi, Roy. http://www.royyamaguchi.com.

The State of Hawai'i Department of Education 2006 Superintendant's 17th Annual Report Appendix C: Data Table 6. Ethnicity of Students and Teachers from http://arch.k12.hi.us/system/sutreport/2006.html.

The State of Hawai'i Data Book 2005, Section 1, Table 1.37—Ranking of Races— 2000 from

Index

PEOPLE INDEX

368